Hegel's
PHENOMENOLOGY
OF
SELF-CONSCIOUSNESS
• *text and commentary* •

Leo Rauch
and
David Sherman

STATE UNIVERSITY OF NEW YORK PRESS

Published by
State University of New York Press

© 1999 State University of New York

For information, address the State University of New York Press,
State University Plaza, Albany, NY 12246

Marketing by Dana Yanulavich
Production by Bernadine Dawes

Library of Congress Cataloging-in-Publication Data

Rauch, Leo
    Hegel's phenomenology of self-consciousness : text and commentary
/ Leo Rauch and David Sherman
        p.   cm. — (SUNY series in Hegelian studies)
    Includes index.
    ISBN 0-7914-4157-1 (alk. paper). — ISBN 0-7914-4158-X (pbk. :
alk. paper)
    1. Hegel, Georg Wilhelm Friedrich, 1770–1831. Wahrheit der
Gewissheit seiner selbst. 2. Consciousness—History—19th century.
I. Sherman, David, 1958–   . II. Hegel, Georg Wilhelm Friedrich,
1770–1831. Wahrheit der Gewissheit seiner selbst. English.
III. Title. IV. Series.
B2929.R38   1999
193—dc21   99-19061
                                                    CIP

1 2 3 4 5 6 7 8 9 10

CONTENTS

Preface and Acknowledgments / vii
INTRODUCTION by David Sherman / 1

PART I
G. W. F. HEGEL
PHENOMENOLOGY OF SPIRIT: SELF-CONSCIOUSNESS
translated by Leo Rauch

1. Chapter IV: The Truth of Self-Certainty / 13
2. Hegel's Summary of Self-Consciousness from the
   "Phenomenology of Spirit" in the *Philosophical Propaedeutic*
   (1809) / 47

PART II
A DISCUSSION OF THE TEXT
by Leo Rauch

3. What is "Self-Consciousness"?: An Overview / 55
4. On Hegel's Aims and Methods / 65
5. Before "Self-Consciousness" / 71
6. Self-Consciousness and Self-Certainty (Para. 1–12) / 79
7. Mastery and Slavery (Para. 13–31) / 87
8. Stoicism, Skepticism, and the Unhappy Consciousness
   (Para. 32–65) / 103
9. After "Self-Consciousness" / 121
10. Early-Twentieth-Century European Criticism / 125

PART III
THE DENIAL OF THE SELF:
THE REPUDIATION OF HEGELIAN SELF-CONSCIOUSNESS
IN RECENT EUROPEAN THOUGHT
by David Sherman

11. Overview / 163
12. Georges Bataille / 167
13. Gilles Deleuze / 179
14. Jacques Lacan / 191
15. Jürgen Habermas and Axel Honneth / 205

Notes / 223
Index / 233

PREFACE AND
ACKNOWLEDGMENTS

In early 1997, I was contacted by Leo Rauch, who offered me the opportunity to co-author a book on the "Self-Consciousness" chapter of Hegel's *Phenomenology of Spirit*. In fact, much of the book had already been written: Professor Rauch had completed his translation of the chapter, a "Discussion" section, and a basic overview of the chapter's reception by various early-twentieth-century European philosophers. My task, quite simply, was to write an Introduction to the book and a section on the chapter's treatment by more contemporary European thinkers. I was pleased to come along for the ride. Sadly, however, Professor Rauch died in the summer of 1997, and the pleasure of seeing this book published is now, unfortunately, mine alone. Although I never had the opportunity to meet Professor Rauch, in my many telephone conversations with him I came to see him as a kind and wise old soul. I hope that this completed work does justice to his original vision.

As with any book, there are many people to whom a debt of gratitude is owed. First, I would like to express my appreciation to Bernadine Dawes, Jane Bunker, and William Desmond for shepherding this book through the publishing process under difficult circumstances. I would also like to express my appreciation to Professor Gila Ramras-Rauch for her continuing moral support. Moving closer to home, I would like to thank Robert C. Solomon, teacher and friend, who made my involvement in this book possible, and reviewed earlier drafts of my contribution to it.

So, too, I would like to thank Kelly Oliver, who reviewed an earlier draft of my discussion of Jacques Lacan. (Needless to say, all errors are mine.) Moving yet closer to home, I would like to express my love and gratitude to my mother and late father, Lenore and Jerrold Sherman. And finally, and most of all, I would like to thank my wonderful wife, Nancy, who makes all things possible.

David Sherman

INTRODUCTION
by
David Sherman

This book deals with chapter IV of the *Phenomenology of Spirit*, which is generally taken to be Hegel's first significant work. This chapter, which is entitled "Self-Consciousness," contains an introduction, "The Truth of Self-Certainty," and two sections, which are called "Independence and Dependence of Self-Consciousness: Mastery and Slavery" and "Freedom of Self-Consciousness: Stoicism, Skepticism, and the Unhappy Consciousness." At first blush, it may appear somewhat odd to devote an entire book to one short chapter of a much larger work, but "Self-Consciousness" is no ordinary chapter. As an initial matter, in a pivotal passage that concludes the introductory part, in which he reviews the gains that consciousness has made in its attempts to better know the world and indicates the advances that remain for it to make, Hegel suggests that chapter IV constitutes the "turning point" in the *Phenomenology*:

> A self-consciousness exists for a self-consciousness. Only in this way is it self-consciousness indeed—for only in this way does it become aware of the unity of itself in its otherness. . . . Since a self-consciousness is the object, it is just as much "I" as it is object. With this we have arrived at the concept of spirit. Still ahead, for consciousness, is the experience of what spirit is—this absolute substance which, in the total freedom and independence of its opposite (i.e., different independent self-consciousnesses), is their unity. Namely, it is the "I" that is "We," the "We" that is "I." Only in self-consciousness, as the concept of spirit, does con-

1

sciousness have its turning point. Here it turns away from the colorful illusion of the sensuous here-and-now and the empty night of the supersensuous beyond, and it strides into the spiritual day of the present. (Para. 12)[1]

Furthermore, the section on mastery and slavery, which follows on the heels of this passage, is, in particular, much more than just the "turning point" in the *Phenomenology*. This section, in which two lone self-consciousnesses meet in the "state-of-nature" and engage in a "fight to the death" that culminates in master and slave, heralded a new approach for understanding ourselves, as well as the ways in which we come to know the world, and heavily influenced generations of subsequent thinkers (including—indeed, perhaps especially—those who most vociferously disagree with its message). As a result, chapter IV also constitutes nothing less than a "turning point" in the history of modern philosophy.

More broadly, the *Phenomenology* itself is basically an assemblage of successive "forms of consciousness." Each form of consciousness, which reflects the world view or *Weltanschauung* of a specific time period (and not merely an individual consciousness), has its own particular way of looking at the world, which means that each form of consciousness has its own truths. But the object of philosophy is "the Truth," according to Hegel, and when the contradictions that inhere in a particular way of looking at the world can no longer be satisfactorily reconciled within the context of that distinctive form of consciousness, a new form of consciousness will emerge that is more adequate to the task. This "dialectical" process does not merely involve a ceaseless, indiscriminate swapping of forms of consciousness and their concomitant truths, however. Instead, inasmuch as the truths for any particular form of consciousness always capture some aspect of the "the Truth," however tenuously, the insights that are associated with a superseded form of consciousness are incorporated into all subsequent forms of consciousness. Consequently, shifts from one form of consciousness to another characterize an expanding, more comprehensive conception of the world. This process of conceptual growth continues until consciousness ascends to that state which Hegel calls "Absolute Knowing," in which consciousness recognizes that its knowledge of objects is ultimately self-knowledge, and that self-knowledge is always conditioned by some existing set of sociohistorical categories. Thus, in spite of its pretentious connotations, "Absolute Knowing" involves the recognition that there is no absolute standpoint from which human beings can reflect upon the world, which means that all thought is necessarily context bound.

Although they inauspiciously arise more than one hundred pages into the *Phenomenology*, the forms of consciousness that correspond to master and slave betoken Hegel's own distinctive philosophical contribution, for the first three chapters of the book, as well as the introductory part of the fourth, are basically a recapitulation of the philosophical failures of Hegel's predecessors. In large part, the first three chapters deal with epistemological concerns, and it is, perhaps, for this reason that the interpretations of important social thinkers, such as Alexandre Kojève (who will be considered later), take off from Hegel's seemingly unrelated discussions of "life" and "desire" at the start of chapter IV. (Indeed, this is precisely where the present translation begins.) But given the fact that Hegel is a deeply historical thinker, and that the *Phenomenology* is a deeply historical work (in the sense that we are dealing with a "logical" characterization of the historical evolution of consciousness), it is a mistake to simply disregard the earlier chapters. For Hegel's discussion of "life" and "desire," which culminates in the "fight to the death" between two stripped-down, "self-certain" self-consciousnesses, is actually not unrelated to the earlier epistemological concerns at all.

The meeting of these two self-consciousnesses, which initially "recognize themselves as mutually recognizing one another" (para. 19), is the "turning point," according to Hegel, because with it "we have arrived at the concept of spirit," which signals nothing less than his repudiation of the philosophical tradition's penchant for approaching epistemological questions from an individual standpoint. Spirit, which pertains to the subjectivity of the human collective, is the interpersonal medium whose basic character both forms and is formed by our personal self-conceptions, which, in turn, condition our conceptions of the world around us. For Hegel, therefore, the concepts that are brought to bear on epistemological questions are intersubjectively generated, and this suggests that the hard and fast distinction that is usually drawn between ethical and epistemological issues becomes much less distinct. But as consciousness marches toward a social reconciliation that is tantamount to "Absolute Knowing," in which it sees that Spirit is "the 'I' that is 'We,' the 'We' that is 'I,'" it is not merely the case that the social concepts drive the epistemological ones, for the socially engendered epistemic concepts that lead us to comprehend the natural world in a particular way reciprocally determine our collective and personal self-conceptions. As we shall see, it is this reciprocal dynamic that leads master and slave to not only be alienated from one another, and thus themselves (inasmuch as social and individual self-conceptions are inextricably interrelated), but also leads them to be alienated from the objects of the natural world. And it is this alienation from self, other, and the objects of the natural world that leads to forms of consciousness such as Stoicism, Skepticism, and the Unhappy Consciousness, each of which finally fails to satisfactorily redress these problems in turn. This failure to reconcile self and other, subject and object, is what drives consciousness past "Self-Consciousness" to "Reason," which is what motivates the forms of consciousness that appear in chapter V of the *Phenomenology*. For our purposes, however, it is necessary to put the forms of consciousness that appear in chapter IV into sharper focus by more clearly delineating the philosophical problems that informed them.

In the lengthy passage from the *Phenomenology* that is excerpted above, Hegel says that in comprehending itself as self-consciousness, consciousness "turns away from the colorful illusion of the sensuous here-and-now and the empty night of the supersensuous beyond, and it strides into the spiritual day of the present." This passage implicitly refers to the philosophy of Kant, who had attempted to make sense of the stark epistemological division that had previously existed between empiricism and rationalism by turning to self-consciousness, but had become enmeshed in his own contradictions, and thus ended up postulating a supersensuous beyond of his own making. The first three chapters of the *Phenomenology*, which crudely correspond to certain versions of empiricism, rationalism, and Kant's so-called "Critical Philosophy," are characterized by Hegel as "Sense-Certainty," "Perception," and "Force and the Understanding," respectively. And, the Kantian turn to self-consciousness in chapter III notwithstanding, these three theories of knowledge are all classified under the general title of "Consciousness," for they all ultimately view the object that one knows as, in some sense, independent of the process of knowing. Thus, in "Sense-Certainty," we are presented with a form of consciousness that thinks that the particular objects it apprehends are immediately given to it—in other words, that knowing the world is nothing more than a matter of attending to the way that objects affect our senses. In Hegel's view, however, there is no direct acquaintance with objects, for all knowledge requires the mediation of concepts. Indeed, without concepts, there can be no knowledge whatsoever, and consciousness is not even in a position to gesture at the object to communicate what it purportedly knows. Consequently, a different view of knowledge must be undertaken in order to overcome this impasse, and the form that it assumes is "Perception." While "Sense-Certainty" approached the object from the standpoint of the object's sensuous particularity but failed because it lacked concepts, "Perception" would tackle the problem by approaching the object from the standpoint of its properties ("sensuous universals")—in other words, the object is viewed as just a collection of its properties. But as a form of consciousness, "Perception" also comes up short, for it fails to connect with the object's sensuous particularity, which essentially falls out of the picture. In the final analysis, then, the one-sided supersensible conceptual approach to the object is no more able to grasp the object in its particularity than the one-sided sensible approach; consciousness is, therefore, impelled to move beyond the two one-sided approaches if it is to actually come to terms with the object.

The form of consciousness found in "Force and the Understanding" involves a series of philosophical and scientific views in which both the sensible and supersensible approaches to the world subsist, implicitly or explicitly, in a more comprehensive explanatory theory. For example, in scientific views on "Force," Hegel contends, there is the notion that force both expresses itself in physical phenomena as they appear and is the impetus that hangs behind the appearance. This dualistic view, which Hegel finds untenable, reaches its highest point of tension in the philosophy of Kant, and it is with Kant's philosophy that the chapter is primarily preoccupied. According to Kant, the empiricists were correct in maintaining that all we can ultimately know is the world of our experience. However, in contrast to the empiricists, for whom this position culminated in the skepticism of Hume, Kant relied upon the rationalists' notion of a priori concepts, but views them as innate to our own minds. These unconditioned universal concepts, which precede experience, are called "categories" by Kant, and they are the foundation upon which all human experience is made possible. In other words, in every person there is "the Understanding," which furnishes the laws and principles that are necessary in order for us to even have an experience. We can therefore depend upon what our senses tell us about the objects that we apprehend because we ourselves "constitute" these objects through the Understanding, which initially synthesizes them. But the shortcoming of Kant's "Copernican Revolution," which, epistemologically, shifts the emphasis from the object to the subject, is that it maintains that there is some way that the object actually is independent of our possible knowledge of it. This implies that a "world-in-itself" hangs behind our "apparent" world, and bears some unknown relationship to it. Once again, therefore, we are left holding the bag in terms of knowing the actual nature of particular objects, a fact that is forcefully brought home by Hegel in his "inverted world" hypothesis. In this reductio ad absurdum, Hegel wryly speculates that a second supersensible world actually hangs behind Kant's supersensible world, and that in this even truer world objects are diametrically opposed to the way in which we apprehend them—that is, what is sweet for us is really sour, what is black for us is really white, what is up for us is really down, and so forth.

To get past this dualism, consciousness seeks to do away with the idea that objects subsist independently of our experience of them, and this brings us to the first form of self-consciousness that appears in chapter IV, which corresponds to Fichte's alteration of Kant's dualistic philosophy. Fichte, who rejected the idea of a world-in-itself, was of the view that all epistemological inquiries essentially take place within a practical context, not a theoretical one. For Fichte, in other words, it is not knowledge, but self-knowledge and action, that is of primary importance. In this way, we move from Kant's notion of the Understanding, which shifts the epistemological emphasis to the subject but still sees the enterprise of comprehending the world in theoretical or objective terms, to Fichte's idea of the engaged subject, for whom the quest for knowledge is inextricably intertwined with life's pragmatic (and moral) concerns. And these concerns are, in part, bound up with our personal desires, which stand in a negative relationship to the otherness of the world. As a result, for Fichte, and to a somewhat lesser degree Hegel as well, our desire-driven attempts to know the world involve a process of conceptualization that would—figuratively speaking—break down and wholly assimilate all objects, leaving no remainder. According to Hegel, however, this voraciousness is without limit, and what Fichte fails to comprehend is that such desire will never be satisfied because "self-consciousness attains its satisfaction only in another self-consciousness" (para. 10). In other words, what Hegel rejects is Fichte's view (or, at least, the view that Hegel attributes to him) that the knowing self is an individual self, for the individual self in Hegel's view is indeterminate: the self-certain self-consciousness of Fichte is only "the motionless tautology of 'I am I'" (para. 2). Only by relating to another self-consciousness can a self-consciousness develop into a determinate self, and thereby attain a truer view of knowledge.

Furthermore, Hegel's difficulties with Fichte are not limited to the latter's characterization of an individual self. Although Hegel agreed with

Fichte's rejection of Kant's world-in-itself, he also thought that Fichte went too far in the other direction, for Fichte's all-encompassing subject sees the natural world only in subjective terms, thus losing the objective perspective of the natural sciences. Fichte thus breaks down the unbridgeable subject-object duality that Kant produces with his introduction of the world-in-itself, but loses the objectivity of the object in the process. Or, in Hegel's parlance, Fichte has merely given us a "subjective Subject-Object." To counteract Fichte's partial perspective, Hegel's draws upon the philosophy of his erstwhile friend, Schelling, whose philosophy of nature affords an "objective Subject-Object" to counterbalance the Fichtean outlook. According to Schelling, whose philosophy greatly influenced the contours of the *Phenomenology*, but, for structural reasons, is not presented until the beginning of chapter V ("Reason"), there is an absolute identity between consciousness and nature since consciousness, despite its pretensions, is only a part of nature. Thus, from the first-person standpoint, we (individually and collectively), as subjective Subject-Objects, are nature, and nature, as an objective Subject-Object, is us, meaning that we can only comprehend ourselves by comprehending nature. Furthermore, the two sides of the equation, each of which grows in a purposive fashion, are unified in a higher order "Absolute," which comes to realize itself in this enormous growth process. And it is because of this identity between consciousness and nature, Schelling contends (according to Hegel's contentious account), that we can come to know the world through (transcendental) intuition. But this is where Hegel and Schelling part company, for Hegel believes that knowledge of the world can only be obtained through "the Concept"; accordingly, in the Preface to the *Phenomenology*, he says that Schelling's "determinateness of intuition" is a "formalism" that is "predicated in accordance with a superficial analogy."

We are now in a position to see that the master-slave section does not reflect a radical shift in the *Phenomenology*, but rather builds upon the earlier chapters, which themselves are prototypal representations of earlier positions taken in the philosophical tradition. This section, in particular, and the "Self-Consciousness" chapter, more generally, symbolizes, in short, a radically different approach for dealing with a variety of problems relating to the knowing self. During the course of the *Phenomenology*, consciousness must surmount the forms of consciousness that correspond to master and slave, for each is alienated from the external world, the other, and, ultimately, himself. (And in terms of this condition of thoroughgoing alienation, the remaining forms of consciousness in the "Self-

Consciousness" chapter—Stoicism, Skepticism, and the Unhappy Consciousness—exhibit only marginal improvement.) A large assortment of forms of consciousness must still be transversed before a situation in which "one [self-consciousness] is only recognized, the other only recognizing" (para. 20) becomes one in which consciousness sees that "it is the 'I' that is 'We,' the 'We' that is 'I'." But with the master-slave encounter, we have reached the "turning point" that has put consciousness on the proper path—the path that will lead to "Absolute Knowing."

Hegel's discussion of the dialectic of self-consciousness (as well as the remainder of his large and varied body of work) had an enormous impact in the years following its publication.[2] In Hegel's immediate aftermath, there were the so-called "Young Hegelians," who were particularly enamored of the radical role that Hegel's historicized reason plays in critiquing existing institutions so as to move beyond them toward an ultimate social reconciliation. These Young Hegelians, as well as Ludwig Feuerbach, whose materialism had inspired them, gave rise, in turn, to Marx, who was strongly influenced by the master-slave section. In his *Economic and Philosophic Manuscripts of 1844*, for example, Marx contends that

> the outstanding achievement of Hegel's *Phenomenology* and of its final outcome, the dialectic of negativity as the moving and generating principle, is thus first that Hegel conceives the self-creation of man as a process, conceives objectification as loss of the object, as alienation and as transcendence of this alienation; that he thus grasps the essence of labor and comprehends objective man—true, because real man—as the outcome of man's own labour.[3]

Although he (somewhat unfairly) goes on to claim that Hegel stands the dialectic "on its head" by holding that "the Idea" creates the "real" world, as opposed to simply being "the material world reflected in the mind of man,"[4] Marx closely adheres to the form of Hegel's "dialectic"; in fact, the structure of *Capital* is patterned after Hegel's *Science of Logic*.

Where Marx unequivocally takes issue with Hegel, however, is in the latter's view of the (bourgeois) State. In the *Philosophy of Right*, which is, arguably, Hegel's most conservative work, Hegel contends that the rational state is the highest social manifestation of Spirit, and that the task of the "universal" class of civil servants that comprise it is to effectively harmonize the various interests in civil society. Unlike modern societies, however, in which particular interests come to dominate the State (which was, in no small part, Marx's criticism of Hegel's view of the State), or come to be alienated from it, all elements of civil society regard the rational State as satisfying both their specific interests and the general public interest. And, according to Hegel, the monarchical Prussian State within which he lived met this ideal. While Marx and other leftist thinkers clearly rejected this conclusion out of hand, a reactionary group known as the Right Hegelians embraced Hegel on these very grounds. The Right Hegelians, many of whom held high office in Prussia, argued that religion and the State were the organic ties that bound a citizenry together, and that the "negativity" within Hegel's philosophy, which was so heavily relied upon by the left, was simply a mistake. Accordingly, they brought back an embittered and now conservative Schelling to teach at the university after Hegel's death in order to bring this point home, and, while there were still many Left Hegelians on the faculty, Schelling was not without his influence. Engels, who was obviously not dissuaded from his revolutionary path, attended Schelling's lectures, along with Kierkegaard, the self-styled Christian who was nominally the father of existentialism.

For Kierkegaard, unlike Schelling (who thought that Hegel stole and then misrepresented his own ideas), Hegel was first and foremost an intellectual nemesis. According to Kierkegaard, who was inclined to view Hegel through the lens of his own religious preoccupations, Hegel was a metaphysician who subsumed religion under philosophy, and, thereby, the moment of faith under the moment of reason. (Indeed, the forms of consciousness that directly precede "Absolute Knowing" in the *Phenomenology* are religious.) For Kierkegaard, however, faith is not simply a matter that is to be dissolved within an overarching, reconciling reason; instead, it is a chosen way of life that is to be lived passionately if it is to be lived at all. Reason can tell us nothing about how to live our lives, much less our faith—a point that Kierkegaard brings home when he recounts the biblical episode in which God tells Abraham to take the life of his son, which would, of course, be in violation of all rational ethical precepts. Like Abraham, we are all ultimately confronted with the decision as to whether we should make an irrational "leap of faith." Even as Kierkegaard attacks the Hegelian "system" in the name of Christianity and "the individual," who would be namelessly subsumed by it, however, he embraces a dialectical method that is akin to the one that Hegel uses in the *Phenomenology*. In *Either/Or*, Kierkegaard posits three "modes of existence," namely, the aesthetic, the ethical, and the religious, and claims that contradictions in each of the first two modes of existence inexorably lead one to choose the religious life. Still, for Kierkegaard, the religious life is an unhappy one, and the form of consciousness that ends the "Self-Consciousness" chapter in the *Phenomenology*, the "Unhappy Consciousness," is an anticipatory caricature of him.

In contrast to Kierkegaard, for whom Christianity involves ceaseless suffering, Nietzsche declares that one should love one's fate. But while proclaiming *amor fati*, Nietzsche also attacks the very notion of "the individual"—at least to the extent that this notion gives rise to the idea that there is a discrete, self-contained "self" that subsists over time, and in its freedom should be held morally responsible for its actions. For Nietzsche, this view of the self is fundamentally "slavish." Accordingly, in the *Genealogy of Morals,* he forcefully argues that the categories of "master" and "slave" pertain to those human beings who are innately stronger and weaker, and that the Judeo-Christian tradition reflects the success of the weak in overturning the rule of the strong through the imposition of their own life-denying, otherworldly values. In contrast to Hegel, therefore, for whom the master-slave encounter gives rise to the notion of selfhood, which will progressively be perfected in society, Nietzsche views the notion of selfhood as one that was basically slavish at its inception. And, at least in this sense, he appears to valorize premodern values (although it must be quickly added that while Nietzsche is hostile toward modern mass society, the superior individuals of whom he often speaks generally take the form of great artists, such as Goethe, rather than the "blond beast"). Nevertheless, in a variety of respects, which cannot be considered here, Nietzsche and Hegel are more alike than not. For our purposes, however, it must be pointed out that more than a few contemporary anti-Hegelian philosophers have used Nietzsche (who died in 1900) as a cudgel with which to attack Hegel, which has tended to unduly diminish the thought of both.

The purpose of this book, which is comprised of three parts, is to revisit Hegel's remarkable "Self-Consciousness" chapter from the *Phenomenology of Spirit*. The first part of the book consists of Leo Rauch's translation of this chapter, as well as a supplement in which he translates the relatively brief self-consciousness section from Hegel's Philosophical Propadeutic of 1809. The second part of the book is comprised of Leo Rauch's extensive discussion of the "Self-Consciousness" chapter and his brief overview of its early-twentieth-century European reception. Lastly, in the third part of the book, I will offer a critical exposition of the chapter's interpretation by those European thinkers whose views on it tend to hold sway today.

PART I

G. W. F. HEGEL
PHENOMENOLOGY OF SPIRIT:
SELF-CONSCIOUSNESS

translated by

LEO RAUCH

CHAPTER IV:
THE TRUTH OF SELF-CERTAINTY

Translator's Note: In working with the text of Phänomenologie des Geistes, *I have adhered to Hegel's paragraphing, but I have taken the liberty of breaking up some of the paragraphs for easier reading. To indicate where Hegel's paragraphs occur, I have assigned consecutive numbers to them. Explanatory words and phrases of my own are in square brackets. Italics are Hegel's.*

[1] In the modes of certainty considered so far, what is true for consciousness is something other than consciousness itself. Yet the concept of this truth vanishes in the experience of it. Whatever the object immediately was *in itself*—whether it was something existing in sense-certainty, the concrete thing in perception, or something the understanding saw as force—the object now turns out to be not truly so. Rather, the *in-itself* is revealed as a mode in which the object is merely so for another. The concept of the object is superseded in the actual object; i.e., the first immediate presentation of the object is superseded in experience, and certainty loses itself in the truth.

Now, however, something arises that was not there in the previous relationships, namely a certainty that is identical to its truth—since the certainty is [now] its own object, and consciousness is the truth for itself. In this there is indeed an otherness; consciousness does make a distinction. But it is a distinction that, for consciousness, is at the same time not something distinct. If what we call the *concept* is knowing in process, while the *object* is knowing as a passive unity or "I," we can see that the object corresponds to the concept—not only for us but for knowing itself.

On the other hand, if what we call the *concept* is what the object is *in itself*, but what we call the object is what it is as *object for an other*, it becomes clear that its being for itself and its being for another are one and the same. This is because the *in-itself* is consciousness, although it is likewise that *for which* an other is the *in-itself*. And it is for consciousness that the in-itself of the object and the being of the object for another are one and the same. The "I" is the content of the relation and the relating itself. The "I" is its own self in juxtaposition to another "I," and at the same time it reaches beyond this other "I," which, for the "I," is equally only the "I" itself.

[2] With self-consciousness, then, we have arrived at truth's own territory. What we must now see, above all, is how the form of self-consciousness makes its appearance. If we consider this new form of knowing, i.e., self-knowledge, and consider it in relation to the foregoing, i.e., knowing something other, we see that the latter has indeed vanished. And yet at the same time, its elements have remained. And the loss consists in that they are still present here, as they are in themselves. The *being* of an opinion, the particularity of a perception (and the universality opposed to it), along with the *empty inwardness* of the understanding—all these are no longer there as realities, but as mere elements of self-consciousness, i.e., as abstractions or distinctions which are at the same time not really there *for* consciousness, are not distinctions but are purely vanishing entities.

Thus it seems [that in self-consciousness] it is only the main element itself that has been lost—namely the *simple independent existence* for consciousness. Yet the fact is that self-consciousness is a reflection out of the existent world as sensuously perceived, and is essentially the return from *otherness*. As self-consciousness, it [this otherness] is movement. But inasmuch as what it distinguishes from itself is *only itself, as* itself, the distinguishing of otherness is *immediately negated* for it. [Thus] the distinction *is not*, and *it* [self-consciousness] is then merely the motionless tautology of "I am I." Insofar as the distinction does not also have the form of *being* for self-consciousness, it is not self-consciousness.

Accordingly, otherness is there for self-consciousness *as an entity*, a *distinct element*—yet it is also for self-consciousness the unity of itself with this distinction, as a *second distinct element*. With that first element of otherness, self-consciousness is there as *consciousness*—and for it the entire expanse of the sensory world is maintained. Yet at the same time [that world] is related only to the second element, the unity of self-consciousness with itself—and hence this world is, for self-consciousness, something existing independently, although this is only *appearance*, a distinction that *in itself* has no reality.

This opposition between its appearance and its truth has as its essence only the truth, namely the unity of self-consciousness with itself. This [unity] must become essential for self-consciousness. That is to say, self-consciousness is *desire* in general. Consciousness, as self-consciousness, henceforth has a double object: one of these is the immediate object which is the object of sense-certainty and perception, although for *self-consciousness* this has the *character of negativity*; the other object is self-consciousness *itself*, which is the true *essence* and is primarily there in opposition to the first object. In this, self-consciousness presents itself as the process wherein this opposition is overcome, and it becomes for itself its own identity with itself.

[3] The object, however, which is the negative element for self-consciousness—whether it is so *for us* or *in itself*—has for its part gone back into itself, just as consciousness has done. Through this reflection into itself, the object has become *Life*. [Thus] whatever it is that self-consciousness distinguishes from itself, as having [independent] *being*, not only has the modes of sense-certainty and perception attached to it (insofar as the thing is posited as existing); but it is also an entity reflected into itself, and the object of immediate desire is a *living thing*. This is because the *in-itself* (i.e., the *general* result of the understanding's relation to the inwardness of things) is the distinguishing of what is not to be distinguished, or the unity of what is distinguished.

Yet as we saw, this unity is just as much its repulsion from itself. And this concept *divides* itself into the opposition between self-consciousness and life: the former is the unity *for which* there is this infinite unity of differences, while the latter *is* merely this unity itself so that it is not at the same time *for itself*. Thus, to the degree that consciousness is independent, to that degree its object is independent *in itself*. Self-consciousness, which is simply *for itself*, and which directly characterizes its object as a negative element (which is why self-consciousness is primarily *desire*), will therefore on the other hand have the experience of the object's independence.

[4] The determination of life—as this determination emanates from the concept or from the general outcome [of the understanding] with which we enter this sphere—is sufficient to characterize it, without our having to develop its nature further. Its sphere is determined in the following elements: *Essence* is the infinitude as the overcoming of all differences, [like] the pure motion around an axis whose self-repose is an absolutely restless infinity; *independence* itself, in which the differences of motion are resolved; the simple essence of time, which in this self-identity has the stable form of space.

The *differences*, however, are just as much there in this *simple universal medium*, as *differences*—since this universal fluidity has its negative nature only in that it is the *overcoming of them*. Yet it cannot overcome the differentiated elements if they do not have an enduring existence. This very fluidity, as self-identical independence, is itself the enduring existence, or their substance wherein the elements are there as differentiated members, [independent] parts *existing for themselves. Being* no longer means *abstract Being*, nor does their pure essentiality mean *abstract universality*. Rather, their being is just that simple fluid substance of pure motion in itself. Yet the difference of these members with regard to one another, as difference, generally consists in no other *determinacy* than that of the elements of infinity, or pure motion itself.

[5] The independent members are *for themselves*. Yet this *being-for-self* is just as much their reflection into a unity as this unity is the division into independent forms. This unity is divided because it is an absolutely negative or infinite unity. And because *it* is the *enduring existence*, the differentiation also has its independence only in that unity. This independence of form appears as something *determinate, for an other*, since the form itself is something divided. And the *overcoming* of the division therefore occurs through something other. Yet the overcoming is just as much a part of that form itself, because the aforementioned fluidity is the substance of the independent forms. This substance is infinite, however. The form is therefore division in its very existence, i.e., the overcoming of its being-for-self.

[6] If we differentiate more precisely the elements included here, we see that the *first* element is the *subsistence of independent* forms, i.e., the suppression of what differentiation is in itself (which means not to exist in itself and to have no subsistence). The *second* element, however, is the *subjection* of that subsistence to the infinitude of the difference. In the first element

there is the subsistent form: As *existing for itself* or in its determinacy as infinite substance, the form makes its appearance in opposition to the *universal* substance—thus belying this fluidity and continuity with it and asserting itself as not dissolved in this universality, but rather as maintaining itself by separating itself from this its inorganic nature and consuming it. Life—in the universal fluid medium, a *quiescent* array of forms—thereby becomes a movement of those forms, becomes Life as *process*. The simple universal fluidity is the *in-itself*, and the differentiation of forms is the other. Yet this fluidity itself becomes the *other* through this differentiation—for it is now something *for this difference*, which exists in and for itself and is thus the endless movement by which the quiescent medium is consumed: Life as a *living thing*.

This *inversion*, however, is for this reason again the *invertedness in its own self*. What is consumed is the essence. That is, the individuality which maintains itself at the expense of the universal and that gives itself the feeling of its unity with itself, thereby overcomes *its opposition to the other, by means of which it exists for itself*. The *unity* with itself, which it gives itself, is precisely the *fluidity* of the differences, the *general dissolution*. Yet conversely, the overcoming of individual existence is also what produces that existence. For since the *essence* of the individual form is the universal life, and since what exists for itself is in itself simple substance, it negates its own *simplicity* (which is its essence) since it posits the *other* within itself. That is to say, it *divides* that unity, and this division of the undifferentiated fluidity is precisely the positing of individuality.

The simple substance of life is thus the division of itself into forms, and at the same time the dissolution of these existing differences. And the dissolution of the division is just as much a division into members. With this, the two sides of the total movement that had been differentiated—namely the formative process quietly articulated in the universal medium of independence, and the Life-process itself—collapse into one another. The latter is just as much a formative process as it is an overcoming of form. And the former, the process of formation, is just as much an overcoming as it is an articulation of members.

The fluid element is itself only the *abstraction* of essence, so it is *actual* only as form. And so that it articulates itself, there is again a division of what is articulated or its dissolution. This entire cycle is what comprises life: being neither that which was expressed to begin with, the immediate continuity and stability of its essence, nor the persistent form and the discrete element that is for itself, nor its pure process, nor yet the simple synopsis of these elements—but rather the self-developing totality, dissolving its development, and [yet] in this movement simply maintaining itself.

[7] Since we proceeded from the first immediate unity, through the elements of formation and process, and through these to the unity of both these elements, and thus have returned to the first simple substance, this [latter] *reflected unity* is different from the first. The first is an *immediate unity*, expressed as an *entity*; and opposed to this, the second is the *universal* unity, containing within itself all these elements as [now] superseded. It is the *simple species* which, in the movement of life, does not itself *exist for itself* as this *simple thing*. Rather, in this *result*, life points to something other than itself, namely to consciousness, for which it exists as this unity, or as species.

[8] This other life, however—for which the *species* exists as such, and which is for itself the [human] species, i.e., self-consciousness—is there for itself, first of all, merely as this simple entity and has itself for an object as *pure* "I." In its experience, which is now to be considered, this abstract object will be enriched for it, and will attain the unfolding we have seen to be associated with life.

[9] The simple "I" is this species, the simple universal, for which the differences are no longer differences—but only because the "I" is a *negative entity* of articulated, independent elements. And thus self-consciousness is certain of itself only through the overcoming of this other which presents itself to self-consciousness as independent life. Self-consciousness is *desire*. Certain of the nothingness of this other, self-consciousness asserts *for itself* this nothingness as its truth [about the other], destroys the independent object [i.e., negates the other's independence] and thereby gives itself its certainty of itself as a *true* certainty, a certainty that has now become explicit for it in an *objective manner*.

[10] In this satisfaction, however, experience [presents] the independence of its object. Desire, and the self-certainty arrived at in the satisfaction of desire, are conditioned by the object, since the self-certainty is [arrived at] through the overcoming of this other. In order for this overcoming to occur, there must *be* this other. Thus, self-consciousness, through its negative relation, cannot overcome the other. [Rather,] it thereby creates it all

the more [in desiring it], along with creating desire. Indeed, it is something other than self-consciousness that is the essence of desire, and through such experience self-consciousness has grasped that truth. Yet at the same time self-consciousness is absolutely for itself, which it is only because it negates the object—and this must become its satisfaction, for it is the truth.

For the sake of the object's independence, self-consciousness can therefore attain satisfaction [only] in that the object achieves its own negation. And it must achieve its own negation in itself, since it is *in itself* the negative element and must be for the other what it is. Since the object is its own negation and is thereby independent, it is consciousness.

In regard to life, which is the object of desire, negation either is present *in an other*, namely in desire, or as *determinacy* in opposition to another indifferent form, or as its *inorganic universal nature*. Yet this independent universal nature (wherein negation is there as absolute) is the species as such, i.e., as self-consciousness. *Self-consciousness attains its satisfaction only in another self-consciousness.*

[11]   It is only in the following three aspects that the concept of self-consciousness is fulfilled: (a) The pure undifferentiated "I" is its first immediate object. (b) Yet this immediacy is itself absolute mediation, only as the overcoming of the independent object, i.e., as desire. The satisfaction of desire is indeed the reflection of self-consciousness into itself, i.e., certainty becomes truth. (c) Yet the truth of this certainty is really a double reflection, the duplication of self-consciousness. [In this,] consciousness has as its object that which posits its own otherness, or asserts the difference to be nothing, and is thereby independent.

The differentiated and merely *living* form does indeed suspend its independence in the process of life, yet with this differentiation it ceases to be what it is. The object of self-consciousness, on the other hand, is equally independent in this negativity of itself; and thus the object of self-consciousness is a species for itself, a universal fluidity in the peculiarity of its distinctness—it is living self-consciousness.

[12]   A *self-consciousness* exists *for a self-consciousness*. Only in this way is it self-consciousness indeed—for only in this way does it become aware of the unity of itself in its otherness. The "I" that is the object of its own concept is in fact not *object*. The object of desire, on the other hand, is merely *independent*, because that object is the universal indestructible substance, the

fluid self-identical essence. Since a self-consciousness is the object, it is just as much "I" [subject] as it is object.

With this we have arrived at the concept of *spirit*. Still ahead, for consciousness, is the experience of what spirit is—this absolute substance which, in the total freedom and independence of its opposite (i.e., different independent self-consciousnesses), is their unity. Namely, it is the "I" that is "We," the "We" that is "I." Only in self-consciousness, as the concept of spirit, does consciousness have its turning point. Here, it turns away from the colorful illusion of the sensuous here-and-now and the empty night of the supersensuous beyond, and it strides into the spiritual day of the present.

A. Independence and Dependence of Self-Consciousness: Mastery and Slavery

[13]   Self-consciousness exists *in* and *for itself* by virtue of the fact that it is in and for itself for another. That is, it exists only in being recognized. The concept of its unity in its duplication—of an infinitude realizing itself in self-consciousness—is an interrelation of many aspects and many meanings. Thus its elements must in part be kept strictly distinct, in part be undifferentiated in that very differentiation, so that its elements are always taken in their opposite significance. The two-sided significance of these differentiated elements must, in the nature of self-consciousness, be infinite, i.e., the direct opposite of the determinacy in which it is posited. Analyzing the concept of this spiritual unity in its duplication presents us with the process of *recognition*.

[14]   For self-consciousness there is another self-consciousness [confronting it]; it has come *out of itself*. This has a twofold meaning: *first*, it has lost itself, since it finds itself to be an *other* entity; *second*, it has thereby negated the other, since it does not see the other as essential, but rather sees *itself* in the other.

[15]   Self-consciousness must overcome its *own otherness*. This is the overcoming of the first of its double meanings, and therefore is itself a second double meaning: first, it must aim at negating the *other* independent entity, in order thereby to become certain of *itself* as essential; *second*, it thereby seeks to *negate* itself, since the other is itself.

[16] This two-sided [i.e., double-meaning] negation of its two-sided other-ness is at the same time a two-sided return *into itself: first*, because in the negation it gets its own self back (since in negating *its own* otherness it once again becomes equal to itself); *second*, however, the other self-con-sciousness equally restores it to itself (since it saw itself in its other and negated *its own* being in the other, thereby setting the other free once more).

[17] This movement of self-consciousness in relation to another self-con-sciousness has been presented, however, as the *action of the one*. Yet this action of one has itself the double meaning of being both *its own action* and the *action of the other*—since the other is equally independent, deter-mined in itself, and there is nothing in it that is not there through its own means. The first does not have its object before it (as merely in the case of desire, primarily), but rather has an object that is independent and for itself, in which there is nothing there for it if the object does not do for itself what the first does to it.

The movement is therefore simply the duplication of both self-con-sciousnesses. Each sees *the other* do the same as it itself does. Each itself does what it demands of the other, and therefore does what it does only because the other does the same. The one-sided action would be useless, because what is to occur can only come about through the action of both.

[18] The action therefore has a double meaning, not only in that it is as much an action *towards itself* as *towards the other*, but also in that it is indivisibly the *action of the one* as well as the *action of the other*.

[19] In this movement we see the process repeating itself that had presented itself earlier as the play of forces, but repeated now in the sphere of con-sciousness. What was there for us in that earlier process is now there for the two poles. The middle-term is self-consciousness, which separates into the extremes. And each extreme is this exchange of its determinacy, and the absolute transition into its opposite. Although it does indeed come *out of itself* as consciousness, it is in its emergence retained in itself, *for itself*, and what is external is something *for it*. It is aware that it *is* and *is not* immediately another consciousness. And likewise it is aware that this other is only for itself in that it negates itself as something existing for itself, and is for itself only in the being-for-itself of the other. Each is the middle-term of the other, through which each mediates itself with itself and com-

bines with itself. And each is for itself and for the other an immediate entity existing for itself, which is at the same time for itself only through this mediation. They *recognize* themselves as *mutually recognizing one another*.

[20] This pure concept of recognition, of the duplication of self-consciousness in its unity, is now to be considered: i.e., how the process of recognition appears to self-consciousness. At first it will show the *inequality* of the two parties, the extension of the middle-term into the extremes—which, as extremes, are opposed to one another—so that the one is only *recognized*, the other only *recognizing*.

[21] To begin with, self-consciousness is simple being-for-self, self-identical through the exclusion *from itself* of everything *other* than itself. For it, its essence and absolute object is "I." And in this *immediacy*, in this *being* of its being-for-self, it is an *individual*. Everything other is unessential for it, an object characterized as the negative.

Yet the other is also a self-consciousness; one individual confronts another individual. In the *immediacy* of this confrontation, they are for one another as common objects, *independent* forms, consciousness immersed in the *being of life* (since the existent object has here determined itself as life). They have not yet achieved *for one another* the movement of absolute abstraction, suppressing all immediacy and existing only as the purely negative self-identical consciousness. They have not yet shown themselves to one another as pure *being-for-self*, i.e., as *self*-consciousnesses.

Each is indeed certain of his own self but not of the other, and therefore his own self-certainty has as yet no truth. It would have this truth only if his own being-for-self were shown to him as an independent object, or if the object had shown itself as this pure self-certainty (which is the same thing). According to the concept of recognition, however, this is not possible unless: as the other is for him, so he is for the other—each only fulfills this pure abstraction of being-for-self through his own action and again through the action of the other.

[22] The *presentation* of itself as the pure abstraction of self-consciousness, however, consists in showing itself as the pure negation of its objective aspect, i.e., to show itself to be connected to no specific *existence*—not at all to the general particularity of existence as such, nor to life itself. This presentation is the *twofold* action—action of the other and action of one's own. Insofar as it is *action of the other*, each aims at the death of the other.

Yet in this there is also the second aspect, *action of one's own*, since the former includes the staking of one's own life. Thus the relation between the two self-consciousnesses is such that they *prove* themselves in a life-and-death struggle.

They must engage in this struggle, since each must have his self-certainty, his *being-for-self*, raised to the level of truth—for the other as well as for himself. And it is only in staking one's life that one's freedom is established, and it is proven that for self-consciousness it is not mere *being* that is the essence—not the *immediate* aspect as it appears, nor one's submersion in the expanse of life. Rather, one proves thereby that as far as self-consciousness is concerned there is nothing in life that is not a thing of a passing moment, that life is nothing but pure *being-for-self*.

The individual who has not risked his life may well be recognized as a *person*. Yet he has not arrived at the truth of this recognition as that of an independent self-consciousness. Similarly, each must seek the death of the other as he stakes his own life—since the other counts no more for him than he himself does. His essence presents itself to him as something other, external, and he must overcome his existence in the external. The other is an existent consciousness, multifariously involved. It must see its otherness as pure being-for-self, as absolute negation [of everything other than itself].

[23] Yet this trial by death thereby negates the truth that was to have emerged, as well as the self-certainty in general. For just as life is the *natural* assertion of consciousness, the independence without absolute negativity, so death is the *natural* negation of consciousness (the negation without independence), which thus remains without the required significance of recognition. In death there is indeed the certainty that both have risked their lives, that each held life in contempt, his own as well as that of the other. But this is not so for those who have survived the struggle. They terminate their awareness placed in this alien reality that is the natural existence; they negate themselves, and are negated as *extremes* wishing to be for themselves.

Yet thereby the essential element disappears from this interplay, that of splitting apart into extremes of opposed characteristics. The middle-term collapses into a dead unity which splits into dead, merely existing but unopposed extremes. And the two do not mutually give and receive one another once again by way of consciousness. Rather, they leave one another free, indifferently, as mere things. Their act is the abstract negation, not the negation by way of consciousness—which *negates* in such a way that it *retains* and *maintains* that which is negated, and thus overcomes its own negatedness.

[24] In this experience, self-consciousness becomes aware that life is as essential to it as is pure self-consciousness. In the immediate self-consciousness, the simple "I" is the absolute object. Whether for us or in itself, this is the absolute mediation, and its essential element is its continued independence. The dissolution of that simple unity is the result of the first experience. Through this, a pure self-consciousness is posited, and a consciousness that is not purely for itself but for another, i.e., as *existent* consciousness, or consciousness in the form of *thinghood*. Both elements are essential. Since they are, to begin with, unequal and in opposition, and their reflection has not yet given way to unity, they exist as two opposed forms of consciousness: the one is independent consciousness, whose essence is being-for-self; the other is the dependent consciousness, for whom the essential thing is to live or to exist for another. The former is the *master*, the latter the *slave*.

[25] The master is consciousness existing *for itself*—but no longer the mere concept of consciousness. Rather, it is a consciousness existing for itself, mediated with itself through *another* consciousness, namely through a consciousness whose nature it is to be connected to independently *existent* things or thinghood as such. The master relates to both these elements: to a *thing* as such, to the object of desire; and to the consciousness for which the thinghood is what is essential. And since (a) as the concept of self-consciousness, the master is the immediate relation of *being-for-self*, yet (b) at the same time, as mediation or being-for-self which is for itself only through another, he relates (a) to both, immediately, and (b) mediately to each through the other.

The master relates to the slave *mediately* [i.e., indirectly] *through the independently existing thing*—for it is this by which the slave is held. This is his chain, from which he could not abstract away in the struggle. And therefore this is what shows him to be not independent, and shows that he has his "independence" in thinghood.

The master, however, is the power over this thing—since he demonstrated, in the struggle, that it counts as no more than something negative. Since the master is the power over this thing, and the thing is the power over the slave, it follows that the master has thereby subjugated the slave.

Equally, the master relates to the thing indirectly, *through the mediation of the slave*. The slave, as consciousness in general, also relates to the thing negatively and overcomes it. Yet the thing is at the same time independent as far as he is concerned. For this reason, his negating activity does not permit him to dispose of it to the point of destroying it—which means that he merely *works* on it.

For the master, on the other hand, the *immediate* relation *becomes* (through the slave's mediation) the sheer negation of the thing, the *enjoyment* of it. What he could not attain in desire, the master now achieves: to dispose of the thing so as to satisfy himself in the enjoyment of it. Desire could not attain this, due to the independence of the thing. Yet since the master has placed the slave between the thing and himself, he is connected only to the non-independent aspect of the thing, and enjoys it purely. The independent aspect of the thing he leaves to the slave, who works on it.

] In both these elements the master gets his recognition through another consciousness. This consciousness is expressed (in these elements) as unessential—both in the working on the thing and in the dependence on a specific entity. In neither of these can consciousness achieve mastery over [contingent] being and arrive at an absolute negation of it.

Thus, there is the element of recognition, here, whereby the other consciousness annuls itself as being-for-self, and thereby does what the other does to it. The same is true for the other element, so that the action of the second party is the first's own action toward itself. What the slave does is actually the master's doing.

For the master, what is essential is only his being-for-self. He is sheer negative power, for which the thing is as nothing. Thus, his is the pure essential action in this relation. The slave's action, on the other hand, is not a pure action, but an unessential action. For recognition proper, however, the element is lacking whereby what the master does to the slave he also does to himself, and what the slave does to himself he also ought to do to the master. This therefore leads to a one-sided and unequal recognition.

] The unessential consciousness [of the slave] is here the object for the master, constituting the *truth* of the master's self-certainty. It is clear, however, that this object [i.e., the slave's recognition] does not match the master's concept [of himself], but rather that the object wherein the master achieved his mastery has become something altogether different from an independent consciousness. It is not an independent consciousness that is there for him, but rather a dependent consciousness, not a *being-for-self* certain of its truth. On the contrary, his truth is rather the unessential consciousness and its unessential activity.

[28] The *truth* of the independent consciousness is, accordingly, the *slave consciousness*. This indeed appears *outside* itself to begin with, and not as the truth of self-consciousness. Yet just as mastery showed that its essence is the opposite of what it wants to be, so slavery, in its culmination, becomes the opposite of what it is immediately: as a consciousness *repressed* into itself, it will retreat into itself and will turn to true independence.

[29] We have seen what slavery is, but only in relation to mastery. Yet it is self-consciousness, and we must now consider, accordingly, what slavery is in and for itself. To begin with, the master is the essential reality for the slave. Thus the *truth* (for the slave) is the *independent consciousness existing for itself*. But it is a truth that the slave has not yet grasped explicitly, although it is implicitly there for him. Slavery possesses *within itself* this truth of pure negativity and *being-for-self*—since slavery has this as part of its *experience*.

   Thus, the slave consciousness has known fear, not for this cause or that, nor for this moment or another, merely. Rather, the slave has feared for his entire being—because he has known the fear of death, which is the absolute master. In that fear, the slave consciousness was dissolved internally: he trembled in every fiber of his being, and everything stable was shaken.

   Now, this pure general movement, the absolute dissolution of everything that is permanent and solid—this is precisely the simple essence of self-consciousness, absolute negativity, *the pure being-for-self*, which is here implicit *in* this consciousness. This element (of pure being-for-self) is also explicit *for* the slave consciousness; to the master it is his object. Moreover, it is not merely this general dissolution as such; rather, in servitude it is brought about in *actuality*. That is, the slave consciousness, in its servitude, negates all attachment to natural existence in all its *particular* aspects, and he dismisses it by working on it.

[30] The feeling of absolute power, however, both in general and in the particular aspect of servitude, is only this dissolution *in itself* [i.e., implicitly]. And although "the fear of the lord is the beginning of wisdom," con-

sciousness is not thereby aware *for itself* that it is *being-for-self.* Yet in work it comes to itself. In the element that corresponds to desire in the master's consciousness, it did seem that the slave's lot was the unessential relation to the thing, since the thing retains its independence [as the slave works on it]. Desire has retained for itself the pure negating of the object and thereby the unmixed feeling of self. For this reason, however, this satisfaction is itself merely evanescent, since it lacks the *objective* aspect, *permanence.*

Work, on the other hand, is desire that is *limited,* evanescence *restrained,* in that it *gives shape* to things. The negative relation to the object becomes the *form* of the object and something *permanent,* since for the worker the object has independence. This *negative* middle-term, the formative *activity,* is at the same time *the individuality,* the pure being-for-self of consciousness—which, only in work, steps out of itself into the element of permanence. Thus, the working consciousness thereby comes to the view of independent being as *its own* independence.

1] The formative activity does not only have this positive significance, however, namely that the servile consciousness therein comes to see itself as *being* pure *being-for-self.* There is also the negative element of fear. For in giving form to things, the slave consciousness becomes aware of its own negativity, that its being-for-self becomes objective only insofar as it overcomes the existent *form* that stands opposed to it. Yet this objective *negativity,* is precisely that alien entity before which it had trembled. Now, however, the slave consciousness destroys this alien negativity and posits *itself* as such a negativity in the element of permanence—and thereby becomes *for itself* something *existing for itself.*

The slave consciousness sees the master's being-for-self as something *other,* something there only *for him* (the master). But in the slave's fear, the element of being-for-self becomes *his own.* And in the slave's formative activity [as well], the element of being-for-self becomes *his own.* He becomes conscious that he exists in and for himself. The form he gives to things in working, being *externalized* by him, is not something other than himself—for this form, too, is his pure being-for-self, which (as externalized) thereby becomes the truth for him. This rediscovery of himself becomes his own *sense of self* precisely in work—where that sense of self had heretofore appeared as *foreign* to him.

Both these elements—fear and service as such (along with the formative activity)—are needed for this reflection, and both of them in a universal sense. Without the discipline of service and obedience, fear remains merely formal and is not extended over conscious reality; without the formative activity of work, fear remains internal and mute, and consciousness does become self-consciousness. If consciousness is involved in formative activity without the initial element of absolute fear, then it is nothing more than an idle self-centeredness—since its form or negativity is not negativity *in itself*, and the slave's formative activity therefore cannot give him a consciousness of himself as essential being. If consciousness has not experienced absolute fear but only some moments of anxiety, then the negative element has remained external, and consciousness has not had its very substance touched by it, through and through. If not all the contents of the slave's natural consciousness have been shaken up, then that consciousness *in itself* remains in the realm of determinate existence [i.e., conditioned by external factors and thus not free]. The sense of self is thus a *self-will*, a freedom which nevertheless remains within the bounds of enslavement. To the extent that the pure form cannot become an essence for such consciousness, to that extent it is not a universal formation, an absolute concept (considered as something to be extended over the world of particulars)— rather, it remains nothing more than a skill that dominates some limited areas, not the universal power and the entire objective realm.

B. Freedom of Self-Consciousness:
Stoicism, Skepticism, and the Unhappy Consciousness

[32] For the independent self-consciousness, it is (on one hand) only the pure abstraction of the "*I*" that is its essence. And (on the other hand) when this abstraction is developed and finds differences in itself, this differentiation does not become an objective and intrinsic essence to it. Accordingly, this self-consciousness does not become an "I" that truly differentiates itself in its simplicity or remains identical to itself in its absolute differentiation. On the contrary, the consciousness that has been forced back into itself becomes an object to itself in seeing its own formative activity, as the form of the thing to which it gives shape—and at the same time, it sees the master's being-for-self as consciousness [i.e., sees in the master's consciousness his being-for-self]. For the servile consciousness as such, however, these two elements fall asunder—namely, the slave's own consciousness *of itself* as an independent object, and its consciousness of this object as being that of a consciousness (and this as its own essence).

Yet since *for us* (or *in itself*) the *form* given to the thing and the *being-*

for-self (Fürsichsein) are the same—and in the concept of the independent consciousness the intrinsic *being-in-itself (Ansichsein)* is consciousness—it follows that the aspect of *intrinsicality (Ansichsein)* or of *thinghood* (which acquires form through work) has no other substantiality than consciousness; and thus we have arrived at a new form of self-consciousness. That is, we have arrived at a consciousness that sees its essence as infinitude, or the pure movement of consciousness, which *thinks* or is free self-consciousness. For what we mean by *thinking* is not the *abstract "I,"* but rather the "I" that also has the significance of being *intrinsically* what it is *(Ansichsein)* as its own object, relating to its objective essence in such a way that it has the significance of the *being-for-self (Fürsichsein)* of consciousness existing for consciousness.

For in *thinking*, the object does not move in [visualized] representations or shapes, but in *concepts*—that is, in a differentiated intrinsicality *(Ansichsein)* which is immediately there to consciousness and is not differentiated from it. That which is *represented*, or *given shape, existent* as such, has the form of being something other than consciousness. A concept, however, is at the same time something *existing (Seiendes)*—and this difference, insofar as it is in the concept itself, is its determinate content. Yet in this fact, that this content is at the same time conceptual, consciousness remains *immediately* aware of its unity with this determinate and differentiated entity—not as in the case of representation, where consciousness has to be reminded that this is *its* representation. Rather, the concept is for me immediately *my* concept. In thinking, I *am free*, that I am not part of another. On the contrary, I am straightforwardly with myself, and the object which is the essence for me is my being-for-self in undivided unity. And my conceptual movement is a movement in myself.

In determining this form of self-consciousness, however, it is essential to keep this in mind, namely that this is a *thinking* consciousness *above all*, that its object is an *immediate* unity of *being-in-itself (Ansichsein)* and *being-for-itself (Fürsichsein)*. The very same consciousness that repels itself from itself becomes for itself an *intrinsically existing (ansichseiendes) element*. But it first is this element for itself only as a general entity as such, not as this objective entity in the development and movement of its manifold being.

3] As we know, this freedom of self-consciousness was called *Stoicism* when it first made its appearance in the history of spirit. The principle of Stoicism is that consciousness is a thinking entity, and that something has reality for consciousness (or is true for it or good for it) only insofar as consciousness relates itself to it in thinking.

[34] Desire and work are directed at life, in its many-sided and self-differentiated extent, its detail and complexity. This multifarious activity has now drawn itself together into simple distinctions which are the pure movement of thought. What is most essential now is not the distinction that sees itself as a *determinate thing*, or as a *consciousness on the part of a determinate natural entity*—e.g., as a feeling, a desire and its goal (whether posited by *one's own* or *an alien consciousness*). Rather, the only distinction that is essential now is the one that is *thought* of, and as such is not differentiated from myself, the thinker.

This consciousness is therefore negative with regard to the relation of master and slave. The activity [of the Stoic consciousness] in the master is aimed at not having his truth in a life that is slave-like; and in the slave, the aim is not to find its truth in the will of the master and in his service. Rather, whether the thinker be on a throne or in chains, the aim of his thinking is to be free of all dependence on his individual existence, and to maintain himself in a lifeless withdrawal from the movement of life, from activity as from passivity, into *the simple essentiality of thought.*

Self-will is [seen as] the freedom that attaches itself to a particularity and remains *within* the bounds of slavery. Stoicism, however, is the freedom that always steps directly out of particularity and returns to the *pure universality* of thought. As a universal form of the world-spirit, Stoicism could appear not only in a time of universal fear and slavery, but also in a time of general culture that had risen to the level of thought.

[35] Now for this self-consciousness, the essence is not in something other than self-consciousness, nor is it in the pure abstraction of the "I," but rather in the "I" that has its otherness within itself (but as a difference that is thought of), so that in its otherness it has directly turned back to itself. Yet despite all this, its essence is at the same time merely an *abstract* essence.

The freedom of self-consciousness is *indifferent* to natural existence, and therefore has *equally let this go free.* The *reflection* is *twofold.* Freedom in thought has nothing but *pure thought* as its truth, a truth that lacks the concrete fullness of life. This freedom is therefore the mere concept of freedom, not its living reality—since for this freedom, it is only the *thinking* in general that is the essence, the form as such, which has retreated from the independence of things to go back into itself. But since the aim had been to show that in the realm of action individuality is really alive, and in the realm of thought to grasp the living world as a system of thought—so it had to be in *thought itself* that the extension had to be found that could provide the *content* of good (as applying to action) and the true (as applying to thought). This was so that *throughout what is present to consciousness*, there would be no other ingredient but the concept, which is the essence. And yet since the concept, as *abstraction*, retreats from the multiplicity of things, it has *no content of its own* but only a content that is given to it. Consciousness indeed destroys the content as an *alien* entity, by thinking it. Yet the concept is a *determinate* concept, and this *determinacy* is what is alien to it.

Stoicism was therefore faced with an embarrassment when asked for what was called the *criterion* of truth as such, i.e., actually the *content of thought itself*. To the question of *what* is good and true, Stoicism's answer was again a *contentless* thought: The true and the good are to consist in reasonableness. Yet this [tautological] self-identity of thought is once again merely the pure form in which there is nothing determinate. The true, the good, wisdom, virtue—which are the general terms Stoicism is left with—are therefore generally uplifting, to be sure; but since they cannot actually lead to an extension of content, they soon become tedious.

5] This thinking consciousness—having determined itself as abstract freedom—is thus merely the incomplete negation of otherness. Having *withdrawn* from existence to go back into itself alone, it has not thereby achieved for itself the absolute negation of that existence. The content does indeed count for it as mere thought, but it also is *determinate* thought and therefore it is also determinacy as such.

7] *Skepticism* is the actual realization of that of which Stoicism was only the concept. It is the actual experience of what the freedom of thought consists in. This freedom is *in itself* negativity, and it must present itself as such. With the reflection of self-consciousness into simple thought about itself, we find that the realm of independent existence—the sustained determinacy that had stood over against that reflection—now in fact falls entirely outside the infinitude [of thought]. In Skepticism, what is now there, *for consciousness*, is the total unessentiality and non-independence of this "other." Thought now becomes the complete process of annihilating the existence of the world in its *many-sided determinacy*. And the negativity of free self-consciousness becomes, for itself, a real negativity toward this manifold configuration of life.

It becomes clear that just as Stoicism corresponds to the *concept* of the *independent* consciousness (which appeared in the master-slave relation), so Skepticism corresponds to the actual *realization* of that consciousness as the negative bearing to otherness, to desire and work. But although desire and work could not achieve the negation on behalf of self-consciousness, the polemical bearing toward the many-sided independence of things will nevertheless succeed, because it is as a self-consciousness already complete in itself that it turns against those things. More precisely, it will succeed because it is *thinking*, it is infinitude in itself, and for it the independent entities and their differentiations are nothing but evanescent quantities. The distinctions which, in the pure thought directed at itself, are nothing more than the abstraction of distinctions, here become the *totality* of distinctions—and all differentiated reality becomes a differentiation of self-consciousness.

[38] In this way, the *activity* in general of Skepticism and its *modes* have been delineated. It reveals the *dialectical movement* which is sense-certainty, perception, and understanding—as well as what is unessential in the relation of mastery and servitude, and what counts as *determinate* for abstract thinking itself. That relation comprises a *determinate* mode, in which moral laws are presented as commandments. The determinations in abstract thought, however, are scientific concepts wherein contentless thought is extended, appending the concept (actually in a merely external manner) to an independent reality comprising its content, and for which only *determinate* concepts count, even if they are pure abstractions.

[39] The dialectical as a negative process, as it immediately *is*, at first appears to consciousness as something that has consciousness at its mercy, as though it did not exist through consciousness itself. As *Skepticism*, on the other hand, that negative process is an element of self-consciousness, to which it does not merely *happen* that the true and the real vanish without its knowing how. Rather, the skeptical self-consciousness is in full certainty of its freedom when it allows that "other" to vanish, although it presents itself as real. Thus, the skeptical self-consciousness does away not only with the objective world as such, but also with its relation to it, since it is in that relation that the world counts as objective and is made objective. And therefore it does away with its own *perceiving*, as well as its

securing of what it is in danger of losing and the truth that *it itself determined* and *established*—i.e., when it indulges in *sophistry*. Through this self-conscious negation it secures *for itself* the certainty *of its own freedom;* it produces the experience of that freedom and thereby raises it to the level of truth.

What vanishes is the determinacy, the differentiation, which, whatever its manner or source, sets itself up as fixed and immutable. It has nothing permanent in it, and *must* vanish before thought—since for something to be differentiated means that it does not have its reality *in itself* but in another thing. Thinking, however, is the insight into the nature of the differentiated; it is the negating function, in its simplicity.

40] In the mutability of everything that would seek to stand secure before it, the skeptical self-consciousness thus experiences its own freedom—as self-given and self-maintained. For itself, self-consciousness is this *ataraxia*, the skeptical impassivity of self-thinking thought, the unchangeable and *genuine certainty of itself.* This self-certainty does not emerge from something alien whose complex development was stored up within itself and is a result of having that process of emergence behind it. On the contrary, consciousness itself is the *absolute dialectical unrest*, this mixture of sensuous and intellectual representations whose differences coalesce as their *identity* is again dissolved—for this identity is itself the *determinacy* in opposition to the *non-identical.*

Yet in all this, the fact is that this consciousness, instead of being self-identical, is nothing but a simply fortuitous disarray, the vertigo of an ever-self-generating disorder. Indeed, *this is how it sees itself,* for it itself produces and maintains this self-propelling confusion. Hence it also admits to this, to being an altogether *fortuitous, individual* consciousness—a consciousness that is *empirical,* directed by what has no reality for it, giving obedience to what has no essentiality for it, doing and bringing to realization what has no truth for it.

Yet all the same, while it takes itself in this way to be *individual, fortuitous,* and in fact an animal life and a lost self-consciousness, it also converts itself once again to a consciousness that is *universal, self-identical*—since it is the negativity that is the negation of all individuality and all difference. From this self-identity, or rather within itself, it falls back again into fortuitousness and confusion—since this same spontaneous negativity has to do solely with what is individual, and is occupied with what is fortuitous.

The skeptical consciousness is therefore this mindless oscillation, swinging from the one extreme of self-identical self-consciousness to the other extreme of the fortuitous, confused, and confusing consciousness. It itself does not unite these two thoughts about itself. *At one time*, it apprehends its freedom in rising above all confusion and all fortuitousness of existence; *at another time*, it equally admits again to falling back into the *unessential* and occupying itself with it. The skeptical self-consciousness allows the unessential content of its thinking to disappear, but in doing so it is the consciousness of something unessential. It affirms the absolute *disappearance* of the unessential, yet the *affirmation is there*, and this consciousness is the affirmed disappearance. It affirms the nothingness in seeing, hearing, etc.—and it itself *sees*, *hears*, etc. It affirms the nothingness of moral realities, yet makes them the power over its own conduct.

Its actions are always being contradicted by its words, and equally it itself has the twofold contradictory consciousness of its immutability and identity, yet of utter fortuitousness and of its non-identity with itself. Yet it keeps the poles of this self-contradiction about itself apart, and relates to the contradiction as it does in its purely negative movement in general. If the *identity* of the poles is pointed out to it, it will point to the *non-identity*, and if it is confronted by what it has just said, it will go back to affirming the *identity*. Its talk is actually like the squabbling of stubborn children, one of whom says A if the other says B, and then says B if the other says A, and who gain pleasure by contradicting *one another* but at the cost of contradicting *themselves*.

[41] In Skepticism, consciousness truly experiences itself as internally self-contradictory. Out of this experience there emerges a *new form* of consciousness, which unites the two thoughts Skepticism had kept apart. The thoughtlessness (on the part of the skeptical consciousness about itself) must vanish, since it is actually one consciousness having these two modes to it. This new form is thereby a consciousness that knows *for itself* the twofold consciousness of itself as self-liberating, immutable, and self-identical, yet absolutely self-confusing and misleading—and in this it is the consciousness of its own contradiction.

In Stoicism, self-consciousness is the simple freedom of itself. In Skepticism, this freedom is realized: it negates the other side of determinate existence, yet rather duplicates *itself* and is now for itself something two-sided. Accordingly, the duality which had earlier divided two individuals—the master and the slave—is now found within one consciousness. The duality of self-consciousness in itself, which is essential to the concept of mind, is thus present—but not yet its unity. And the Unhappy Consciousness is the consciousness of itself as dual, a merely contradictory being.

[2] This *Unhappy Consciousness—divided against itself*—must, in that one consciousness, therefore have the other as well—since its own contradictory essence is for it the content of the *one* consciousness. And thus it must immediately be driven out of each, while it imagines that it has succeeded in coming to a peaceful union with it. Yet its true return into itself, or its reconciliation with itself, will present the concept of a spirit which has come to life and entered into existence—because as one undivided consciousness it is already dual. That is, the Unhappy Consciousness itself *is* the seeing of one self-consciousness in another. It itself *is* both, and the unity of both is for it the essence of consciousness as well. Yet it does not grasp this *explicitly*, namely, that its essence is to be the unity of both.

[3] Since, at first, the Unhappy Consciousness is merely the *immediate unity* of both, yet regards the two as opposites, not as the same, it takes only one of them (i.e., the simple and changeless consciousness) as the *essence*; while it sees the other (i.e., the many-sided and changeable consciousness) as the *unessential*. From its viewpoint, the two are alien to one another. And because the Unhappy Consciousness is itself the consciousness of this contradiction, it sees itself on the side of the changeable consciousness and therefore sees itself as unessential. Yet as conscious of the changeless, or of simple essential being, it must likewise aim to free itself of the unessential—which means that it must free itself from itself.

For although it certainly sees itself as only changeable, and the changeless as alien to it, *it itself* is simple and is therefore changeless consciousness—which it is therefore aware of as *its* own essence, although in such a way that *it itself* does not see itself as being this essence. The position it assigns to both cannot therefore be that of mutual indifference—that is, it cannot itself be indifferent to the changeless. Rather, it itself is both of them, directly. And for the Unhappy Consciousness *the relation between* the two is a relation of the essential to the unessential, so that the latter is to be negated. But inasmuch as the two are equally essential to the Unhappy Consciousness and are mutually contradictory, that consciousness is merely the contradictory movement in which the opposite does not come to rest in its opposite, but only generates itself anew in it as an opposite.

[44] With this there is a struggle against an [inner] enemy, against whom any victory is a defeat, since what the one consciousness gains it loses in its opposite. The consciousness of life, of one's existence and activity, is merely the painful awareness of that existence and activity—since it is a consciousness of the opposite as the essence, a consciousness of one's own nothingness.

In raising itself out of this, it becomes a consciousness of the changeless. But this elevation is itself this consciousness [of the changeless, while undergoing change itself] and it is therefore the immediate consciousness of the opposite, namely of itself as a [changeable] individual. The element of the changeless, which enters into consciousness, is thereby touched by individuality, and is present only when it too is there. Thus, instead of individuality having been suppressed in the awareness of what is changeless, it comes forward in that awareness all the more.

[45] In this process, however, consciousness has the experience of just this *emergence of individuality in the changeless*, and of the *changeless in individuals* [i.e., of the particular in the universal, and vice versa]. Consciousness becomes aware of individuality *as such, in* the changeless essence—and at the same time it sees *its own* individuality in it. This is because the truth of this process is just the *unity (Einssein)* of this dual consciousness. *Above all*, however, *this unity becomes for consciousness such that the difference* between the two consciousnesses is the predominant element.

For consciousness, therefore, there are three ways in which the element of individuality is linked to the changeless: One way is for individual consciousness to come forward once again as opposed to the changeless essence, and it is thus thrown back to the beginning of the struggle, which remains the basic element of the entire relation. At another time, however, the *changeless* itself has the element of *individuality* attached *to it* (for consciousness), so that all individuality becomes a form of the changeless, and the totality of existence goes over into it. Finally, consciousness finds *itself* as this individual in the element of the changeless.

In the first instance, the changeless is (for consciousness) nothing but the *alien* entity that judges the individual. Since, in the second case, the changeless is a *form* of *individuality* itself, consciousness becomes, in the third case, Spirit, in which it has the joy of finding itself and becomes aware of itself—its individuality now reconciled with the universal.

46] What is presented here as the mode and relation of the changeless element, was given as the *experience* of the divided self-consciousness in its unhappiness. Certainly, this experience is not a *one-sided* process of *its own*, since it itself is changeless consciousness and therefore is an individual consciousness at the same time. The process is just as well a movement of the changeless consciousness, which appears as much in that movement as in the individual consciousness. That is because the process passes through these moments: one, the Changeless [God] is opposed to the individual consciousness in general; then, *qua* individual, the changeless is opposed to another individual consciousness; and finally, it is one with it.

Yet this consideration, insofar as it is ours, is out of place here—because until now we have had before us only the changeless element as the changelessness of consciousness. For that reason it was not the genuine changelessness, but was still burdened with an antithesis. That is, it was not the changeless, *in and for itself*, and therefore we do not know how that would conduct itself. All we know is that for the purposes of consciousness (which is our object here) the indicated determinations appear to the changeless consciousness.

47] For this reason as well, the changeless *consciousness* in its very form retains the character and basis of dividedness and being-for-self, as against the individual consciousness [which is united]. Accordingly, it is for the individual consciousness a [contingent] *happening*, that the element of the changeless takes on the form of individuality—just as it also merely happens to *find* itself opposed to it, and thus had this relation *through its own nature*. Finally, that this individual consciousness does *find itself* in the changeless—this seems to it as due in part to its own efforts because it itself is individual. Yet a part of this unity, in its origin and existence, seems due to the changeless—and the antithesis remains in the unity itself.

In fact, it is because the changeless has taken on a definite form that the element of the beyond not only remains but is more firmly secured. This is because, on the one hand, if the beyond seems indeed to have been brought nearer to the individual consciousness through the form of an individualized reality, it is, on the other hand, as an opaque sensuous *One* that it henceforth stands against that consciousness with all the stubbornness of something *actual*.

The hope of becoming one with this *One* must remain a hope, without fulfillment or present reality—for between the hope and the fulfillment there stands absolute contingency, fortuitousness, immobile indifference, and this lies in the definite form itself, the basis of hope. Through the nature of the *existing One*, through the actuality it has acquired, it necessarily happens that it has vanished in time, and having been remote in space it simply remains remote.

[48] If at first the bare concept of the divided consciousness was marked by the aim of overcoming its particularity and becoming the changeless consciousness, it henceforth strives to nullify its relation to the purely *formless* element of the changeless and to relate only *to the Changeless* as *formed.* Thus the *being-one (Einssein)* of the individual and the Changeless is from now on the *essence* and the *object* for this consciousness—just as in the bare concept it was only the formless, the abstract changeless that was the essential object. And the relation of this absolute division of the concept is what it must now avoid. However, the initially external relation to the formed Changeless as an alien reality it must now elevate to the absolute becoming-one *(Einswerden).*

[49] The process in which the unessential consciousness strives to achieve this oneness is itself *threefold*, according to the threefold relation that it will have to its informed Beyond: once as *pure consciousness;* another time as a *particular individual* relating to the actual world in desire and work; and finally as *consciousness of its own being-for-self.* We must now see how these three modes of its being are present and determined in that general relation.

[50] To begin, then, by regarding it as *pure consciousness:* the formed Changeless seems to pure consciousness to be what it is, in and for itself—although as such it has not yet come into existence, as we said. In order that it appear to consciousness for what it is, in and for itself, the effort must rather come from it than from consciousness. Thus, however, its presence is only one-sidedly due to consciousness, and for this reason—it is not perfect and genuine but rather remains burdened with imperfection, i.e., an antithesis.

[51] Yet although the Unhappy Consciousness is thus not in full possession of this presence, it has at the same time gone beyond pure thinking—insofar

as this is either the abstract thinking of Stoicism (which *ignores individuality* as such) or the merely *restless* thinking of Scepticism (which is in fact mere individuality in the form of unrealized contradiction and its restless movement). The Unhappy Consciousness has gone beyond both these. It unites pure thought and individuality, and keeps them united. But it has not yet risen to that level of thought *for which* the individual consciousness is reconciled with pure thought itself. Rather, it stands at the middle point where the abstract thought makes contact with the individual consciousness *as* individuality.

The Unhappy Consciousness *is* this contact, the unity of pure thought and individuality. And this thinking individuality or pure thought is also there *for* that consciousness—and the Changeless itself is in essence individuality. Yet the Unhappy Consciousness is not aware that this its object (the Changeless, which essentially has the form of individuality for that consciousness) is *its own self*, that it itself is the individuality of consciousness.

[52] In this first mode, therefore, wherein we regard it as *pure consciousness*, the Unhappy Consciousness does not *relate* itself as a thinking consciousness *to its object*. Rather, since it itself is *in itself* pure thinking individuality, and its object is this pure thinking (although their *interrelation itself* is not *pure thought*), it merely goes *toward* that thinking and thus it is *devotion*. Its thinking as such remains the discordant jangle of bells or a warm fog of incense—a musical form of thinking that does not get as far as the concept, the only immanent and objective mode of thought. This infinite pure inner feeling certainly does come to have its object, yet it is not grasped conceptually and therefore appears as something alien.

What we have, therefore, is the inner movement of *pure* heart, which *feels* itself, but as painfully divided. It is the movement of an infinite *yearning*, having the certainty that its essence is such pure heart, a pure *thinking* which *thinks* of itself *as individuality*—in the certainty that it will be known and recognized by this object precisely because the object thinks of itself as individuality. At the same time, however, this essence is the unattainable *Beyond*—elusive just as it is being grasped, or is already gone. It is already gone because it is in part the Changeless, which thinks of itself as individuality—and in it, consciousness thereby arrives directly at its own self: that is, at *its own self*, but as *the opposite to the Changeless*. Instead of grasping the essence, it merely *feels*, and falls back into itself. Since, in attaining itself, consciousness cannot keep at a distance from itself, it has grasped nothing more than the unessential (rather than the essence). Just as, on one hand, it grasps only its own divided existence while striving *toward itself in the essence*, so, on the other hand, it cannot grasp the "other" as *individual* or as *actual*. Wherever the "other" is sought it is not to be found, since it is meant to be a *Beyond* which cannot be found. When it is sought as an individual it is not a *universal* individuality that can be grasped in thought, not a concept, but rather as an *individual* which is there as an object, as *actual*. It is an object grasped in immediate sense-certainty, and for that very reason it is merely something that has already vanished.

Accordingly, consciousness can come only to the *grave* of its life, as its present reality. Yet since this grave is itself something *actual*, and nothing actual can be possessed permanently, the presence of this grave signifies a struggle which must be lost. Since experience shows consciousness that *the grave* of its *actual* changeless essence has *no actuality*—that the *vanished individuality* is no true individuality because it has vanished—consciousness will give up the search for the changeless individuality as something actual, or give up the attempt to hold to what has vanished, and only then is it capable of finding individuality as something genuine or universal.

[53] Above all, the return *of the feeling heart to itself* is to be taken to mean that, as an *individual*, it has *actuality*. It is the *pure* heart which—whether *for us* or *in itself*—has found itself and is inwardly satisfied. For although, as far as that feeling is concerned, its essential being is separated from it in its feeling, this feeling is, in itself, a feeling of *self*, having felt the object of its pure feeling—and this object is the feeling itself. It therefore presents itself here as self-feeling, as independently existing actuality.

In this return into itself its *second relation* appears to us, that of desire and work, which confirms for consciousness its inner certainty of itself, the certainty that it has attained for us by overcoming and enjoying an alien thing existing independently. Yet the Unhappy Consciousness *finds* itself to be merely *desiring* and *working*. It is not aware that what underlies this is its inner self-certainty, and that its feeling of the alien thing is this self-feeling. Since it does not have this inner self-certainty *for itself*, its inner life remains the fragmented certainty of itself. The self-confirmation it would have received through work and enjoyment is therefore equally *fragmentary*. Thus the Unhappy Consciousness must itself nullify this self-confirmation, in order that it may thereby find the confirmation of its own dividedness.

54] The actuality to which desire and work are directed is no longer a *nothingness in itself* for this consciousness, to be overcome and consumed by it. Like that consciousness itself, it is an *actuality broken* in two: From one standpoint it is in itself nothing. Yet from another standpoint it is also a sanctified *world*—the form of the changeless, since it has retained individuality in itself; and since as the changeless it is universal, its individuality has in general the significance of all actuality.

55] If consciousness were aware of itself as an independent consciousness, and the actual world were nothing in and for itself as far as that consciousness were concerned, then it would achieve a feeling of its own independence in work and enjoyment by virtue of the fact that it itself had nullified the actual world. But since this actual world has the form of the changeless as far as consciousness is concerned, it is unable to nullify it on its own. On the contrary, since consciousness gets as far as negating the actual world and enjoying it, this occurs for it essentially because the changeless itself has *surrendered* its [embodied] form and *leaves* it to consciousness to enjoy.

Similarly, consciousness on its part appears here as an actuality, but equally as internally fragmented. And this division presents itself in its work and enjoyment as divided between a *relation* to *actuality* or *being-for-self*, and a *being-in-itself*. That relation to actuality consists in the *changing* of it or the *working* on it, the being-for-self belonging to the *individual* consciousness as such. Yet in this relation it is also *in itself*: this aspect of intrinsicality belongs to the changeless Beyond, although in consciousness it comprises abilities and powers as gifts from an alien source, which the changeless likewise leave to consciousness to utilize.

56] Accordingly, consciousness in its activity involves a primary relation of two extremes: On one side it is actively *here*, confronted on the other side by a passive reality. The two are related to one another, although both have gone back into the changeless essence and thus stay what they are. From either side, only a superficial element is let loose to enter the interplay of motion between them.

The extreme of a [passive] reality is overcome by the active extreme. On its side, the [passive] reality can be overcome only because its own changeless essence negates it, repelling it from itself, and surrendering it to activity. The active force appears as *the power* wherein the [passive] reality is dissolved. For that reason, however, as far as this consciousness is concerned (for which the *intrinsic*, the essence, is something "other," its object), this power—making its appearance in the sphere of activity—is the Beyond of itself.

Thus instead of returning from its activity back into itself with the confirmation of itself, consciousness really reflects this movement of activity back into the other extreme, which is thereby presented as the pure universal, as the absolute power, from which the movement emanated in all directions—and which is the essence of the self-dividing extremes as they first appeared, *as well as* of their interchange itself.

[57] In that the changeless consciousness *renounces* its [embodied] form and *surrenders* it, while the individual consciousness gives thanks for it—i.e., *denying* itself the satisfaction of being conscious of its own *independence*, and assigning the essence of its activity to the Beyond rather than to itself—through these two elements of *reciprocal self-surrender* on the part of both, consciousness is certainly aware of its *unity* with the changeless. Yet at the same time this unity is affected by the division, again fragmented in itself, and from it there emerges once more the antithesis of the universal and the particular.

For indeed consciousness does renounce the *appearance* of satisfying its self-feeling, yet it does achieve the *actual* satisfaction of it—since it *was* desire, work, and enjoyment, because as consciousness it *willed, acted,* and *enjoyed.* Equally, its act of *giving thanks* (in which it acknowledges the other extreme as the essence and negates its own self) is *its own* act, which counterbalances the other extreme by meeting the other's self-sacrificing good deed with an *equal* act of its own. If the other offers only its surface [i.e., the outer side of its reality], this consciousness *still* gives thanks, by surrendering its action, i.e., its *essence*—and thereby it actually does more than the other, which merely sheds a superficial aspect of itself.

Thus the entire movement is reflected not only in the actual desiring, in the working and enjoying, but even in the giving of thanks, wherein the opposite seems to occur, in the *extreme of individuality.* Consciousness therein feels itself as this particular individual, and is not taken in by its own seeming renunciation—for the truth of the matter is that it has not really given itself up. What has come about is only the twofold reflection into the two extremes—and the result is the repeated division into the consciousness of the *changeless* and the opposed consciousness of willing, achieving, enjoying, and self-renunciation itself, i.e., the *independent individuality* in general.

[58] With this there has appeared the *third relation* of the movement of this consciousness. This proceeds from the second in such a way that it has genuinely proven itself independent through its willing and its accomplishment. In the first relation there was merely the *concept* of actual consciousness, or the *inner feeling*, which is not yet actual in its action and enjoyment. The second relation is this actualization as external action and enjoyment. Returned from this activity into itself, however, it is a consciousness that has *experienced* itself as actual and effective—a consciousness aware that its own being, *in and for itself*, is its *truth*.

Yet in this the enemy is revealed in his truest form. In the struggle of the emotions, the individual consciousness is nothing more than an abstract musical element. In work and enjoyment (where this unessential being is made real), this consciousness can directly forget *itself*—and its own *individual role* in this realization is suppressed by thankful recognition. Yet this suppression [of the individual role] is really a return of consciousness into itself, and indeed as the genuine reality for it.

[59] This third relation, in which this genuine reality is one pole, is the *relation* of that reality (as a nothingness) to a universal essence. The movement of this relation is yet to be considered.

[60] Let us begin with the relation of consciousness in its opposition, wherein it regards its *immediate reality* as a *nothingness:* What that consciousness does is a doing of nothing, and its enjoyment becomes a feeling of its misfortune. In this, the doing and the enjoyment lose all *universal content* and *significance*—for if there were such, they would have a being in and for themselves. Both retreat into the particularity to which consciousness is directed in order to negate them. Consciousness is aware of itself as *this actual individual* in its animal functions. These are no longer a matter of indifference, as nothing in and for themselves, performed without any special importance or essential significance for the spirit. Rather, since it is in them that the enemy shows himself in his characteristic form, they are really the object of earnest effort and they take on the greatest importance.

The enemy thrives on his defeat, however. And consciousness, in focusing on him, sees itself as permanently defiled, so that it remains involved with him instead of freeing itself from him. At the same time, it sees this content of its effort as the lowest instead of as something essential. It sees itself as the most peculiarly individual being, instead of as the universal—limited to itself and its small activity, brooding on itself, so that what we see is a miserable and impoverished personality.

[61] Yet to both these elements—the feeling of one's misery and the poverty of one's actions—there is equally linked the consciousness of one's unity with the changeless. Thus the attempt at the direct negation of one's own actual being is *mediated* by the thought of the changeless, and it occurs in this *relation* [to it]. The *mediated* relation comprises the essence of the negative process in which consciousness is directed against its own individuality—although as a *relation* it is equally positive *in itself* and will make consciousness itself aware of this unity with the changeless.

[62] This mediated relation is thus a syllogism, in which this individuality—at first fixed in its opposition to the *in-itself*—is connected to this other pole only through a third term. By means of this middle term, the pole of this unchangeable consciousness [i.e., God] becomes present to the unessential consciousness [i.e., man], just as the latter relates to the former only through this middle term [i.e., the church]. That is, the middle term presents these two to one another, serving each [i.e., ministering to each] as it relates to the other. The middle term is itself a conscious entity, for it involves activity which mediates consciousness as such. The content of this activity is the suppression of individuality, undertaken by consciousness.

[63] In this mediating element, therefore, consciousness frees itself from its activity and enjoyment, heretofore considered as *its own*. As one of the extreme poles existing *for itself*, consciousness rejects the essence of its *will*—and it throws upon the mediating element or its servant [i.e., priest] the role and freedom of decision, along with the *responsibility* for action. This mediator—who is considered to have a direct connection to the Changeless Being—serves by *advising* of right [so far as doing or willing are concerned]. One's action, with respect to one's doing or *willing*, ceases to be one's own, since it follows from the decision of another.

There still remains the *objective* aspect of action, for the unessential consciousness, namely the *fruit* of its labor and the *enjoyment* of it. These are equally rejected by consciousness—and as it renounced its own will, so it renounces the *reality* it has won in its work and enjoyment. That is, it renounces them, partly on the basis of the truth that it has gained of its own self-conscious *independence* (to the extent that what moves here is something utterly strange, speaking and representing what is senseless to it), partly as *external property* (in giving up something of the possession acquired through work), and partly as the *enjoyment* it has had (in denying itself that enjoyment through its fasting and mortification).

64] Through these elements of surrender—first, of its own right of decision, then of property and enjoyment, and finally through the positive element of carrying on what it does not understand—it truly and completely denies itself the consciousness of inner and outer freedom, of reality as its own *being-for-self*. Consciousness has the certainty of having truly alienated its own "I," and of having made its immediate self-consciousness into a *thing*, an objective entity.

The self-renunciation could be demonstrated only through this *actual* sacrifice. For only in this way does the *deception* vanish that rests on the *inner* acknowledgment of gratitude through heart, sentiment and word. This is an acknowledgment that indeed disavows for itself all the power of an independent existence and ascribes it to a gift from above. Yet in this disavowal itself, it nevertheless retains for itself its *outer* identity in the possessions that it does not give up, its *inner* identity in the awareness of the decision that it itself has made—and in the awareness of its own content, which it itself has determined, which it has not exchanged for something foreign to it, which would be meaningless for it.

65] Yet in this sacrifice actually achieved, consciousness has nullified its *action* as its own and has thereby achieved, *in principle (an sich)*, the remission from its *unhappiness*. That this remission has happened [only] *in principle* is due to the action of the other pole of the syllogism, the self-existing Being (*ansichseiende Wesen*). Yet that sacrifice on the part of the unessential pole was at the same time not a one-sided action, but rather contained within itself the action of the other pole. Thus the surrender of one's own will is negative from only one aspect: According to *its concept* or *in itself*, it is at the same time positive—namely in positing one's own will as the will of the *other*, and decidedly of a will that is not individual but rather universal.

From the standpoint of this consciousness, the positive significance of the negatively posited individual will is the will of the other pole—which, precisely because it is "other" for it, becomes present to the Unhappy Consciousness not through itself but through the action of the mediator in the role of counselor. For *consciousness*, accordingly, its will certainly becomes a universal will, existing *in itself*—yet *it itself* does not regard itself as this *in-itself* (*aber es selbst ist sich nicht dies Ansich*). The surrender of its own will, as *individual*, is not in line with its concept of what is positive in the universal will. Similarly, its surrender of possession and enjoyment has merely the same negative significance—and the universality which thereby becomes present to consciousness is not regarded as its *own doing*.

This *unity* of objectivity and being-for-self lies in the very *concept* of action [although it is not that concept itself], and it thereby becomes for consciousness the essence and *object*. Just as, for consciousness, this unity is not the [whole] concept of its action, so this unity does not actually become an object for consciousness directly through its own effort. Rather, it permits the mediating minister to express this fragmented certainty: that only *implicitly*, or *in principle* only, is its unhappiness the opposite (i.e., its activity a self-satisfying activity or blissful enjoyment); that likewise its impoverished action is only *implicitly* its opposite (i.e., an absolute action); and that according to the concept of action, it is only individual action that is action at all.

For consciousness itself, however, its own actual activity and activity as such remain impoverished, its enjoyment remains pain—and the overcoming of these is [already] a *Beyond* in a positive sense. Yet in this object—wherein its activity and being (as belonging to this *individual* consciousness) are being and activity *in themselves*—consciousness has become aware of *reason*, of the certainty that in its individuality it is absolute *in itself*, it is all reality.

2

HEGEL'S SUMMARY OF SELF-CONSCIOUSNESS FROM THE "PHENOMENOLOGY OF SPIRIT" IN THE *PHILOSOPHICAL PROPAEDEUTIC* (1809)

Translator's Note: In preparing this translation, I have consulted the 1841 edition. The paragraph numbers are of that edition.

22] As self-consciousness, the I regards itself; and the pure expression of this is "I = I," or: "I am I."

23] This statement of self-consciousness is without any content. The motive of self-consciousness is to realize its concept, and in all things to give itself a consciousness of itself. Accordingly, it is active: a) in overcoming the otherness of objects and equating them with itself; b) in externalizing itself from itself, thereby giving itself objectivity and existence. The two are one and the same activity. The becoming determined of self-consciousness is at the same time a self-determination, and vice versa. It brings itself forward as object.

24] In its development or movement, self-consciousness has three stages: a) Desire, insofar as it is directed at things other than itself; b) the relation of mastery and slavery, insofar as this self-consciousness is directed at another self-consciousness that is unequal to itself; c) the universal self-consciousness, which recognizes itself in another self-consciousness and indeed as its equal, just as that other self-consciousness recognizes the first as equal to itself.

Desire

[25] Both aspects of self-consciousness—the positing and the negating—are thus immediately united with one another. The self-consciousness asserts itself through the *negation of otherness* and is *practical* consciousness. Thus, if in the actual consciousness—which is also called the *theoretical*—the determinations of itself and of the object were to be altered *in themselves*, this now occurs through the activity of consciousness itself and is there *for* consciousness. Consciousness is now aware that this negating activity belongs to it. In the concept of self-consciousness there lies the determination of the as yet unrealized difference. Insofar as this difference puts itself forward at all in it, self-consciousness has the feeling of an otherness within itself, a negation of itself—or, the feeling of lack, a *need*.

[26] This feeling of its otherness contradicts its identity with itself. The *felt necessity* to overcome this antithesis is the *drive*. The negation or the otherness presents itself to it as consciousness, as something external to it, different from it—yet as something that is determined through self-consciousness: a) as *commensurate* with the drive, and b) as something *negative in itself*, whose subsistence is to be posited as negated by the self and as identical with it.

[27] The activity of desire thus transcends the object's otherness in its subsistence, and unites it with the subject, whereby the *desire* is *satisfied*. Accordingly, the desire is conditioned as follows: a) through an external object, indifferently juxtaposed to it, or through consciousness; b) its activity achieves its satisfaction only through the nullification of the object. Self-consciousness thereby arrives only at its *self-feeling*.

[28] In desire, self-consciousness relates to itself as *individual*. It relates itself to a selfless object that is, in and for itself, something other than self-consciousness. This self-consciousness thereby arrives at its identity with itself in respect to the object, only through the nullification of the object. As such the desire is: a) *destructive*; b) in its satisfaction it therefore arrives at nothing more than the self-feeling of the subject's being-for-itself as individual—at the indeterminate concept of the subject in its connection to objectivity.

Mastery and Slavery

[29] The concept of self-consciousness as that of a subject that is at the same time objective, implies the relation whereby there is, for self-consciousness, another self-consciousness.

[30] A self-consciousness that exists for another is not there as mere object for the other, but as *its other self.* The I is no merely abstract universality, in which (as such) there is no differentiation or determination. Thus, inasmuch as the I is object for the I, it is (according to this aspect) the same as what it itself is. In the other it sees itself.

[31] This self-regard of the one in the other is a) the abstract element of *self-identity (Diesselbigkeit);* b) yet each one also has the characteristic of appearing to the other as an external object—and to that extent as an immediate, sensual, and *concrete existent;* c) for itself, each is absolute and individual toward the other, and also demands of the other (as absolute and individual) that it be such and count as such for the other, so that each can see in the other its own freedom as that of an independent being— i.e., to be *recognized* by the other.

[32] In order to make itself count as *free* and to become recognized as such, the self-consciousness must present itself to the other as *free of natural existence* [i.e., independent of its life]. This element is as necessary as that of the freedom of the self-consciousness in itself. The absolute identity of the I with itself is in essence not something immediate, but rather something that makes itself such through the nullification of its sensual immediacy, and thereby presents itself to an other I as free and independent of the sensual world. It thereby shows itself to be equal to its concept and it must be recognized because it gives reality to the I.

[33] Yet *independence* is not so much the freedom *from* (and external to) the sensual, immediate existence, but rather a freedom *in* that existence. The one element is as necessary as the other, although they are not of the same value. To the extent that the element of *inequality* enters (so that for one of them what counts as essential is freedom vis-à-vis sensual existence, while what counts as essential for the other is that sensual existence rather than freedom), what enters into the determinate reality, along with the shared desire for recognition, is the relation of *mastery* and *slavery* between

the two—or that of *service* and *obedience*, to the extent that this difference in independence prevails through the immediate relation of nature.

[34] Inasmuch as, in two juxtaposed self-consciousnesses each must strive to show himself toward and for the other as an absolute being-for-self—the one who enters into *slavery* is the one who *places life over freedom* and thereby demonstrates that he is not capable, on his own, of abstracting from his sensual existence in favor of his independence.

[35] This purely negative freedom, which consists in the abstraction from natural existence, does not correspond to the concept of freedom—for this is self-identity in otherness, partly of the intuition of oneself in the other self, partly of freedom, not from existence but in existence as such, a freedom that itself has existence. The *one who serves* is *selfless* and his selfhood is in an other self, so that he alienates himself in the master as an individual I, and is nullified and sees his essential self as an other. The *master*, on the other hand, sees in the servant the other I as nullified, and sees *his own individual will as maintained*. (See the story of Robinson Crusoe and Friday.)

[36] The servant's own individual will, regarded more closely, dissolves itself however in the *fear of the master*, in the inner feeling of his negativity. His *work* in the service of an other is an *alienation of his will:* Partly it is so in itself; and partly it is (along with the negation of his own desire) the positive *forming of external things* through work, by means of which the self converts its own characteristics into the form of things and regards itself as objectified in its work. The alienation of *unessential caprice* constitutes the element of true obedience. (Pisistratus taught the Athenians obedience, thereby introducing the laws of Solon into reality; and after the Athenians had learned this, a master was superfluous for them.)

[37] This alienation of individuality as self is the element whereby self-consciousness makes the transition to the universal will—the transition to positive freedom.

The Universality of Self-Consciousness

[38] The universal self-consciousness is in the regard of itself as not something particular, differentiated from that of another, but rather as the self-exis-

tent *universal self.* In this way it recognizes itself and the other self-consciousnesses in itself, and is recognized by them.

39] In accordance with this its essential universality, the self-consciousness is real for itself only insofar as it knows its reflection in the other (I know that others know me as themselves)—and knows itself as *essential self*, as the pure spiritual universality of belonging to one's family, one's homeland, etc. (This self-consciousness is the foundation of all virtues, of love, honor, friendship, courage, all self-sacrifice, all fame, etc.)

PART II

A DISCUSSION
OF THE TEXT

by

LEO RAUCH

3

WHAT IS "SELF-CONSCIOUSNESS"?:
AN OVERVIEW

How do we arrive at self-consciousness? What is its peculiar content? Why is self-consciousness necessarily conflicted? We might try to answer these questions from the standpoint of psychology (in terms of one of its ortho-doxies or another)—but that would lead us away from the direct *experi-ence* of self-consciousness itself. In order to grasp that experience, our approach must be phenomenological rather than psychological. That is to say, in addressing ourselves to these questions in psychological terms, we would be considering one or more causal factors external to self-con-sciousness—e.g., stimuli producing certain attitudinal responses; the action of the superego, etc.—and while such factors might or might not "explain" self-consciousness satisfactorily, we would still be far from hav-ing grasped it in descriptive terms, as lived. To do this, we must direct our attention to the structure of self-consciousness, as experienced; and in illuminating our experience in this way we would be revealing its univer-sal features.

Hegel speaks of phenomenology as a "science of the experience of consciousness." In phenomenological terms, what would turn us to *self-* consciousness would have to be something internal to consciousness, some problematic aspect of experience that would lead us to think about our thinking, to be conscious of our consciousness itself. This is rather out of the ordinary, almost an anomaly in the natural order. For if it is natural for consciousness to be directed "outward," at anything but itself, then there would have to be something disturbing indeed to get us to direct our gaze inward, at ourselves.

For Hegel, what leads us to thinking about ourselves is that we are puzzled by our immediate experience, especially in trying to delineate the reference to the words *this, here,* and *now.* These index-words (the term is Gilbert Ryle's) are peculiar because they are reflexive: *this* refers to whatever I am pointing to when I utter the word *this; here* refers to whatever place I am at or in when I utter the word *here; now* refers to the moment at which I utter the word *now,* and so on. We can see that "I" plays a crucial role in all this; and indeed, "I" is itself an index-word, referring to whoever happens to be uttering the word *I.* That self-reflecting function is the key to the problematicity of "I"—as well as of self-consciousness in general. For here it is "I," the knower, who am the known.

In phenomenological terms, therefore, our initial puzzlement about our immediate experience leads us to turn inward to question ourselves. And then, having embarked upon this self-consciousness, the problematic feature is that the thinking *subject* is also the *object* of our thinking. One can almost feel, here, the tension between the freedom of the subject and the fixity it tries to impose upon the object that is itself, in trying to know it. And yet the "I" is neither of these, neither subject nor object, in any fixed way, but oscillates between the one pole and the other.

That is why Hegel speaks of consciousness as "the absolute dialectical unrest." It is therefore difficult to define—if definition is a way of putting an idea to rest. It is also difficult to define because of the dialectical aspect: Self-consciousness is not a static thing like a faculty, but rather a process, variable in content and form, and free to generate conflict, even contradiction. Indeed, it *must* generate them if it is fully active. A succession of thoughts that are self-aware must go that road.

Self-consciousness is infinite, not only in its freedom but in its complexity. How, then, is this infinitude to be defined? How is the unlimited to be given limits? Self-consciousness itself is ultimately also the resolution of contradiction. Such resolution *should* be one of the main functions distinguishing self-consciousness from consciousness in general. If so, this reveals a further dialectical aspect: Self-consciousness is the source of paradox, and it is also where such paradox makes its peace. Yet we shall see that such "resolution," although fervently aimed for, is not attainable by self-consciousness.

In addition, self-consciousness is the basis of selfhood; it is where selfhood is registered. This is problematic as well—which is why Kierkegaard adopts the Hegelian locution to say, cryptically: "The self is a relation which relates itself to its own self." Cognition normally takes its object as something "other" than consciousness. How, then, can it turn back upon itself and know itself as not other? As we shall see, it is this very paradox that generates selfhood and civilization, in Hegel's view.

Hegel says that such paradoxical self-return is emblematic, not only of self-consciousness but of all spiritual activity: The human spirit projects itself out into the world and returns to itself by way of thought, culture, and society. Spirit works its way through consciousness, self-conscious-ness, various social forms, and art, religion, and philosophy (where it comes home to full self-awareness). Self-consciousness, in its going out and return, is therefore the microcosm of the entire cultural world.

But let us go back to a more primordial stage: the "subject" beginning to see itself as "object." At one point, it will leave its inertness and become associated with the idea of Life. As Hegel says: "Through this reflection into itself, the object has become *Life*." With this, there will be introduced a dynamic, developmental aspect. That is, the mind's own concern with itself and with its processes will make this leap necessary. But there is a fur-ther leap, when Hegel abruptly replaces the abstract "object" with a living object that is *another* conscious (and indeed *self*-conscious) subject!

The reason for this second transition is entirely phenomenological: Self-conscious selfhood begins to see itself as the basis of its life. Since its experience is fluid, it tries to see itself as the stable center of life: i.e., that center as the self-conscious subject itself. But the self has not yet found its security in this. Its self-questioning is very disturbing. I therefore turn to another individual for aid and comfort, so that the "other" (as the ordi-nary object of the knowing subject) now becomes an "Other" (as a rival consciousness, another self having its *own* sense of being the center of its experience). Yet there cannot be two selves, *each* of whom is the center of the experienced world. I therefore deny *you* the place of subjective cen-trality of *my* world.

Thus, I gain and enhance my sense of self through opposition to another self. Indeed, selfhood must be an adversary relation at this pri-mordial stage. Here, Hegel presents a model of an interpersonal relation, and sees a pattern of culture emanating from it. The struggle for identity, through clash and combat, becomes the theme of all subsequent history. The interpersonal relation is marked by conflict because the selves involved are conflicted to begin with. But in addition, there is the very real struggle between the two—a struggle to the death. I am willing to risk my life in order to achieve recognition for myself as person; you are ready to do the same. This is because my objectification of you is resisted by you. You see yourself from within, as subject, not as "object" (thing) for another. Likewise, I will resist your objectification of me. This standoff is the aboriginal source of conflict, the struggle for freedom that is exemplified in history and is replicated at all levels. The aboriginal struggle is embodied in the Master-Slave scenario.

This microdrama can be seen as a retelling of a quasi-Hobbesian state-of-nature story. But in phenomenological terms, it is the passage from innocence to experience. With its conclusion, the conflict over selfhood is internalized. Culture is the ultimate response to this inner conflict. This is a strange and provocative view of culture—and, as a phenomenological account, it is at variance with Hegel's quasi-metaphysical view of Spirit manifesting itself in the world. Rather, the microdrama of Master and Slave stems from a clash of egos, and as such it represents a necessary stage in the growth of self-awareness; and this depends on one's view of oneself as free Subject, while one sees the other as unfree Object. This occurs for no psychological reason, but solely for the phenomenological reason that one *is*, necessarily, the center of one's own relatedness to the world. I attempt to make that centrality independent of everything, even independent of my life—and that is why I am ready to put my life at risk. One of us wins in this struggle; yet the loser cannot be killed, for then the victor would be denied the recognition he wanted. The victor therefore allows the loser to live, but enslaves him.

The Slave now has no alternative but to internalize his sense of self: Nothing in the outer world offers any support for his ego. With this internalization, the ego curls inward, only to recoil outward in forms as varied as Stoicism, Skepticism, and that medieval Christian worldview Hegel calls the Unhappy Consciousness. Culture therefore proceeds by way of the Slave.

What the two had struggled over was recognition—nothing more than a matter of ego. Yet this is a deadly serious thing, and the struggle had to be a struggle to the death since we achieve personhood only at the risk of life itself. *Each* one wanted to be recognized as person, and each one knew that his own personhood must crowd out the other's. Ego, selfhood, personhood, recognition—these, then, are the "materials" of all subsequent culture.

The struggle to the death is resolved in favor of life. The fact that the victor lets the vanquished live, but enslaves him, is a symbolic reflection of the fact that Life is the ultimate residual continuum. No matter what our struggles are, and death-bound though we are, the life-context that is culture survives us all. But that Life retains the elements of the struggle—along with the persistent vectors toward liberation or enslavement.

Our two aboriginals have come a long way: From abstract epistemological puzzles, they have begun the discovery of selfhood; they have gone into and out of a life-and-death combat, and into the formation of a primordial minisociety involving only the two of them. Moreover, these steps are shown to be the dialectically necessary stages in the evolution of consciousness. Self-consciousness, then, is not a benign advance. On the contrary, it introduces an element of strife that we will never be free of. We have emerged out of Nature and have entered the realm of Spirit. The return to Nature (the inert, the "in-itself," without self-consciousness) is an enticing dream, but it is an impossibility. That humanization (via self-consciousness), once attained, is irreversible.

We said that culture proceeds by way of the Slave—because he embarks upon a series of internalizations that manifest themselves externally. First, he must tell himself that, despite everything, he is a free soul in his heart and mind. Since he finds no ego-support in the outer world, he must seek that support within. Again, this happens for phenomenological, rather than psychological, reasons: Since his earlier attempt at selfhood has been thwarted, he is driven inward, to find selfhood there. The driving element is not some psychological force, but the press of logical necessity. Thus, the internalization and its contents are the dialectical outcome of the ego struggle itself.

Once the Slave has told himself that although he is enslaved he is nevertheless free in heart and mind, this view is externalized as Stoicism: I now see all values as subjective creations, ego-relative. Recognition by another is now seen as an illusory goal. Now it is I who bestow personhood upon myself. The difference between being a master and being a slave is also seen as illusory, since I now see both of us as sharing in "mankind." Yet the Slave remains enslaved, and so his concepts of "mankind" and "inner freedom" remain abstract; the external circumstances of his life are never negated entirely. That is why the Slave (as an egological prototype) must proceed to a higher resolution, Skepticism. Here, the entire world—with all its social standards and political arrangements, etc., along with the entire gamut of human possibilities—is rejected as being unknowable, unreal, without value. Thus the knowing ego is utterly detached from the world, and in that sense is free. Yet in rejecting the world as unreal and valueless, we render all our action in that world unreal and valueless as well. Thus, every gain is a loss: We have detached ourselves from the world, yet our selfhood is not any the more secure—and in our hearts there is nothing left beating but doubt.

Because all this is so unsatisfactory, the Slave goes over into Christianity. And yet these doubts go with him. Christianity is therefore as much a projection of these doubts as it is a "resolution" of them. That "resolution," as it turns out, is neither satisfying nor complete; for if it were, there would be no impetus toward the further spiritual progress that actually does take place after medieval Christianity has run its course. As it happens, the medieval worldview that Hegel calls the Unhappy Consciousness is such that its contradiction is irresolvable. This is because *in essence* that consciousness is divided against itself. And that is because the earlier duality—externalized in the Master and Slave—is now internalized in the one Christian psyche. Yet it is more than this that produces the division.

Consider this: Christianity is an attempt at reconciling that spiritual division through the mediation of a divine Spirit that has come into the world and has become human. Yet this produces the further division whereby the self-consciousness of the believer sees itself in the self-consciousness of another (the God-become-man). This leaves the consciousness of the believer feeling so much more inadequate and incomplete—and consequently unhappy. Therefore, the so-called "mediation" leaves the believer as remote as ever from the desired fulfillment—and the gap between man and God is greater than ever.

For example, if we try to characterize spirit as such, and we say that the very essence of spirit is its immutability—i.e., the unchanging realness that is the nature of God—then the human spirit sees only its own mutability, the endless changes and variations that render its own life unessential and unreal. The same sort of inequity plagues this consciousness in countless other ways. Whatever is ascribed to God is denied to man—and we can feel, here, a foreshadowing of the Feuerbachian statement: "In order that God may be everything, man must be nothing." In this respect, the Christian self-consciousness undergoes an unending struggle in trying to assert itself while it negates itself. Christianity is a "critical" religion—in the literal sense of the Greek word *krisis,* which is judgment. The self-judgment and self-struggle are intertwined. All this is an echo of the aboriginal struggle earlier on, except for the ironic reverberation in the fact that the previous struggle did end, while this one (involving two sides of one psyche) cannot find a way out. In this combat of self-consciousness with itself, therefore, every victory is a defeat.

The reason for all this is phenomenological, not theological. That is to say, the psychic division exemplified in Christian consciousness stems from the paradoxicality of self-consciousness itself: The fact that the ego has made itself the object of its own awareness—this is the source of the division and contradiction. As self-conscious subject-and-object it is free and yet determined, particular and also universal, mutable although eternal, and so on. Indeed, this seems so inescapable a feature of human self-consciousness that we now can see a phenomenological justification for positing a God: If it is inevitable that I am free and yet determined, mutable although eternal, etc., then I will conceive of a God who is immutable and eternal, and so on—as a way for *me* to overcome, vicariously, the division I see persisting within me.

This self-division is as far as self-consciousness can go (short of making way for a higher Reason). And this is why self-consciousness here *must* be unhappy. It sees and feels its own problematicity mirrored everywhere around it—and it lacks the Reason that would allow it (self-consciousness) to construct its own resolution to the problem. For the time being (i.e., the medieval Christian era), self-consciousness is overcome by the Changeless God on one side, and by the undervalued and changing world on the other—and both are seen as diametrically opposed to the essence of self-consciousness itself.

In time (and in the realm of logical transition), the troubled stage that is self-consciousness will give way to Reason. The bipolar tension we saw, in the relation of self-consciousness to God (on one side) and to the world (on the other), now drops off—and then the *individual* consciousness is seen as in itself the Absolute Essence. It is then that Reason can enter, because with the focus on the individual consciousness we come to see how the psyche constitutes its world—and even God! Only then does man himself begin to be the supreme being, and man's reason begins to feel its dominion of the world. Only then will the human spirit begin to find itself reflected in the world, as it sets about making its world as rational and as real as spirit itself now is. (Hegel does not stop here. Reason will have a career all its own—and then it will give way to yet another stage, which Hegel calls Spirit; this will have even more complex and bizarre configurations when Hegel takes it through phases such as the Enlightenment and the French Revolution.)

The theme that unites the "Self-Consciousness" chapter is that of alienation. This underlies self-consciousness itself from beginning to end. To begin with, there is a marked ambivalence, for the Master and Slave, in regard to the *thing*. The Master appropriates what he does not himself produce; the Slave produces but does not possess the thing he works on. Hegel believes that the Slave's work is, in effect, a form of liberation—and I shall be discussing that point later on, to show that it is mistaken. In any case, the Slave is *not* free to reject the thing, and therefore his labor is an incomplete negation of it. On the other hand, the Master has separated himself from all meaningful work by putting the Slave between himself (the Master) and the natural world of things. This means that each one is alienated from the world in his peculiar way.

As we have seen, the subsequent cultural forms—Stoicism, Skepticism, and Christianity—only extend that alienation. What they urge (in their various ways) is our separation from the world. But such separation can never be a conquest of the world. In one way or another, that conquest is what the ego has been aiming for. Yet to tell itself that it does not need the world, that the world is illusory, or that there is a God-man who has transcended the world altogether if we cannot—all these are false "conquests." We can see, here, the negative roots of these cultural forms: they are ways of getting back at the world for what it has done to us (as Slaves).

The idea that Christianity is the product of the Slave mentality is repeated by Nietzsche, with the idea that Christianity is the outcome of "the slave-revolt in morals." The difference is that Hegel foresees no Master mentality to supplant it (since the Master needs none of the brooding sensitivity produced by internalization). Nietzsche, as we know, sees Christianity as the product of the slave's *ressentiment*: As his revenge upon the world of power, the slave makes the world tolerable by using Christianity to emasculate it. For Hegel, on the other hand, it is the Slave's Christianity that emasculates him, the result being "the feeling of one's misery and the poverty of one's actions." Despite their differences, however (as phenomenology vs. psychology), the views of Hegel and Nietzsche are remarkably close. What they share is the nineteenth-century preoccupation with the theme that our creations (God, culture, political society, art) come to dominate us and to make creatures of us. We find this theme in *Frankenstein*. We find it in Goethe's *Faust* (line 7003): "Am Ende hängen wir doch ab von Kreaturen die wir machten" ("At the end, we are dependent upon the creatures we have made"). The idea is the same in Marx's discussion (in the 1844 Paris manuscripts) of the alienation involved in the work process. For Hegel, the only resolution of this bizarre fact is in the advent of Reason. Only when *we* are shown to be fully responsible for our world can we see ourselves as being free to change it. The fact that the more recent changes the world has undergone have been depraved, even pathological, should indicate that the world and our egos still have some distance to go before the Rational becomes the fully Real.

4

ON HEGEL'S AIMS AND METHODS

There are two places in his book where Hegel gives us a capsule-statement of what he takes the phrase "phenomenology of spirit" to mean: In his Introduction, it is the "science of the experience of consciousness" (*Wissenschaft der Erfahrung des Bewusstseyns*). On the last page of the book, he speaks of phenomenology as "the science of knowing [in the sphere of] appearance" (*die Wissenschaft des erscheinenden Wissens*). Now, a science aims at certainty; yet experiences and appearances are contingent, anything but certain. The crucial issue, then, is the questionable certainty of that science vis-à-vis the contingency of experience, i.e., appearance.

This is a question Hegel comes to grips with in his Preface and Introduction. Directly and indirectly, he raises the question concerning the extent to which our knowledge can achieve a grasp of the absolute. It seems that the psyche is more elusive the closer we get to it. In one sense, the challenge is to find a *Ding-an-sich* that is *not* unknowable. For Hegel, this challenge is met—in the view that phenomenology is precisely the science wherein we come to know the mind *in itself* through the study of its outer manifestations. These "outer Manifestations" are thought patterns, interpersonal relations, cultural configurations, and other expressions of the human spirit—here studied in the ways they follow from one another in their logic, as *essences*. Phenomenology is, in other words, the study of the noumenon which is penetrable, nothing less than the noumenon as phenomenal!

65

We are being asked to *see* phenomenologically, and this begins with an element of doubt regarding our ordinary mode of cognition. Ordinarily, we presuppose that there is a "distance" between the knower and the known. Here, that presupposition is placed in abeyance, since the knower *is* the known, the subject is the object of his own knowing.

Yet in order to arrive at this stage, i.e., self-consciousness, we must detach our "object" from our latent presuppositions concerning "distance." We must also detach it from what we usually take as "explanation"—i.e., an account that is given in terms that are causal, deterministic. Thus, we must suspend our reliance on the "evidence" presented in such terms. As phenomenologists, therefore, we begin with a skepticism toward the entire range of phenomenal experience as *usually* understood. It is this skepticism that sets us to examining our experience for its truth. Yet this means that phenomenology is beset by the unavoidable difficulty of having to reject phenomenal knowledge (qua knowledge), while taking its experiential content very seriously indeed.

In Hegel's phenomenological approach, then, both the "external" world *and* our knowledge of it fall within the sphere of consciousness. Instead of conceiving of an "independent" world to which our consciousness must conform in its knowing, we now see that it is consciousness itself, in its self-subsistence, to which both our consciousness and our world must conform. Thus, consciousness itself becomes the standard by which it measures that which it knows.

Even if we try to think of an object as independent of consciousness, as it is in itself, that "in-itself" is already there *for* consciousness. The true, then, for Hegel, is the being-for-consciousness of the in-itself. This seems to be an equivocation, as though we are speaking (epistemologically) of the actual subjectivity of what we mistakenly think of as objective. Yet Hegel is not a Humean phenomenalist. From the fact that the transcendent world (i.e., transcendent of the stream of consciousness) is posited in an act that is immanent to consciousness, it does not follow that the transcendence itself is *dependent* upon that immanent act. Rather, if the true is the being-for-consciousness of the in-itself, then the result is an object of a new sort, one that excludes from our consideration all reference to the in-itself status of the object, so that we may then see how our experience has modified the object (which is unquestionably there). As Hegel says, "It is what experience has made of it."

Hegel is not out to replace earlier philosophies as though this were to replace error with truth. Rather, he thinks of himself as standing at the end of a development in which each previous philosophical standpoint is a moment of the whole. As a new science, however, phenomenology can lead to one or another extreme, an overemphasis of form or of content—and he sees a danger in the fact that the one extreme can exist without the other. Such polarization could lead to a formalism that remains unfulfilled, or a contextualism which remains formally unfounded. Without the completion of the formal foundation, he says, the various contexts amount to little more than repetitions of bald formulae—so that the unfounded contextualism is a formalism of sorts, a mass of data in a "monochromatic formalism."

Hegel claims that his approach achieves a synthesis in which the true is seen not only as *Substanz* but also as *Subjekt*. We might ask whether this is at all a phenomenological (as distinct from a metaphysical) synthesis. *Substanz* embraces the immediacy of knowledge as well as being *for* knowledge. In this, he addresses the great mystery of how the ego acts to posit and project a world as something other than itself. He suggests this in the concept of self-alienation—"the mediation of self-othering with itself" (*die Vermittlung des Sichanderswerdens mit sich selbst*). This is but one half of the total process Hegel has in mind, however, for he asks that we show how the self returns to itself by negating the otherness of the constituted world. The circular movement of self-alienation and its negation, along with the completion of formal by means of contextual syntheses—all this is epitomized by him in the principle that "the true is the whole" (which is an attempt at combining the phenomenological with the metaphysical).

What Hegel offers, therefore, is the systematic knowledge of how the world can be the creation of the human spirit. We begin by abandoning the idea of the simple thereness of the world (as independently existing), along with the attitude that sees it as devoid of spirit. Rather, science is to provide us with the means by which we may see spirit as world-constituting. Yet first we are shown a series of configurations that consciousness must go through as the detailed history of the education of consciousness, now brought to the standpoint of science.

This is not a mere refinement, to be added casually onto the body of scientific knowledge. We can see the importance of this point if we consider the relation inhering in the traditional dichotomies of world vs. thought and nature vs. spirit: In this outlook, ideas and thoughts are not a part of the natural order. In looking at things and thinking about them, we take them out of their immanent environment. Thinking is an intrusion, an interruption of the natural context. Hegel says thought is the power of the negative, of the pure "I." It is understanding wrenched out of its ordinary connection to the world, undergoing a death, yet thereby attaining Truth.

In the modern era, we have no trouble in coming up with abstract thoughts, as Hegel points out. We find abstractions everywhere around us. They are fixed and solid, and they can be volatilized only when we relate them to the ego that posits them—so that the abstractions are thereby made to take on the unconditioned character of the ego itself. Thus, the notion of the ego is what our universal science must take account of, and what makes such a science complete.

Our relatedness to the "outer" world occurs "within" the ego, by means of an "internal" act that posits its object as "other" than itself. Hegel sees this as an antithesis, especially in the fact that the elements of that antithesis are themselves the shapes of consciousness. Not only is the so-called objective world to be seen as the work of the constitutive ego, the ego is itself to be made the object of its own observation. The ego thereby becomes an "other" to itself. Yet it suspends that otherness—just as, in reverse, we live in a world of objects whose otherness we begin with, take as given, and must neutralize, so that we may thereby return to the ego that constitutes them. (I have used, here, the terminology of twentieth-century phenomenology; yet I do not regard Hegel's phenomenology as very far removed, in aim, from the phenomenology of more recent times.)[1]

We can say, therefore, that for Hegel the phenomenological problem is impelled by the metaphysical dichotomy between ego and world. This dichotomy (like all others) is to be overcome. The path of elucidation is to show how the ego fashions its world. The same holds true for the dichotomy between essence and existence. The essential *is* the actual, and thus contains existence within its concept. This is human consciousness in contact with itself—and here, fulfillment involves essence qua existing.

Here, then, is where philosophy and phenomenology can be seen to coalesce for Hegel—namely in the characterization of philosophy as a *process* that both begets and surpasses its productions, and comes to see them as moments in the movement towards ultimate truth. The half-truths are, in Hegel's view, necessary and essential elements of the truth. His conception of philosophy requires this, and in his view phenomenology is to display this in actuality. We have, then, the philosophic truth as the goal as well as the partial truth on the way to it—which he so vividly characterizes as a bacchanale. Accordingly, Hegel's program (as presented in the Preface) can be seen as philosophic in its remote and final links, but phenomenological in the means to that end.

Any phenomenological discussion must eschew two poles: metaphysics and psychology. Hegel does not entirely succeed in avoiding them. The proposed aim of seeing Substance as Subject can fall prey to either of these extremes. Indeed, we can say that in Hegel it is the tension exerted by these two that acts as an antidote to both—and keeps his discussion in the middle area, which is phenomenology. We avoid the extremes when we return to the knowing self as the true self-identity *in* otherness.

Hegel embraces the metaphysical idea that the self-identity of a thing is in the fact that its being is in its concept *(in seinem Sein sein Begriff zu sein)*, and to see in this the logical necessity of it. Yet this is the material of speculative philosophy, and he admits that this carries only an anticipatory, not a complete, assurance. The suggestion is that we *can* avoid metaphysics and psychology, and that the only assured path is in phenomenological exposition and the display of concepts in their concrete evolution—as "the detailed history of the education of consciousness . . ." *(die ausführliche Geschichte der Bildung des Bewusstseins)*.

We thereby use the self as a hothouse of ideas, a microcosm of culture wherein we allow ideas to develop in their essential and implicit ways—without editing or interfering with them, but only observing their careers in nonhistorical time. Such self-restraint is part of the concept itself, he says, and the conceptual content of truly dialectical thinking consists in the return to the subject. All this is phenomenological in tone and method—the philosopher's ego serving as the proving ground of humanity in its self-education.

5

BEFORE "SELF-CONSCIOUSNESS"

In focusing our attention on the fourth chapter alone of Hegel's *Phenomenology* we are doing something un-Hegelian. If "the True is the whole," then it can hardly be correct for us to extract one chapter from its wider context, especially as that context is important and revealing on its own account.

Each of the chapters concerns a stage of human awareness. As such they are interconnected, each one emerging from the one before and leading to the one after. Even more to the point, each stage presents a distinct conflict in awareness, and every such conflict is resolved in the stage that follows. Thus, our chapter IV is to be seen as the resolution to the problem posed in chapter III, and as presenting the problem to be resolved in chapter V.

For any *one* part of the *Phenomenology* to be treated adequately, then, we would have to have a book discussing all of the *Phenomenology*. But I suppose we could extend that principle and say that the *Phenomenology* itself ought to be discussed only in the context of Hegel's entire body of works—if we are aiming at any measure of adequacy in our discussion. However that may be, we shall be discussing chapter IV alone, and we shall try to make up for the missing context by considering some ideas leading up to, and following from, that chapter.

The first two chapters—which are included under the general heading of "Consciousness"—display the problematic nature, the conflicted character, of ordinary "sense-certainty" and perception. Thus, for example, I perceive *this* table, yet that perception has that meaning only because I perceive the table as being a member of a class called "table." Every noun (other than a proper noun) refers to a class of objects. How, then, can the specific aspect, the "thisness" of the table be expressed in language, if the only terms available express such generality? One way of answering this question is to say that the term "table" refers to a universal form. This is of little help, however, since the universal is unconditioned. Nor do we usually see the part we ourselves play in conditioning it. As Hegel says, consciousness does not yet recognize *itself* in its intellectual object.

Only when we look upon all this from a higher viewpoint do we become aware that our consciousness is involved in the development of its intellectual object. This is not grasped at the level of ordinary perception, the level at which we are immersed in the immediacy of experience. Nor, we might add, is it grasped at the level of philosophical perception if the philosopher seeks to give the universal an objectivity such that his own consciousness plays no part in creating it (Plato). For Hegel, this is "consciousness still retreating from what has emerged, so that this is the essence for it as objective." The content of thinking, here, is the objective essence, not consciousness as such. We are still at the level at which we assume that there is an insuperable dichotomy between the knower and the known, between subject and object. We do not as yet recognize the world as the product of our own thinking and making. That is, we do not yet see that the *self* is the *truth of everything*, as Hegel declares.

Ordinary consciousness may well have arrived at an intellectual understanding of the world, but it is not yet the understanding in which consciousness actually sees itself participating. It stands aside and watches itself, as a thing apart but not in the light of its creative activity. We may have got so far as to posit the difference between form and content, or between a unifying whole and a many-sided multiplicity. Yet one side of every such distinction merges easily into the other and back again—and this is the sort of fluctuation that marks thinking that is merely abstract. Throughout this process the two sides (of any distinction you may wish to think of) are distinct yet identical. All this is the display of an underlying force, or perhaps an inner being of things, but it is not yet an objective opposition. We therefore see that such abstract intellectual distinctions do not succeed in establishing the reality of what it is they distinguish; on the contrary, they introduce an element of unreality into the world.

For related reasons, the independence we ascribe to universals (in our abstract way of looking at them) is a spurious independence. The universal ought first to be seen as a human creation, and only then as independent, i.e., with the personal aspect having been overcome. So long as this difficult step has not been taken, what we see is merely a multiplicity of universals, nominally independent of one another but not objectively independent of our thinking. We see their multiplicity, but we also see them as part of a domain of universality. That is, we see them as diverse but also as unified—so that we undergo an incessant to-and-fro motion in our thinking, from diversity to unity, and back.

In our becoming aware of this motion, we are led to posit a psychological "force" (another abstract concept), which seems to govern the intellectual movement from diversity to unity and back. That force is seen as expressing itself by going outside itself and yet remaining self-enclosed. We see the difference in the movements, yet we see one force persisting behind them all. Force, then, is another unconditioned universal, and we can give it almost any content we please: It is difference *and* identity, it is being-for-another *and* being-in-itself. (This is why the concept of Force fails to serve our needs, and why we must eventually reject it.) What we have to see, first, is the independent self-identity of that force, and only then can we see it as self-differentiating. Only then do we see the two movements as aspects of *one* force, coming out of itself *and* going back into itself *at the same time* (as in, e.g., consciousness expressing itself and returning to itself in its self-expression)—i.e., these are movements independent of one another, yet overcoming the difference between them to achieve unity.

What all this signifies is the objectification of subjective activity. And what is problematic in this, as Hegel sees it, is that the subject and the object, or the perceiver and the perceived, are a unity and yet are distinct. We may see them united as aspects of one force, and yet the force itself is disunited by extending itself into these two poles. The result is that we see the movement between them as not genuinely objectified, but merely as the inner aspect of things (and this marks a failure to resolve the problem).

The objectification of subjectivity is what our chapter IV is all about. In chapter III, Hegel reflected on some inadequate attempts to do just that, as with the concept of a Force, conceptualized as expressing itself, yet as self-contained. The point is, however, that this division is itself a part of the Force. In the same way, the materiality upon which it acts is supposedly outside it, and yet this too is part of Force, the unconditioned universal. These distinctions oscillate in this way because they are abstract. Ultimately, they will be made concrete in something as real as an interpersonal relation—and this we see in chapter IV.

So long as these different and conflicting aspects are all of them a part of the one Force, the concept has not yet emerged from its purely conceptual form. Moreover, since the concept splits so easily into opposed aspects, we see that as a concept this Force is not the unifying entity we might have thought it to be. Thus, there is an element that "solicits" Force, and there is the Force being solicited *(sollizitiert)*—both, again, aspects of the supposedly unifying Force. These two disparate aspects are mutually determining and yet opposed. They seem to be mutually independent, yet they turn out to depend upon one another. Each is *other* to the other, yet each is its own self and is Force itself. Here we have the epitome of the Hegelian dialectic: two entities opposed to one another, yet identical to one and the same thing. This appears to violate the Law of Contradiction, and Hegel's critics have made much of this. Yet when Hegel says that A is both A and not-A, he is not giving the same denotation to the two A's, and thus there is no contradiction here; the seemingly opposed terms are not actually opposed. Each *is* what it is through the other, so that each is not what it appears to be in itself. The differences collapse into a unity—but this unity is nothing more than a concept, and moreover a concept that (since it is inadequate) is there to be superseded.

In the light of these apparent contradictions (and others that are real), we are driven back into ourselves. We try to see the contradiction as *there*, but we also come to see it as the mere appearance of things, something on the surface. What we must decide is whether we will take the appearance as *all* there is. On the level of appearance, we see things becoming their opposites. But this leads us to consider consciousness itself as the mover and shaper of the antithesis—and here we approach being-for-self. We do not as yet arrive at that being-for-self, however, since we have not yet grasped that concept.

In turning to ourselves, we conceive of a real world beyond the appearances, a world of permanence beyond change—and this is taken to be the essential nature of things. Yet in conceptualizing such a realm, we have a concept that is empty of content because (as Hegel says) consciousness does not yet find itself in it. Since such a "realm" is beyond the concrete world, it is also beyond consciousness. It is the empty void of the mystics, a supersensible Beyond, a spiritual vacuum that could be filled by anything we like. Yet that supersensible Beyond is now supposed to have come into being, and although it is posited as being beyond appearance its content is precisely that appearance. Hegel emphasizes the point that this is not a grasp of the concrete empirical world, but rather the supersession of that world in favor of an "inner" world. How concrete is it? It too is empty, in-itself, universal—at least for the time being. Here again we have an incessant oscillation of contraries—a tennis game without a net, ball, rackets, or players, yet with spectators turning their heads back and forth! All determinations become their opposites, and we shuttle from one side to the other. What we have is mere difference and flux without content. Opposed to this flux there is the concept of scientific or philosophic law, as "the stable image of unstable appearance" (*dem beständigen Bilde der unsteten Erscheinung*). In this light, the supersensible world is "a tranquil realm of laws" (*ein ruhiges Reich von Gesetzen*) that is beyond the perceived world as well as present in it.

To some degree all laws are indeterminate—which is why there must be an indeterminate number of them to cover the full diversity of appearances. This *multiplicity* of laws thwarts the *unity* that our understanding seeks in setting up a system of laws. There is a tendency toward economy: one law is to cover the greatest number of phenomena. But what such a law gains in generality it loses in specificity, until the law is so general that it becomes identical to the concept of law itself. Thus laws have opposed tendencies toward unity and diversity. This can lead to a polarization such that the two extremes are indifferent to one another. What unites them is the understanding, which embraces the differences. But in this, the understanding introduces the element of necessity, which we might be tempted to see as a subjective product, or something merely verbal. Thus, we tend to reduce all phenomena to these "subjective" principles in what is taken as explanation. But since this is nothing more than the understanding feeding upon itself, as it were, the explanation is tautological and empty.

From another point of view (shared by Hegel) this can be seen in a positive light: Since, as it turns out, self is the truth of everything, all explanation involves (at least implicitly) the self-consciousness that constructs both the *explanandum* and the *explanans*. As Hegel says, explanation is consciousness communing with itself, enjoying itself—and although it seems to be concerned with an "object" it is in fact occupied only with itself!

For both these reasons (the negative and the positive), the so-called objectivity we are after is a spurious objectivity after all. We are still enmeshed in subjectivity at this stage (i.e., prior to Self-Consciousness), primarily because we are not as yet aware of the part played by subjectivity. The element of self-consciousness (better: the *stance* of self-consciousness) has not yet fully emerged. That is, we do not as yet know how to account for the role of subjectivity in the formation of *our* "objective" view of the world. We have not as yet achieved the reconciliation of objectivity as such with objectivity as "ours." For this reason, the distinctions fashioned by the theoretical understanding are spurious distinctions. Because the understanding is merely partial rather than all-embracing, its distinctions are artificial, false. As Hegel says, "differences arise which are no differences." Once again we see the mark of such artificiality in its oscillation: "like becomes unlike and unlike becomes like," and supposed differences cancel each other.

To all this, there is another possible response. It is the view that besides the all-inclusive tranquil realm of laws there is yet another realm—an intelligible realm containing the distinctions set up by the understanding. Since the first realm is inadequate to contain all there is in the phenomenal world (in all diversity *and* unity), we must posit another realm, which is the opposite to the first. Yet in opposing the first, this second realm is an "inverted world." The first realm had no place for change and alteration; the second makes a place for it, but in inverted form (i.e., so that what is permanent in the one is impermanent in the other, what is real in the one is illusory in the other , etc.).

The theme of the "inverted world" is discussed at length and much illuminated by Gadamer.[1] The general problem Hegel addresses is to show how consciousness becomes self-consciousness—and this is where such "invertedness" comes in. Hegel shows that we cannot merely begin with our consciousness of the objective world, expect that consciousness to satisfy our explanatory needs, and then expect that consciousness to turn its attention automatically to self-consciousness and *become* self-consciousness. This is because consciousness is individual and subjective, and what we must find is a way of overcoming both the individuality and the subjectivity if we are to arrive at a genuine objectivity. That is, we are to show why consciousness *must* lead to self-consciousness—but that "must" is logical, not psychological (i.e., deterministic). Because consciousness is intrinsically problematic, its problematic character can be resolved (logically) only in self-consciousness, in a logical supersession of consciousness as a level at which we function.

Hegel's itinerary, then, begins with the ordinary sense-certainty we enjoy with regard to physical objects, to show such "certainty" to be riddled with conflicts. The conflicts are not merely implicit, immanent, but manifest themselves, so that we become aware of them and we are led to try to overcome them. We therefore go from sense-certainty to a consideration of perception, only to encounter further conflicts. This leads us to a consideration of the Understanding. It is in this third stage that we posit a theoretical entity such as Force, but this too is conflicted (as we saw).

What we must do, then, is to return to the world of appearance, but to see it *as* appearance, not as the epiphenomenon of a deeper force. Nor is it to be seen as appearance as opposed to reality, but appearance is seen as real. From the world of appearances we extract the concept of law. If such law is "the stable image of unstable appearance," opposed to appearance, then it is inadequate to encompass it—since, as stable, it cannot account for change. Where Plato finds the phenomenal world inadequate in approximating the pure forms, Hegel finds the forms (laws) inadequate to embrace the phenomenal world. This is why we need an inversion of the formal realm of laws, i.e., a world in which change and development are now realities. That inverted supersensible world now contains the phenomenal world, but inverts it as well. That is, the phenomenal world is inverted (or perverted: *verkehrt* has both meanings) because no instance is a pure case of a law, as Gadamer reminds us. Indeed, the vital reality of an instance, or phenomenon, consists precisely in the perversion of law. But in its perverse character, the phenomenon turns to itself, back into itself—and this (in my view) is the turn that is executed by consciousness in its becoming self-consciousness. The inversion is ontological, but it is also the key to a process that is epistemological.

As Gadamer points out, Hegel does not intend "inversion" to be construed as "wrongness." What he means by inversion is the dialectical reversal, so that the true world is not the tranquil realm of laws but precisely the reverse, the untranquil sensible world of change. And from that reversal we go back to say that the *super*sensible world, too, is precisely that mutable world!

Thus, the Platonic division between the intelligible and the sensible worlds no longer obtains. We have *one* supersensible world driven back upon itself—as both the law *and* its "perversion" in concrete instances. It is that inverted world that exists "above" the appearing world—as a theoretical construct adequate to contain the phenomenal. But that is not the end of the matter. The Platonic division between the intelligible and the sensible worlds leads directly to the Platonic dichotomy between the universal and the particular. According to Plato, the particular entity "participates" in the universal, yet the line between the two realms is decidedly a division: the one is real, the other illusory. For Hegel, that division is itself illusory, the product of mere theoretical Understanding; higher Reason will overcome these distinctions, so that we *see* the universal in the particular, the particular in the universal. Christianity has embodied this in symbolic terms: God becomes this particular Man. In this, the dichotomy is in some ways overcome, but not in terms that fully satisfy reason. What philosophy must do (by way of phenomenology) is to see the dichotomy overcome entirely, and in terms expressive of the higher insight of Reason, so that the universal *is* the particular, and the particular is grasped *as* universal.

Self-consciousness is the arena in which that overcoming takes place: here we achieve the reinversion of the inversion, and with this we overcome all other dichotomies. It is on these grounds—i.e., in view of the operation of self-consciousness—that Hegel rejects the Platonic juxtaposition of the intelligible and the sensible. As Hegel says, the true supersensible world contains both the intelligible and the sensible, and by *its* dividing itself into this opposition it relates itself back to itself—and yet (or thus) is one. The inverted world *is* the real world, relating itself to itself and differentiating itself from itself—which is precisely the characteristic activity of self-consciousness!

6

SELF-CONSCIOUSNESS AND SELF-CERTAINTY
(Para. 1–12)

Self-consciousness carries with it a set of problems (even contradictions) all its own. On one hand, it would seem that in being conscious of myself I have the opportunity of knowing what no one else can know, or know as well. Thus, consciousness *of* consciousness would seem to guarantee a degree of certainty achieved in no other form of awareness. On the other hand, it is precisely the element of self-reference that introduces the factor of *un*certainty: in self-consciousness, the object is identical to the subject, yet is distinct from it. The self is (paradoxically) the relation to the self; but (even more paradoxically) it is the negation of the self. As Hegel says, "The ego determines itself insofar as it is the relating of negativity to itself."[1]

How, then, can we argue for any sort of *certainty* in connection with self-consciousness? It will not do to say that self-consciousness has a *degree* of certainty relative to consciousness in general, and a greater uncertainty with respect to pure reason. We must not think the answer comes in saying that we now have a "greater" certainty in comparison to what has gone before, but that we have not as yet attained the degree of certainty that characterizes what lies ahead—as though there were an uninterrupted and graduated continuum. On the contrary, what Hegel aims to show is that there is a quite determinate certainty attached to self-consciousness in itself—despite the problematicity that must lead us to subsequent (i.e., higher) stages of consciousness.

In the *Phenomenology* the broad heading of "Self-Consciousness" comprises only the fourth chapter: "The Truth of Self-Certainty." The two titles have the same reference (i.e., the same set of pages), but do they also have the same meaning? What sort of certainty is involved here?

There are numerous ways in which self-consciousness differs from consciousness in general. For one thing, consciousness in general involves an object that consciousness relates to as something other than consciousness, and such objectivity is to that extent impersonal; self-consciousness, on the other hand, not only has consciousness itself as its object, but that consciousness is its own. It is *in* that consciousness *of* itself that it grasps its personhood. Moreover, the so-called *sense*-certainty about ordinary objects is problematic, conflict-ridden and not certain at all; *self*-certainty, on the other hand, seems secure because consciousness has directed itself to its own activity. Turned outward to the world, consciousness cannot find its footing; turned inward, it has certainty since it knows itself as nothing else—and as it can know nothing else!

When we direct our attention to external objects and are "certain" of them, we take them to be what they are in themselves. Yet this "taking" (the German word for "perceiving" is *Wahrnehmen*—literally, "taking [for] true") is a *mis*taking: the supposed object in itself is only what it is for another, the Perceiver. The erstwhile "certainty" must therefore give way to truth. Hegel has expressed this in the formula: "Self-consciousness is the truth of consciousness."[2] Not only does this mean that the contradictions of ordinary consciousness are here overcome; it also means that the "certainty" of ordinary consciousness is here shown up as a *false* certainty. (This is another feature of the "inverted world.")

In self-consciousness, however, certainty is identical to truth. This certainty itself is now its own object, thereby providing its own truth. Here the known object corresponds to the concept by which it is known: consciousness qua object (i.e., for another, for the consciousness that knows it) is identical to what it is in itself. The knowing "I" is the knower *and* the known.

If all this seems paradoxical, it is nothing less than the paradoxicality inherent in all self-consciousness per se. As we saw, the self *is* nothing but the relation to the self (a thought echoed by Kierkegaard at the beginning of *Sickness Unto Death*). That is, the self *is* self-awareness. Of course, the self will seek to overcome this paradoxicality about itself by trying to base its selfhood on recognition by another, so that the other person bestows my selfhood upon me. Thus, the two sides of the individual have become two individuals (a leap that Hegel makes no attempt to justify). Yet this means that the self is not merely a self-relation but an adversary-relation: the recognition of oneself requires the recognition of others; my recognition of another involves the recognition of difference; the recognition of difference leads to the question of who is superior, who will dominate; and this leads to a test by open conflict, a life-and-death struggle.[3] In theory, then, self-consciousness is complete in itself. In practice, it looks for support elsewhere, and in seeking support it finds strife.

There are further elements of paradox. As we saw, the ordinary perception of objects involves both the particularity and the universality of the object. (*This* table is *a* table, i.e., an instance of a type.) There is also "the empty inner" (*das leere Innere*) of the understanding, whereby its content entails vacuity, at least the vacuity of passive receptivity as an aspect of its activity. Moreover, as we saw, its positing is a negating. All these elements of ordinary consciousness, problematic as they are, are carried over into self-consciousness and become even more problematic there. (Thus, what happens if I say that *this* consciousness of mine is *a* consciousness? Can I *experience* it as an instance of a type? And can I genuinely speak of an empty inner, here?) Hegel sees these distinctions as abstractions that have no reality *for* consciousness itself, but he does see them as persisting into self-consciousness as residues, and (moreover) as residues that have become formidably substantial.

His way out is to see self-consciousness as a *process* whereby we return to ourselves from the experience of otherness—otherness being superseded in the tautology, "I am I." Yet that tautology is itself to be superseded because of its abstractness. It is superseded by the concreteness of the life-process, which embraces consciousness *and* the world, subject and object as one.[4] In the ordinary mode of consciousness, the object is otherness; here it is unity (the subject *is* object). And now the former difference between knower and known is no difference; the unity becomes explicit.

Yet in that unity there is duality, since self-consciousness also has the world as object while it has itself as object. But just as consciousness has turned back to itself, the world too has turned to itself—at least in our eyes. We ascribe to it that same autonomy we accord to ourselves, when we think of the world as ongoing life. *Life* therefore stands opposed to oneself and to one's self-consciousness. The growth of self-consciousness therefore entails a heightening of this opposition. Life looms in one's awareness as one becomes more *self*-aware. One sees one's own independence—but one also sees it increasingly limited by the independence of everything and everyone else. Yet in my own independence, stemming from my return to myself, I achieve a self-reflection that amounts to infinitude.

This infinitude is the motionless center of all else revolving around it. As such it overcomes all differences—even though the components of those differences persist as entities independent of consciousness! Indeed, it is their independence that lends to self-consciousness an independence of its own as a self-contained movement. Juxtaposed to this, there is the constant movement of life, taking one shape after another and presenting the material upon which consciousness is to act. Life is an incessant process of expression, of differentiation and consumption, of fragmentation and coalescence, of inertness and formative activity—a process of self-maintenance in its own dissolution. In proceeding from its simple unity to its differentiation and back to unity, life points to consciousness, since this is the process that consciousness itself undergoes. Consciousness thus turns its attention to life, to observe it. The observation is as yet abstract, and it has to be enriched; but in turning to life as its object, consciousness approaches the concept of "I." In thinking of life, consciousness thinks of itself and therefore of the self.

In this way we have arrived at the concept of selfhood. In essence it is a simple universal. As such it seeks to overcome difference, primarily the difference between itself and its other. Juxtaposed to it there stands a multitude of independent entities, and the ego truly becomes aware of itself by superseding its "other." Not only is the ego opposed to the other, it is also opposed to the other's independence and seeks to overcome it. This is why Hegel can say, quite simply, that consciousness is desire. The aim of desire is to overcome the otherness, the independence of that other. Remember that the positing is a negating, the ego's self-assertion is at the same time a denial of the other. By negating or destroying (*vernichten*) the other, the ego bestows certainty upon itself, a self-certainty that is now explicit.

Yet as much as it seeks to negate the other, it needs the other—if only in order to have something to negate. (There is much that is akin to the character of Don Juan in all this, as Kierkegaard describes him in *Either/Or*.) But I also need the other to give me my human identity, to recognize me as person. (If this seems unreal, think of it as it is reflected in the problem of private language and in the problem of solipsism. I cannot emerge from my egocentric predicament by my own effort. Descartes needs God to help him out; Hegel's man needs another person.) Thus, the ego needs this negating activity in order to become aware of itself as ego, and this means that the other must be there for it (and be there for it *as* ego)—to be negated, yet not negated! Because the other cannot be negated (not finally), it remains, and desire persists. Self-consciousness thus comes to realize that there is more in desire than self-consciousness alone—much as it continues in that desire.

The way out of this impasse is for the ego's object to cease to be an object, to negate itself as mere object. This seems rather strange—namely, that it is up to the object to do this to itself—but since the ego is incapable of achieving the negation (in any ultimate sense), only the object itself can achieve this. It does not annihilate itself but negates its status as object. That is, it ceases to be the *mere* object it has been, and now it asserts itself as independent—and then it is recognized as a consciousness and a self-consciousness. The outcome is that the self-consciousness achieves its satisfaction only in *another* self-consciousness. The ego *becomes* an ego only by recognizing the egohood of another.

Here we have the bridge to all that follows in the *Phenomenology*. It seems a constructive basis for an interpersonal relation. Yet this stage, necessary though it is, is fraught with conflict, even a struggle to the death. Let us bear in mind the point noted earlier, that the self-relation is an adversary-relation. This becomes even more apparent in the relation between two egos.

The main point is that the relation between egos, or between the ego and its object, is that of negation. My own independence is (for me) equivalent to the negation of the other's independence, of the other's otherness. We now know why this cannot succeed (i.e., I need him there to give me my selfhood), and thus why it is that the attempt at achieving a complete (i.e., independent, solipsistic) self-consciousness cannot succeed at this stage. I cannot realize *myself* as an ego if I see *you* as nothing more than an illusion or dream of mine, or (worse) as something inanimate, inert, impersonal. The solipsist cannot exist as a person.

We have made the transition, here, not only from consciousness to self-consciousness, but from consciousness to society. In my self-consciousness, the object of my consciousness (myself as well as the other) *becomes* ego through that consciousness. The "I" becomes "We"—and this is where the realm of human spirituality begins. The next step is to see what it is for the "I" to *experience* the "We."

Before we go on to discuss the passage on Mastery and Slavery, there is much to be commented upon in the passage discussed so far (and we can here take up only a few of the main points). To begin with, we ought to bear in mind that what Hegel is giving us is not metaphysics but phenomenology. That is, he is not concerned (here in chapter IV) to expound a metaphysics of absolute idealism, which purports to demonstrate the career of reason in the world, as it makes its way through Nature and Spirit. Rather, he is concerned here with the *experience* of consciousness, and with its problematic character *as* it is experienced. The divisions a metaphysics might offer do not present themselves to experience *as* divisions, and therefore they are not the subject matter of phenomenology.

From the standpoint of *most* metaphysical systems, there is no special ontological status to be accorded to *self*-consciousness (as distinct from consciousness as such)—so long as there are vestigial divisions such as subject/object, knower/known, etc. For Kant, the transcendental unity of apperception is a function of self-consciousness, but only insofar as it makes possible our consciousness of an object as something other than consciousness.[5] This is diametrically opposed to Hegel's view, which holds not only that consciousness of a thing is possible only for self-consciousness, but that self-consciousness alone is the truth of the various shapes that consciousness takes on.

Because self-consciousness occupies no special ontological status in most metaphysical systems, and yet the subject/object distinction prevails in one form or another, the concept of truth continues to pose an almost insoluble problem. It seems that there is no "place" for truth in the world-inventory (which is perhaps why, in medieval philosophy, truth had to be accorded the status of a "transcendental" category). Hegel nevertheless can and does declare that self-consciousness is truth's own territory. Truth is no longer an area foreign to consciousness, hopefully to be penetrated under favorable conditions, i.e., when the mind conforms to reality, or the subject conforms to the "independently existing" object. On the contrary, since the object *is* the subject (in self-consciousness), the objective truth apprehended by consciousness is identical to subjectivity as well. Phenomenology, as the study of the experience of consciousness, therefore examines the area in which truth is manifested and is self-consciously grasped.

A further point: The *Phenomenology* has presented a rather dry exposition so far—altogether theoretical and more often than not obscure. Yet with the phenomenological concern with self-consciousness, along with the attention given to life and desire, it is inevitable that the theoretical exposition should lead into a scenario, a script in which these complex elements are given concrete embodiment. We have gone from the formal to the contextual; from philosophy to something like drama, as its fulfillment. (Hyppolite speaks of the *Phenomenology* as a philosophical novel.)[6]

Now, quite apart from the dramatic value of the master-slave episode, we may well wonder to what extent it is consistent with what has gone before, and is a necessary development of the foregoing. In discussing the special nature of self-consciousness, along with the problems it generates, we may well ask whether that discussion is at all illuminated by the "dramatization." As we saw, Hegel goes from a division within the individual to an opposition between individuals (i.e., the psychological "other" becomes the "other" person). What makes for consistency between the exposition and the dramatization is the fact that there are the parallels we have discussed: life extending itself and returning to itself, as consciousness does; consciousness itself going—characteristically—from abstraction to concreteness; and consciousness going from itself to a consciousness *of* itself, then to self, and then to another self. What is central, however, is that Hegel ceases discussing the ego in isolation. To discuss it as functioning at all is to discuss its relation to its object; but this *must* lead to further discussion of it in relation to another ego as object. Thus, there seems to be an epistemological necessity in what Hegel is doing. The implication is that any attempt at a discussion of the isolated ego must lead to solipsism, which is as untenable as a theory as it is in reality. It therefore follows that a confrontation of egos is the next inevitable step in the discussion.

We saw that a self-consciousness relates (properly speaking) only to *another* self-consciousness. This is where the paradoxicalness of its self-relatedness is overcome. The ego, in its autonomy, would no doubt prefer solipsisim. We have seen why solipsism is impossible. It is impossible not only because the ego's view of itself leads nowhere if merely directed inward, but because all *self*-consciousness is simultaneously directed outward as a way of returning to itself and its own selfhood. Only another ego grants me my selfhood—by reflecting mine. What follows this insight of Hegel's is the dialectical playing-out of the tension between the ego's autonomy and its dependence.

A further question can be asked: What relation is there between the philosophical concept of self-consciousness and a social relation?[7] The question points to the problematic relation between subjectivity and intersubjectivity. A possible answer is forthcoming if we take note of the arguments against social solipsism (and its ramifications, as in the private language problem). Ego expresses itself in desire, and desire subsists in mutual recognition. Thus, all having to do with the ego involves other egos, just as all social interaction involves self-consciousness (qua ego). Being-for-self *is* being-for-another, and vice versa. The in-itself is that *for which* another is in-itself. This too is paradoxical, for how can another person's identity in itself depend upon its being there for another? This is the overarching paradox that is posed by the notion of self-consciousness, and which the master-slave episode is intended to resolve.

MASTERY AND SLAVERY
(Para. 13–31)

This section begins with a paradoxical statement that sums up what has gone before: "Self-consciousness exists *in* and *for itself* by virtue of the fact that it is in and for itself for another." (*Das Selbstbewusstsein ist an und für sich, indem und dadurch, dass es für ein anderes an und für sich ist.*) Self-consciousness exists only in being recognized—i.e., recognized as the expression of personhood. But the recognition of my personhood is forthcoming from another. The other, who is to bestow personhood upon me, must be an independent person himself—yet he cannot be independent because he looks to me to accord personhood upon him. (One way out of this impasse, I suppose, is to conceive of God as altogether independent and needing no prior recognition in order to bestow personhood upon us all.) Among human beings, then, personhood must be what it cannot be. This is its special ontological status: the only *independent* self-existence the ego can have is precisely in its *dependence* on another ego!

Independence and dependence are what this section is about, its full title being "Independence and Dependence of Self-Consciousness: Mastery and Slavery." (I use the terms *master* and *slave* rather than *lord* and *bondsman*, because the latter terms carry a feudal connotation, which plays no part in Hegel's discussion.)[1]

We have arrived at the peculiar concept known as *recognition*. Although its application appears altogether individual and subjective, it provides the objective basis for social existence. The status bestowed involves no more than a spiritual predicate, yet that status is more binding than any natural property or physical predicate could be. The recognition is as *person*, and Hegel builds his view of culture on that concept.

We may therefore feel that there are two linked questions to be asked: First, how can mere self-consciousness lead to recognition as person (i.e., how can form produce content)? Second, how can the individual concept of person lead to the collective concept of culture? The answer to the second question is presented in the discussion of Stoicism, Skepticism, and the Unhappy Consciousness, where we are made to see that what characterizes these cultural expressions is their emergent views of the individual. In answer to the first question, Hegel gives us a scenario wherein recognition emanates from the clash of egos, and that clash involves a competitive struggle for selfhood.

As to the link between the two questions, we may well appreciate the insight of George Armstrong Kelly, to the effect that the master-slave episode is essentially Platonic, because what is involved here is the primal cleavage in the history of society *and* the history of the ego.[2] That is, Plato's approach to the state and the soul as parallel—i.e., the state as "the soul writ large"—is here reflected in the master-slave episode taken as a microcosm of society. Thus there is one struggle operating on two planes—which is why that struggle must be seen in broader than psychological terms. The recognition does not emerge as the effect of psychological causes alone; rather, it is seen to emerge in a phenomenological framework, wherein that concept arises in the *experience* of self-consciousness and in the clash of such experiences. Once the psychological fence has been breached, we can see the episode as the bridge to a human history.

What Hegel is presenting here is a microsociety composed of two members. The only basis for their interrelation is the desire for individual recognition—the desire on the part of each for the acknowledged status as person—and, as we saw, this leads to mortal combat between them. Not only is this status the issue being fought over, it is the one and only value to be assigned. Thus, we are not dealing with a merely aggressive creature (as in Hobbes), nor with a naturally acquisitive creature (as in Locke), and certainly not with a primordially solitary creature (as in Rousseau). In and of themselves, none of these models would necessarily produce a *humanized* individual through combat. For Hegel, however, it is precisely that status of humanness that is at issue in the primal struggle. From this (in Hegel's view), all other social values and devices will follow. Everything stems, originally, from desire. But it is a desire aiming not merely at the acquisition of some inert object.[3] Rather, what it is aiming at is the union of the "I" with itself. And in desiring its own selfhood, self-consciousness is thus providing a basis for an interpersonal relation and eventual social life.

In the ego's initial confrontation with another ego (such that its independence is precisely in its dependence), the ego has come out of itself and has thereby lost itself (i.e., lost its self-enclosure), but it now sees itself reflected in the other. Now, in this twofold identification (i.e., for itself and for another), the self-conscious ego wants to eliminate the other in order to establish its own independence. But if it succeeds in this it will be eliminating itself, because the other *is* itself (i.e., the source of its selfhood). As a result, the ego returns to itself—but then the other withdraws and returns to *it*self.

All this is further complicated by the fact that what we have just seen is not a unilateral action of one ego with respect to another. Rather, it is an action of total reciprocity, so that each of the two is seen as acting in the same way toward his other. Each must be understood to be totally unhindered in his actions at this point—otherwise, what happens next could not take place. I say "unhindered," not "free," since neither one is genuinely free at this point; if he were, he could provide his own recognition. The two egos are "unhindered," even though they are entirely locked into the scenario that is being played out.

Another complication is that each one's action is as much directed at himself as it is directed at the other—so that what we have is a manifold duplication and reduplication of stances: Each one is unhindered, yet is determined by the other (since each one is dependent upon the other). Each is what he is, yet becomes the other (since the action of each is duplicated by the other). Each ego comes out of itself, yet it is in itself *because* it is for itself (since each is autonomous in its desire, and is to that extent self-enclosed). Each is for itself, yet it is for the other (since each is self-aware in its desire, yet looks to the other to satisfy it). Each is for itself precisely in the other's being-for-itself (since its own autonomy is reflected in the autonomy of the other). Each is a being immersed in the immediacy of its existence, yet is mediated (since in the immediacy of each there is a self-mediation in which the other is the middle term).

Thus, each sees that he *is and is not* the other! As Hegel says, "They *recognize* themselves as mutually *recognizing one another*." *(Sie anerkennen sich, als gegenseitig sich anerkennend.)* We could add to this, that they recognize themselves *in* mutually recognizing one another. It is a toccata and fugue—in which each theme is echoed in stretto and then a fifth lower, and so on and on, except that the counterpoint *is* the harmony, and vice versa. Through it all, there is the figured bass of the growing self-consciousness; and the resounding diapason is the emergence of man as human. (The analogy to art is too tempting to resist. As we saw, Hyppolite speaks of the *Phenomenology* as a philosophical novel; Kelly sees the master-slave scenario as a *Bildungsroman.)*

One would like to imagine that the conflict could be avoided if one party were to *begin* by unilaterally recognizing the other—since, in any case, they could not simultaneously become mutually aware. But in the struggle for recognition, no recognition has as yet been accorded by either one. To that extent, they are equals before the struggle commences. Afterward, the positions are not at all comparable. There can be no unilateral recognition before the struggle takes place, however, because each self-consciousness is absorbed in itself and thereby excludes all else. Each is the individual "I" who is not yet "We." All else (the world of objectivity, as other) stands to the ego in a negative relation, as that which is "not I." Yet what happens when the realm of the "other" includes not merely the external object but another self-consciousness making its own claim to selfhood? It must reject *me* as "other" as I reject it, and in this we have the seed of the eventual confrontation.

To begin with, they seem to one another as "common objects, independent forms," each immersed in the concerns of its own life. They do not as yet appear to one another as self-consciousnesses having the power to negate. Neither ego has as yet expressed itself as a being-for-itself. Each is certain of itself, but since neither one has as yet recognized a similar self-certainty in the other its own self-certainty is ungenuine. As yet, neither one is for the other what the other is for itself. To this extent, therefore, they are not equal, and neither one sees himself as such. The genuine self-certainty has not yet been grasped—and only if it were, could they see themselves as equal, i.e., as equally human.

We have come to another impasse. What would be needed in order for us to escape it? How can self-consciousness develop on its own so that it could then enter into the relation that would develop it further? Since desire is identical to self-consciousness itself—and in self-consciousness one rises above one's day-to-day existence—we are eventually able to get a perspective on life, as such, and thus to set it up as a concept. We then are able to see Life as a composite entity—and thus detach ourselves from it, even negate it.[4] But self-consciousness has not as yet developed the ability to operate in conceptual terms (since this requires intellectual interaction, which is impossible for the isolated ego). All is as yet immanent. Instead of operating in conceptual terms, the ego can only procure its selfhood by means of its activity *and* the mediating activity of others. Since such cooperation is not forthcoming, the only sort of interrelation that remains is that of combat.

If the ego were sufficiently developed before the combat took place, it might have enough of the element of negation in it to reject its dependence on objective circumstances as particulars. It would thus see itself as an autonomous universal. Then it would show that it is not at all attached to its own particular life. (We can see here the germ of the Stoic/Christian idea, but it is even more interesting to see in this the germ of an adversary-relation between man and God, with man negating the life given him by God.) Let us say that each has caught a glimpse of what its own immortality would mean—shall we call it a paleolithic *Bushido*? Yet this is by no means something that could be conceptualized at this point.

Thus, each is ready to stake his own life for the sake of his personhood. The point, however, is that in glimpsing one's own selfhood as independent of one's immediate life, and thereby staking one's life, one does not intend to procure one's own death. On the contrary, one seeks the death of the other *in* one's own willingness to stake one's life! The result is that each one seeks to prove himself in a life-and-death struggle.

At this point there occurs a quantum leap; the two egos go into overdrive. The change is from the implicit self-consciousness, and the potential standoff, to an express self-assertion and overt clash. This is because the two must intensify their quest for self-certainty. As Hegel says, each must raise his self-certainty to truth—each one having that truth as something that is both a truth for the other and a truth for himself. What is at stake is nothing less than full freedom (not yet achieved) and ultimately the full realization of one's personhood. And since this is the ultimate of personal goals, it involves an act that must have everything riding on it, i.e., life itself. Man is not free by nature; rather, he must become free by his own act.[5] Yet this is not achieved through a unilateral act of independence, since it requires recognition. Independence without recognition is empty; recognition without the contextual element of superiority is blind; and superiority that is not gained at the risk of life is meaningless.

This freedom, then—i.e., independence, self-realization, autonomy—is achieved only by staking one's life for it, and only in confrontation with another who is staking his life for a similar goal. One is to take that freedom by force—wrenching one's selfhood and self-awareness out of the mundane life in which these had been buried all along, and then confronting that selfhood directly. There is much that is erotic, certainly, in the idea of the forceful taking of life, freedom, and selfhood. In Hegel, it reflects the prevailing cultural attitude of *Sturm und Drang*, foreshadowing the view later expressed by Goethe at the very end of *Faust* II: "He alone deserves freedom, and life, who each day must conquer them anew"—and these words are pronounced by Faust, at the end of a long and second life, as "wisdom's ultimate conclusion" (*der Weisheit letzter Schluss*).

Those of us with a sound grasp of ourselves may not much sympathize with this outlook, and perhaps even dismiss it as excessively *romantisch*. Yet there are those of us who—so immersed in the details of life as to have lost all mastery over it—know what it is to want a way out of that immersion, in order to find one's individual identity and freedom. The literature of all eras is filled with this theme. And the language of struggle is not at all inappropriate here.

What Hegel is saying goes beyond this, however. He says not only that our individuality is attained through struggle (since this could be a struggle against oneself or against one's circumstances). Rather, our individuality is genuinely achieved only by *combat*—and that this must be a combat with another ego also seeking individuality. It may well be, he admits, that the individual who has not risked his life may nonetheless be recognized as a person—but such recognition is not genuine, since the individual has not arrived at the truth of it as an independent self-consciousness. We may go further and admit that individuals may arrive at their individuality in many ways—for example, asserting individuality in the face of danger, where danger is presented by the horn of a bull, or the mountain that must be scaled because it is there, and so on. But although one may have an altogether worthwhile opponent in one's own self (as the matador and the alpinist do), the most intense struggle is presented by the confrontation with another ego—precisely because the other seeks what you seek, and in *its* seeking it *you* are being limited, even set upon.

Here we might ask: Why can't there be a compromise? Why can't two individuals achieve individuality and realize themselves in a symbiosis? The answer is that a compromise, a concession, means giving something up: I must make room for you, not only in my space but in my awareness as well, and then I am not altogether independent of you. Accordingly, *my* individuation entails *your* restriction; the assertion of my individuality means the negation of yours. This is why my self-assertion requires me to stake my life.

Hegel goes even beyond this, however, to an even more remote and stark point. Just as each must stake his own life, so each must seek the other's death. This is because the self is restricted in the other, and the mirror image to the concept of asserting one's own self is the concept of negating the other's self—that is, in eliminating the otherness of the other, since the other's selfhood is in turn the negation of oneself.

This certainly seems a specious argument, *as* argument. There is in it something like Spinoza's conflation of two different senses of infinitude: since God is infinite, he is the subject of an infinitude of predicates, and then there is nothing that is not an aspect of God and nothing that is not God. This is an equivocation in the meaning of "infinite," which is taken from a qualitative to a quantitative sense. In a similar vein, Hegel is saying (1) that the self is "infinite" in its self-reflection, and that therefore (2) the self is "infinite" in its aim of asserting and extending itself, and that therefore (3) the self aims at the infinitude of its extension—so that, presumably, there is nothing that is not ego, and nothing that is not *my* ego.[6] This means that (for me) every *other* ego is a limitation of *my* infinitude. But as soon as we see the equivocation in the qualitative and quantitative senses of the terms *infinite* and *infinitude*, the ego's demand for exclusivity no longer has a basis.

A further difficulty in this equivocation stems from the fact that (for Hegel) the ego *is* infinite, yet *seeks* infinitude. In its search for infinitude (as though it did not have it), we see the roots of the ego's *essential* inclination toward solitude: it can bear no otherness, and cannot bear being other for another, because it wants to be infinite or nothing—and this is not a function of individual psychological peculiarity but is rather the essence of selfhood. (Perhaps this is why men have conceived of God as a person who is altogether *alone*.)

If every other ego is a limitation of my own, why can't I resign myself to that? Is it not reasonable to accept the fact of our coexistence, limiting though it is? Yet we must realize that here we are not speaking of the ego as *rational*, but rather of the ego in the "infancy" of its human career, prior to the evolution of social values such as accommodation and moderation. Yet we ought not to take the term *infancy* in a temporal sense, as though we were pointing to a time in the historical past. We are speaking, rather, of the ego in its *essence*—stripped of all sociocultural accretions. Take away (theoretically) all that has been acquired and transmitted by way of social experience, and you have an ego that is solitary and "infinite." And there cannot be two "infinite" egos—if, that is, we go along with the equivocation we spoke of (just as, for Spinoza, there cannot be two infinite entities in any sense). What this means is that this world just isn't big enough for the two of us—and therefore combat is inevitable.

This, then, serves to explain (specious though the explanation may be) why each ego must—in the light of its essence—be pitted against its other. Another way of putting this is to say (with Hobbes) that without the restraints imposed by a social order, men would give vent to their natural hostility. But such a statement involves causal assumptions (psychological and other) that are beyond the purview of phenomenology. Thus, Hegel is not saying that presocial man is naturally aggressive; what he says is that a presocial ego would be (*per impossibile*) limited by nothing, and would fill out its world completely, infinitely. A confrontation (again, *per impossibile*) between such an ego and another one just like it would necessarily involve encroachment, the limitation of the infinite. This is why there must be this mortal combat between them. We have seen why the aim must be death. Yet the death of either party would thwart the aims of both. With the death of either, neither one achieves recognition. The lone survivor has no one to accord him the recognition of his superiority. If he were capable of bestowing that recognition on himself, and if such a bestowal were genuine, then he would not have had to fight the other in the first place.

Recognition involves a negation wherein independence is achieved. But this requires consciousness, and death is therefore a negation without such independence being achieved. In the eyes of the survivor, it is not enough for him to have staked his life; he also wants this acknowledged (by the other), so that he may then become (supposedly) a fully independent being-for-himself. But that acknowledgment could not be forthcoming if the vanquished were to die. Recognition demands conflict, and this is a form of contact. And if death puts an end to that conflict, it also puts an end to the contact and subsequent recognition. In death, the parties are unopposed, but there is no mutuality either. Whatever negation there is in death, it is not the conscious negation such that the clash would be genuinely superseded *and* the supersession would be retained in the memory of both parties.

Thus, each one, in seeking the other's death, is implicitly seeking to frustrate his own aim: to be recognized as individual, as person. The *search* for personhood itself thus seems to rule out its *realization*. We may ask, therefore: Is the goal itself self-contradictory? If it were, then social life would be pointless. Yet social life does have as its implicit aim the resolution of that "contradiction."

Since death provides no solution in this life-and-death struggle, the victor will have to allow the vanquished to live. As Hegel says, "self-consciousness becomes aware that life is as essential to it as is pure self-consciousness." The reasons are obvious. But the loser cannot simply be set free, for then no recognition could be demanded or expected. He must therefore be enslaved, to be left alive and yet not be free, and the victor will be his master.

Both have made a choice in favor of life: the victor has granted life to the vanquished because the victor needs the consciousness of the vanquished; the vanquished has chosen to live in defeat rather than die, and that choice is part of his defeat. The crucial question now arises as to what sort of recognition the victor can get from the vanquished.

Prior to the struggle it was possible to speak of a unified consciousness, unified in the fact that its being in itself *is* its being for another. In our primary experience, however, that unity is shattered, and we become aware that the consciousness in itself is not the consciousness for another. That is, I now see the difference between my inner and my outer life, between my inner and my outer identity. But as soon as there is an outer identity it can become an object for the other person. He can regard it as a thing, and thereby *make* a thing of it (and of me). Thus, the situation of consciousness now is that of disunity, fragmentation—with one side of me as in itself and independent, while the other side is for another and dependent.

These are mere aspects of one consciousness. Yet the two aspects also *are* (and reflect) the status of the master and the slave, respectively. They are the embodiments of consciousness, as though these two individuals were sides of one consciousness that is divided against itself.[7] The argumentative weakness here is that Hegel is speaking on two levels at once—the literal and the metaphoric—i.e., of aspects of consciousness and of masters and slaves. He exploits this ambiguity: the situation is as described, but it also stands for something else. But in addition to these two distinct levels, Hegel also speaks as though these two are identical. Thus, the master *is* consciousness existing for itself, as well as being the figurative embodiment of such consciousness. But that consciousness is for itself *in* and *despite* the fact that it is mediated through the consciousness of the slave. Thus, it is for itself by means of that otherness. And that otherness (the slave) now is a consciousness whose nature it is to be connected to thinghood, to independent objects, the things it will be working on. The master now has the things he wants, procured for him by the consciousness and activity of the slave. Thus, the master is a being-for-self, but he is *also* a being-for-self whose being is mediated through another.

Again we find a duplication and reduplication: In regarding the master's selfhood and otherness (or independence and dependence), we see that he himself is related to both these extremes immediately (i.e., directly) *and* mediately (through the activity of the slave). The master relates to the slave mediately (holding him enslaved through, say, the use of an object such as a chain, or through other means such as threats). The master also relates to objects (e.g., his food) in this way, through the slave's mediating activity.

The slave, on the other hand, relates to the thing that is independent of him, and whose independence he wishes to negate; yet he cannot negate it altogether, cannot surmount it, cannot make it entirely his own, since he merely works on it and does not consume it. Through the slave's mediating activity, the master's relation to a thing is in the fact that he enjoys the use of it *and* negates it. When we desire a thing, it is because it resists us, is independent of us. This is now a problem that is overcome as far as the master is concerned: the slave is interposed between the master and the thing desired; the slave obtains it for him, and the master now enjoys it; whatever independent aspect there remains to the thing, this is a problem for the slave to handle in his work on it.

Hegel's aim, in all this intricate dialectic, is to lead back to the question of just what recognition the master can get. The answer can be seen in (a) the respective relations of the master and the slave to the material thing, and (b) the reification of the slave, his suppression to the status of thing. (These factors do not, however, *determine* that recognition.)

The slave, in working on the thing, does not negate it entirely (since he does not both produce and consume it). The slave's negating activity is therefore incomplete, and with this there is an incompleteness to his selfhood. He cannot look upon himself as man-the-maker-and-consumer, one who depends on nothing but his own effort and ingenuity. This lack suggests that he must give up some essential piece of the self-image he may have been hoping for. On the contrary, he sees himself as not in control of his surroundings or of his destiny. He is not his own being-for-self. But that is just how the master saw him, to begin with. Thus, as the slave abrogates his own being-for-self, he does to himself just what the master had done to him earlier: seeing him as less than a man. The slave cannot even regard his actions as his own; his actions are the master's.

The master, as being-for-self, negates the thing. In negating it and being independent of it, he is what consciousness itself is in its essence: free of objects and of the objective world. Hegel regards this relation as pure and essential (and, by contrast, the slave's relation to objects as impure and unessential). This hinges, once again, on the idea that the ego's essential relation to the environing world is that of negation.

This view is disputable, surely, and we see in due course that Hegel himself does not accept the matter so simply and without further ado. That is, the man-thing relation—in the case of the master and of the slave—need not necessarily be taken only in emblematic terms. Nor need we regard negation as *the* characteristic function of consciousness, to the exclusion of all others, such that the mastery and the enslavement are measured thereby. Certainly, there is considerable ambiguity attached to the term *negation*. Moreover, there are all sorts of ways (destructive, constructive, etc.) of saying that the world is nothing to me: e.g., the way of the mystic, the detached cynic, the committed revolutionary, the jaded epicure, the phenomenological observer, etc.—and we would be hard put to say that one of these is the *essential* relation (and the others unessential) merely because it involves negation. It certainly seems as though Hegel is using the term "negation" in an abstract way at this point—and the fact that he will be giving content to that term in the discussion of Stoicism, Skepticism, and Christianity does little to mitigate the emptiness of its use here.

As to the content of recognition, Hegel suggests that genuine recognition would mean that what the master does to the slave the latter does to himself, and what the slave does to himself he does to the master. But this manifold relation does not necessarily obtain. There is only the situation (as we saw) of the slave doing to himself what the master had already done to him. In the absence of that many-sided relation, there is only a partial and unequal recognition.

Yet the relation is even more problematic than this. The struggle for recognition involved (at least) the tacit assumption that whoever won, the recognition of the victor's superiority would be forthcoming from the other party, and that that recognition would be freely given by a free and independent individual. How else is recognition to be of any value? The selfhood of the victor was going to be assured by just such recognition. Yet we now know that although the parties were unhindered prior to the struggle, they were by no means free; on the contrary, their respective free-dom was as yet to be established by the struggle (demonstrating that each, in staking his life, is free of its particularity). The outcome, however, is anything but this—since a new interrelation is established now, linking the two in a mutual dependence that leaves them anything but free.

A similar fate befalls their equality: Let us remember that the battle begins with the parties being equal, and each wishing to prove his superi-ority (and thus his *inequality*) with respect to the other. And now, after the enslavement of the vanquished, the master finds that the recognition he is getting is *not* from an equal. Recognition from an equal is the only recog-nition worth having, and he cannot have it, because he has made the slave his inferior. (Thus, the aims of proving superiority and of gaining recog-nition are incompatible.) As a result, the victor's own sense of selfhood suf-fers. Instead of the truth of self-certainty, he is aware that in receiving recognition from someone who is now his inferior, his own consciousness and action are now unessential and ungenuine. The victory is hollow.[8]

The master had thought of himself as independent. This was how he saw himself in his power of negation. That self-image now turns out to be a false one (which is why I pointed out that Hegel does not accept the equation of consciousness and negation without further ado). The master's "independent" consciousness now sees its truth in the dependent con-sciousness of the slave. As dependent, it is not a genuinely free self-con-sciousness. And to the extent that the slave's dependent self-consciousness is not genuine, the master's self-consciousness (which depends on the slave's for recognition) is doubly dependent and inauthentic. The master's nature has therefore turned out to be the reverse of what he aimed for: He wanted recognition from someone who is his equal. We have seen why the element of equality is ruled out. He also wanted the other's recognition as an outward recognition freely given; but the slave is free in only an inward sense—and as "free" in that special sense, no recognition can be demand-ed of him from that inward source.

The slave, in being suppressed, turns inward into himself and becomes independent in that way (i.e., in his thoughts). Up to a point, then, the independent master is the slave's reality, pervading what he thinks and does. But here the master's power is not infinite; the slave does have an inner area of independence. But then the slave grasps the idea that independence, per se, is the ultimate value, i.e., of being-for-self with the capacity of negation. The question now is whether he can apply this idea to himself. In any event, the slave does *experience* this independence when he is in danger of death: he has found himself in such fear and uncertainty that nothing remains stable and sure for him; in the fact that his life is completely in the hands of the master, usable at the will of the master, the slave has become a mere "object" for the master; but *then* everything melts away in this terror and suppression, so that the slave is left with nothing but his own being-for-self and the power to negate—precisely the characteristics of the master!

In other words, the slave is driven to the point at which he has nothing further to lose—and then he is free, he is the master of everything. He may or may not have arrived at an explicit grasp of his own being-for-self and his capacity to negate; yet they are implicitly there in his experience as slave. These facets are implicit, also, in all consciousness as such, insofar as it is free of all external circumstances, and finds its autonomy in negating all its ties to the environing world.

Hegel says that the slave negates his ties to the world through his work—thereby, in a sense, liberating himself from it (but only in a sense, since he cannot surmount the object's independence completely). Certainly, the slave has no ties to the world in the sense of owning anything in it. Yet (in my view) neither of these forms of negation is in any way a liberation. What we have here is not, for example, the negation that is achieved by the prisoner in Plato's cave, in his spiritual/intellectual ascent to a higher reality. The difference between Plato's prisoner and Hegel's slave is that the negation attained by the former involves a freedom grasped in an all-embracing vision, while for the latter any "negation" of the world is merely piecemeal and only emphasizes his enslavement wherein nothing of the world was his to begin with. The former rejects the reality he has had; the latter never *had* anything to reject. To say, therefore, that the slave's work is his liberation, that it frees him or dignifies him, is (in my view) to speak more myth than truth. Labor frees and dignifies when it *is* free and dignified.

There is another way of looking at this: When Hegel speaks of the liberating effect of work, we might want to read him as speaking *in the person of* the slave. Then the view expressed need not be taken as Hegel's own, but as a characterization of how the slave looks upon his own work. Presumably, the slave (not Hegel) would eventually come to see how false this view is—and this realization would explain his need to go on to Stoicism, Skepticism, and Christianity. This interpretation *seems* sensible, and it exonerates Hegel of the mistaken view that the slave's work, as such, is liberating. It is in any case very uncharacteristic of Hegel to adopt that view, since it is so formalistic. It ignores the contextual aspect of the purpose of the work, the setting in which it is done, and so on. I have no way of assuring myself that the alternate interpretation (namely that we are hearing the slave's thoughts, not Hegel's) is a viable one. Certainly, there are other reasons why the slave goes on to Stoicism, etc. Yet if this interpretation is cogent, then we could possibly excuse other apparent myths as myths held by the slave.

A further myth is that the slave, in working on a thing, makes it his own because he has put "himself" into it. True, the slave gives shape to the thing by working on it, and this "shaping" is all the more permanent the more independent the thing. Further, it may well be true that the slave's *praxis* is tied up with his individuality. But this does not warrant the conclusion Hegel draws, namely that the slave thereby comes to see his *own* independence in the independence of the object he works on. On the contrary, the object's independence *of* him (in a material and a socioeconomic sense) only emphasizes, once again, the slave's situation of enslavement.

It is true that the master's relation to the thing is evanescent and that the slave's is more real since he has worked on it. But this in no way justifies *our* belief that the thing is somehow his—any more than it would justify *his* belief to that effect. His enslavement drives him inward, and perhaps gives him a more intense awareness of himself—but this is also an awareness of his captivity.

We are thereby led from the grotesque view tacitly embodied in the slogan, "Work makes free," to the even more grotesque implication that "Slavery makes free." Note that when we speak of work here, it is not the fulfilling work of the independent and creative craftsman; on the contrary, the work of the slave can be expected to be anything but the creative "shaping" Hegel speaks of, and rather the simple and repetitive work that is soul-destroying to the slave, and that only accentuates his enslavement (as I have argued).

I suppose that the slave *could* derive some satisfaction from the fact that he can "manage" in a way the master perhaps cannot: that is, the slave knows how to light a fire and cook food, and in this regard the master is helpless without him. This might be seen as diminishing the enslavement by giving the slave a say in regard to what and how to cook, etc. Yet liberation is two-valued: you are free or you are not—and being able to work with natural objects does not, in and of itself, confer freedom or make you a free *agent* in any respect.

In Hegel's view, the slave arrives at an awareness (of his selfhood) that is altogether unique. His enslavement has made him conscious of what the terms *freedom* and *dignity* mean—and in an appreciation the master cannot match. The slave knows these as the achievements of spirituality and inwardness, as the master never can know them. Further, the shaping the slave gives the thing is the expression of his own pure selfhood, while the master has never (presumably) experienced this relation to a thing. Moreover, the slave is the one who, by discovering what selfhood is, has discovered what spiritual freedom is. It is he, then, who can surmount his situation (i.e., in a spiritual sense) and create culture. It is he alone who can give shape to history, and surmount that as well.[9]

Hegel has given us a picture of man as self-creating, through work and *praxis*. Yet this is not, in Hegel's view, a process in one direction (outward) only. Rather, man is also seen as self-creating in directing himself inward. And if, paradoxically, the self is a relation that relates itself to its own self, then we become human by *knowing* that we are human. What is valuable and important in this section is the way Hegel has shown us the genesis of humanness. (We might do well to consider some of the parallels and contrasts between the slave and Adam: Adam has acquired a component of humanness: moral guilt; the slave has acquired humanness itself. Adam's acquisition is, of course, sinful, and is therefore mediated by the presence of God; the slave's achievement is entirely his own, not even mediated by the master, and as his own it is human all the more.)

We are shown, also, that humanness is ephemeral, emanating from a very indeterminate recognition, as evanescent as spirit itself. Further, we are shown that recognition is the essential feature and bond in all social relatedness, and as such it is entirely dialectical. That is, it is self-contradictory, arising in its conflict with itself and opposition to its aims, and thus pressing us toward a resolution at a higher level of awareness. Above all, recognition is shown to be not a merely mechanical nexus between automata, but rather the acknowledgment, between humans, of humanness.

It is Hegel's achievement to have shown us how this must arise—almost in spite of itself, yet with a logical necessity—out of the human social setting. The higher stage of that humanness is arrived at through inwardness, as the opening to freedom.

We must now go on to consider the forms that process—the slave's internalization and liberation—can take.

STOICISM, SKEPTICISM, AND
THE UNHAPPY CONSCIOUSNESS
(Para. 32–65)

The *Phenomenology* presents a "natural history of consciousness"—in the sense of recapitulating the essential stages it has passed through.[1] Of course, the term *natural history* is not at all to be taken in its conventional sense (e.g., a scientific depiction of man's transition from Paleolithic to Neolithic technology). Rather, we are given a phenomenological picture of the career of consciousness as it meets its contradictions and overcomes them. Thus, the picture is unified by the element of dialectic. The patterns of conflict and resolution, nascent in consciousness, are here made explicit. The structure of the ego's relation to the world, to another ego, and to itself are here exposed.

That is why the master-slave passage is presented in the form of a scenario: certain essential relations (and their consequences) are displayed *and* their inner logic is revealed. The picture shows its content, but shows it as a sequence whose steps are linked by necessity. Thus, we take something like the concept of desire, we see that this is implicit in all self-consciousness as such, and then we present it in its explicit unfolding through a clash of personalities. These personalities are altogether removed from any particular sociocultural matrix: they are neither Apollonian nor Dionysian, neither ancient nor modern.

The objection might be raised that there *are* no such isolated individuals—since all men are members of one society or another. Yet that objection is not a telling one, once we realize that psychology (for example) studies behavior as such—and it need not even be human behavior, let alone behavior in a particular social or cultural setting. What Hegel is doing, then, ought to be accepted as perfectly respectable, even from the standpoint of the social sciences of our own time. He is directing our attention to certain *essential* aspects of human consciousness and interaction, quite apart from accidental details of culture, place, or time. Moreover, we are shown these essential aspects in the process of their logical development (as I said). What the *Phenomenology* presents, then, is what I would call the "trajectory of essences."

Perhaps the most important part of that "natural history of consciousness" involves the evolution of the ego. In its *essence*, the ego evolves in the struggle of consciousness with itself—represented in the struggle of self-consciousness with its "other." As we have seen, it is a moot point whether the two parties to the struggle are (for Hegel) two sides of *one* self-consciousness or *two* individuals. The master-slave episode is the struggle between two egos *and* between subject and object within self-consciousness itself!

The point we have reached is the subjugation of one of these parties by its other. We have seen that the victor does not achieve selfhood: the recognition he receives is unsatisfactory, yet he is not driven inward into his own psyche, to seek recognition there (since nothing external compels him inward). On the other hand, the slave has been forced into his own psyche (since he is oppressed by external factors). The master cannot accept the slave's recognition—not only because it comes from an inferior, but also because the master senses that the slave has an inner side, and that whatever recognition is forthcoming will not be a genuine expression of the slave's feelings. Thus, recognition from the slave is unacceptable, and not merely because it isn't from the heart; it is unacceptable because there *is* a "heart," an inner life to which the master has no access.

The slave's inner life is still rudimentary, however. His psychic structure stands somewhere between Freud's version of the ego and the superego, i.e., between the reality principle and the subsequent internalization of the ego ideal. Thus, the slave has not yet arrived at full selfhood, although the materials are there. What matters is how the slave will synthesize his selfhood out of these materials. What part of that material is conceptual? What part concrete? What part is rational? What part emotional?

Slave consciousness, with its weak grasp of its own selfhood, does not yet have a firm concept of the "I," such that it (his consciousness) would see its various aspects as those of one ego and see that ego expressing itself in a multiplicity of ways. What is missing in the slave, therefore, is a perspectival conception of his own ego in its unity and diversity. The conception he does have is diffuse—and we may regard such world outlooks as Stoicism, Skepticism, and Christianity as attempts to respond to that problem: namely, how to focus the concept of the ego so that we see its many-sided aspects as expressions of one central consciousness. Eventually we will see self-consciousness in its full freedom, as it comes to take concern with itself, seeks self-recognition within itself, and is not content with recognition from its erstwhile "other."

Hegel deals with these world outlooks as held (theoretically) by any human being who has been driven inward to face his consciousness when his outer world gives no support to his selfhood. Selfhood includes independence, and if slave consciousness needs any examples of what independence means, it finds it reflected (albeit inadequately) in the artifact it has made. This object is inert, self-enclosed, in itself; it has an enviable durability and is impervious to pain. There is also the example of the master—although the master's independence is not fully real. Both examples are merely partial ones: the object is self-enclosed, but is not self-conscious; the master is "superior," but he has not attained inwardness. The slave has not as yet come to unify his own self with a notion of selfhood he could conceptualize; he does not as yet think of himself as something to be thought about.

We, however, as phenomenological observers, know that the self and its thought of itself are coextensive. The slave must find a way of attaching his selfhood to his thinking about himself. When the self thinks of itself, and is aware that that thought about itself is the essence of its selfhood, then it has attained genuine infinitude and freedom. Formally, it is the subject becoming an object for itself, *and* being identical with itself, *and* seeing this as the essence of its identity. But it is not merely a formal relation. On the contrary, it is a concrete mode of self-relatedness: its content is the ego, which is there as knower, as known, and as knower knowing its own self-knowing, but in a way that bears on its activity in the world. This is why Hegel speaks of it as "a new form of self-consciousness" (*eine neue Gestalt des Selbstbewusstseins*). This is what must come about. Heretofore, the slave has *lived* the problem of self-consciousness—in terms of confrontation, struggle, and submission. From here onward, he is no longer only a *living* self-consciousness, but a *thinking* self-consciousness.[2]

This must be grasped in existential terms, however. We are not concerned here with the abstract *ego cogito* and the epistemological claims it can pose. Rather, our concern is with self-consciousness directed at its own being-for-self, and in such a way that the self can grasp its own self-consciousness and freedom *as* the essence of its being. Thus, the process of internalization is such that the slave is now aware of himself as a *thinking* being, and he sees this as the basis of his freedom.

This is an evaluative concept, not a purely theoretical one. Even when we say (in purely formal terms) that the subject is its own object, we mean that it is immediately present to itself and that this presentness is its freedom. Thus, its *formal* self-presence provides a *content* for its thought about itself: I am human, and as such I am free. This unity—of subject and object—occurs first in thinking, where being-for-itself and being-in-itself are one (even if this unity is, to begin with, conceived only in broadly universal terms).

What we are seeing is not only the ego's effort to break out of its servile consciousness; it is also the ego's first faltering attempt to concentrate itself and thus bring itself into being as a self-reflecting identity. One way to achieve that concentration is to isolate the ego from everything extraneous to it. Presumably, by stripping the ego of all its social accretions we are left with nothing but the ego itself—an onion-layer model, where the ultimate center is emptiness and freedom.

a) When we spell this out in theoretical and moral terms, we find that it is precisely the outlook of *Stoicism*. In that view, consciousness *is* thinking, and as such it is free of all determinants and is a law unto itself. Nothing is good or bad, but thinking makes it so. There is no objective good or evil; all values stem from consciousness alone. Everything other than consciousness is regarded as unessential to consciousness. All social differences—especially the difference between master and slave—are rejected as illusions. The one and only reality is the individual consciousness. The idea that one's selfhood is to depend upon recognition by someone else is now seen as a totally false idea, since every consciousness is autonomous.

Underlying this outlook is the belief that there is a common humanity shared by all mankind, a human nature; and therefore everyone ought to act in accordance with that humanity and with nature. The idea of a shared humanness is one obvious way of transcending the difference between master and slave—and it is significant that in Stoicism's later period its two leading proponents were a freed slave (Epictetus) and an emperor (Marcus Aurelius).

For Stoicism, the highest value is freedom (i.e., inner, psychological freedom)—and all men, master or slave, face the fundamental problem of how to attain it. Existentially, this freedom is manifested in the negation of all prior relations.[3] Conceptually, freedom is defined as indifference (*apatheia*), whereby we have overcome all concern with externals, so that the self can retreat into its own thought. Will and desire are marks of attachment to the world, a spiritual enslavement—and it is from this enslavement that Stoicism seeks to release us.

Hegel points out that historic Stoicism could appear only at a time of "universal fear and slavery," but that this was also a time when thought was sophisticated enough to conceive of an answer in broadly philosophical terms. This historic expression of Stoicism is not the phenomenological stage he is here considering, i.e., the stage into which the slave is emerging in its slowly evolving grasp of human selfhood. Obviously, Hegel is not saying that historic Stoicism is in any sense the philosophy of primitives trying to get their egos together, or that all slaves will necessarily come to adopt this philosophy as their characteristic attitude. We can even say that his argument does not depend upon the historical existence of the Stoic movement, since we are not speaking of history but of essences. Perhaps it is best to say that Stoicism happens to coincide with the development of the ego so far—and that if there were no Stoicism there for it, it would have been necessary to invent it. In any case, Hegel does not presume to encapsulate the entire 500-year history of Stoicism—with its physics, logic, and ethics—as a phenomenon answering to the contingent needs of some developing persons. What is important is that the Stoic outlook embodies the next essential stage in the itinerary of consciousness.

The trouble with the Stoic outlook (as Hegel sees it) is that when it regards everything besides consciousness as irrelevant to it, the ego itself is regarded abstractly. It is what it is, no matter what. Recognition, on this account, is a false basis for a shared life, since it asks us to seek our self-definition in a source other than ourselves. Stoicism errs in the opposite direction: nothing delineates the ego but the ego alone; the "otherness" is within the ego itself. Yet this is grasped in abstract terms only, withdrawn from one's immediate situation and from concrete life.

For this reason, the freedom that Stoicism proposes is (in reality) only an abstract freedom, since it says that one's actual enslavement is irrelevant. The slave is told: You are free in your thoughts. But this is a freedom that is not fully materialized—since the slave remains a slave, and thus cannot truly be the originator of his own actions. The genuine freedom is that of the free agent, who acts by no directives but his own—a luxury that no actual slave can attain. If (following Kant) what characterizes us as human is that we can give ourselves a moral law and then act upon it, then the slave has not yet realized his humanity.

Stoicism could not provide a thought content for that theoretical freedom (apart from the thought that we are free). Its values were merely reduced to another abstract value: i.e., reasonableness. But this too is without content. It is one of those wire armatures that have yet to have clay put on them, to be fleshed out, and this never happened in historic Stoicism. Its abstractness makes it tedious, Hegel says. Accordingly, Stoicism's "other" is (ultimately) the content that remains forever outside its own formalism. That otherness is the entire world, and it is never negated entirely, as the Stoics had wished.

b) *Skepticism* is able to realize in a concrete way what Stoicism grasped only abstractly. Thus Stoicism spoke of freeing the mind of all attachment to externals, but Skepticism actually put this into practice, by showing that the mind can know nothing fixed or definite about the world. Stoicism preached an indifference *(apatheia)* that is emotive. Skepticism goes beyond this, to speak of an impassivity *(ataraxia)* that is cognitive. What Skepticism has arrived at, therefore, is a negative knowledge, knowing that it cannot know—and in this an even fuller freedom is attained. The thinking ego has thus withdrawn even farther into itself: the external world is now unknowable, in addition to being irrelevant.

We can see a reciprocal relation here: the sense of selfhood is inversely proportional to one's attachment to the world; and if the detachment operates not only on evaluative but also on epistemic grounds, then the sense of selfhood is correspondingly intensified. Thought does not merely negate the world, it annihilates it (in Hegel's phrase) by seeing no possibility for us to make affirmative contact with the world, let alone encompass it.

We can therefore say that Skepticism makes a twofold contribution to the development of self-consciousness: first, Skepticism emphasizes the ego's focus on itself by severing the ego's evaluative and epistemic connection to the world (i.e., nothing is objectively good or evil; nothing can be known definitely); and second, in its negation of those ties to the world, Skepticism echoes the negating capacity of consciousness itself.

For Skepticism, then, there are no objective distinctions in knowledge *or* values; the only distinctions are those made by the thinking consciousness. The freedom of self-consciousness is therefore all the greater.

Thought is close to infinite here, since—by comparison—its "other" (the world) is minuscule in the light of what the ego can know of it. This is a peculiar and startling reversal of Platonic rationalism: instead of the mind being infinite because it encompasses all reality, it now is infinite because it is totally disconnected from reality.

Surely, historic Skepticism never saw itself as the fulfillment of Stoicism. Yet Hegel treats Skepticism in this way because *in essence* it fulfills Stoicism by going farther (along the same path of negation) than Stoicism had gone. In each of the previous stages in the itinerary of consciousness—beginning with our doubts about sense certainty and going up to the master-slave episode—Hegel has exposed the implicit contradictions. What has served to connect the stages (as I have indicated) is the dialectical movement leading from the doubts of one stage to their resolutions in the next. Each contradiction has led to a higher stage of awareness, but each in turn has had its contradictions as well. It would seem, therefore, that a global skepticism would be the inevitable (and final) outcome of all our thinking and experience.

After Skepticism's conceptual annihilation of the world, self-consciousness is left with nothing but its own freedom (as we saw)—even if this means the annihilation of what it itself knows with any determinacy. Ultimately, this would lead to a sophism such as: There is nothing we can know, not even that we cannot know. The sentence denies what it says. And if this is taken as the acme of knowledge, then all determinacy is at an end. One cannot therefore be a Skeptic successfully.[4]

Thus, there is a price to be paid for this extreme doubt: One falls prey not merely to the inconsistency embedded in it, but (in addition) one suffers the inability to function in the world on the basis of one's beliefs about it. True, the ego may thereby have achieved a more intense self-concentration and freedom, but its doubts about the world leave the ego incapable of coping with it. Those doubts backfire—it is here that consciousness becomes what Hegel calls "the absolute dialectical unrest." Differences turn out to be identities, identities are differentiated—since nothing is what it is. As a result, the expected self-certainty of the self-centered self-consciousness becomes a mind-emptying whirl. Worse, the ego knows that it is to blame for its chaos. It knows only that it is *free*—and that it is therefore moved by nothing it can take to be real, essential, or true!

Thus, all I know is that I am a free-thinking but contingent individual with an animal life. These I cannot reconcile. I am what Hegel calls a "lost self-consciousness." Indeed, the dialectical element of retaliation in all this (i.e., achieving freedom at the price of one's sanity) suggests something out of the *Inferno*—but Dante's "lost people" are individuals together, while our Skeptic is entirely isolated and knows that it is his own doing.

And yet there is a positive side: In this isolation, the ego returns to itself as universal and self-identical, thus seeing itself as the living opposite to all particularity and difference. This would seem to be the self-concentration that was sought. If we are doomed to suffer the madness of the "lost self-consciousness," then let us at least have the consolation of a Promethean solitude, the heroic stance of universality and self-identity. Yet once again the ego emerges from this and goes back into contingency and chaos, because its negating capacity is concerned precisely with contingent particulars (i.e., it is this sum of money, this impending honor, this bit of knowledge it rejects). The result is a dizzying swing (again, like something in the *Inferno*)—a vertiginous shuttling back and forth, between universality and contingency, between self-identity and chaotic diffusion of the ego, without a hope of getting itself together. Thus, the initial aim of securing one's selfhood is altogether frustrated.

The ego sees that everything is in flux, and therefore *it* lacks the certainty within itself with which to say even this with any certainty. Thus, the ego is the master *and* slave of what it believes. It is an internalization—with a vengeance! No unifying synthesis takes place: the ego denies what it asserts, and asserts what it denies. Hegel gives us the image, here, of children squabbling endlessly, merely for the sake of squabbling, so that where one says day the other says night, and then the reverse. But what is worse, the squabble occurs inside oneself. It is a self-consciousness that is permanently self-divided instead of self-focused and self-certain. Whatever dichotomy is proposed—e.g., permanence vs. change, certainty vs. contingency, reality vs. appearance—the ego now occupies both sides at once. Whatever metaphysical division there is, or that can be thought of, the dividing line runs right through the human soul!

Yet (on the positive side) self-consciousness can now *see* its own self-contradictoriness—and see that as the defining characteristic of self-consciousness itself—even if it is incapable of overcoming it. It now *knows* itself as divided, in essence as well as concretely: instead of two distinct persons (master and slave), we now have one person who *is* the two. This insurmountable division is the basis of the *Unhappy Consciousness*.

c) When Andre Malraux speaks of El Greco's *View of Toledo* as "the first Christian landscape," we grasp more about Christianity in that remark than about the painter or the painting. The Christian outlook is *in essence* problematic, dialectical—i.e., in conflict with itself, as all self-consciousness is, and seeking a synthesis at a higher level of knowing—and the painting reflects this in its brooding sky warning of imminent judgment. Christianity is a *critical* religion, in the sense of the Greek word *krisis* (judgment). And although such judgment cannot be fully and conclusively forthcoming, because of the inner division in the Unhappy Consciousness, it is already there because that division is what evokes the judgment in the first place.

In very general terms, we can say that a religion embodies the moral code of an era and sanctifies it into a rigid (at times even deathlike) permanence. Christianity, on the other hand, is timeless to the extent that it goes beyond a particular ethos and speaks in universal terms. In this light, we must see it not as representing the attitudes of one historic era, but as an outlook that goes beyond this or that time or place.

In discussing the Unhappy Consciousness *after* Skepticism, Hegel is decidedly not saying that Skepticism is the sufficient condition for the emergence of Christianity (so that with the former as causal antecedent, the latter had to follow as the inevitable outcome); nor is he saying that Skepticism is its necessary condition (so that without it there would have been no Christianity). On the contrary, he is not speaking of a deterministic historical sequence at all. Rather, by directing our attention to the Unhappy Consciousness (qua consciousness), he shows that he is speaking of a frame of mind, quite apart from its embodiment in a particular *cultus*. That frame of mind is seen as a transhistorical process. It is as though, in our attempt to understand it, we were to strip away all of its historic details—even the life and death of its founder!

Thus, the Unhappy Consciousness is an inevitable stage in the itinerary of consciousness, and Christianity is the inescapable expression of that unhappiness.[5] As a *mode* of consciousness, then, the Christian outlook is a divided one, and it has that division constantly before it. It is therefore conscious *of* that divided consciousness, but it is conscious of that division in a unified way. Thus, it is divided and united. Yet as consciousness it can stay in neither mode—as it shuttles from that basic consciousness to the consciousness of that consciousness, and back. Hegel says, therefore, that *as* a unified consciousness it has a dual nature. This is *essentially* true of that consciousness, even if it does not itself see this in any given era.

I would venture to say that the tendency of religion, in general, is toward simplicism and a unified consciousness. We want to feel safe and certain of ourselves. Yet religion misses its own essence to the degree that it overlooks or ignores its own contradictoriness. Let us keep that point clearly before us: the essence of all advanced religion is paradox, uncertainty, insecurity. The acceptance of this may give discomfort to the ordinary religionist, who may well try to turn his religion around to consistency (so that all is right with the world and his own soul is unified). But that is neither here nor there. To the degree that we evade that essential paradoxicality, to that degree the essence of religion has escaped us.

As we see from Hegel's foregoing discussion, the root of the paradox is in the ego's reference to itself—the ego-subject placing its object (the ego itself) at a distance, yet being at one with it. Thus we seek self-division and self-identity at the same time. For Russell, it is semantic self-reference that is the source of paradox, so that all paradoxicality is a function of the structure of propositions. But however much that problem may have been resolved in the theory of types and the awareness of the levels of language, it remains unresolved (and insoluble) in regard to the levels of selfhood. For Hegel, therefore, paradox is a function of selfhood relating to itself— so that self-consciousness *is* paradox, and is paradox by necessity. Now, what any consciousness might attempt to do, in the light of that paradoxical goal of simultaneous self-division and self-identity, is to seek unity with another soul: God, the Unchanging. What we cannot find in ourselves, we seek beyond us. In that quest, however, consciousness must fail. Such union cannot be achieved. This brings us back to the element of division in the Unhappy Consciousness.

That division *is* its unhappiness; and the irresolvability of that division is the triumph as well as the tragic challenge of Christianity. But in the respect that the division represents all consciousness, as active and aware, *all* consciousness is unhappy, as Merleau-Ponty says.[6]

Accordingly, in discussing the divided consciousness, Hegel is not directing our attention to Christianity in its contingent historical aspect, but rather to Christianity as the embodiment of all consciousness—to the degree that *any* consciousness is self-relating, dialectical, divided. In view of that division, consciousness posits for itself the difference between permanence and change—and sees its own essence to be in permanence, while it sees its own mutability as the unessential aspect of itself. Yet since it is *conscious* of the division in its own self, and sees itself as mutable and unessential, it also sees its essence as remaining forever beyond it—hence its unhappiness. There is no easy choice between one side or the other. The two are equally present and inescapable—and they are irreconcilable. Whatever is gained by one aspect of consciousness is lost by the other. And even if consciousness tries to align itself with the unchangeable, as the universal that is its essence, its ever-present particularity must frustrate the choice.

Consciousness does, however, see its *individuality* as permanence, i.e., as an ongoing identity despite change. And yet, although consciousness may see its identity as a unity, it is aware of itself as a unity of differences: e.g., permanence versus change. It thereby shuttles between seeing itself as universal and as particular, and it finally comes to something like a synthesis of the two by seeing its own individuality as this particularity *in* the universal. Here we have the classic triad—universal, particular, singular—in which the antithesis of universal versus particular is overcome in a synthesis whereby the individual sees his selfhood as one of a kind, a universal all its own, a class of one. This is the traditionally Christian idea that each individual is a microcosm, altogether unique.

All this shuttling and variability in that consciousness is the mark of its profound unhappiness: it tries to grasp at this or that idea about itself, this or that characterization, but each of these is thwarted by its opposite. True, it is a consciousness undergoing change; equally true, it is a consciousness with a permanent identity. Yet each time that this consciousness believes to have attained repose and to have rolled its stone up to the summit of unity, it is pushed back toward division and the abyss, as Jean Wahl says.[7] Further, it is both universal and particular; yet since these aspects appear to consciousness alone, what we have is not genuine universality or permanence.

This is a consciousness that is uncertain, perturbed. By contrast, the Skeptic could at least hope to achieve a benign *ataraxia*. At least he knew that there is nothing to know. But the Unhappy Consciousness has gone beyond the spurious comfort of Skepticism, because it *experiences* in itself its own desperate shifts from doubt to affirmation and back. Thus it knows that it itself is nothing but what it is: limited, fallible, doomed. And yet it knows that it is more: spirit, and the locus of infinitude. On one hand it knows itself as utterly dependent, contingent on externals; on the other hand it knows that whatever it itself is, it is the result of its own nature. Unlike the Stoic, who feels that we ought to pursue and embrace our nature, the Christian feels that our nature is already there, and that it is there to be overcome. Unlike the Skeptic, who has found a way of avoiding judgment, the Unhappy Consciousness judges itself constantly in its situation of *krisis*—but with no sure view of itself to base a judgment on!

The self, in seeing and suffering its division, yearns for its resolution and overcoming, instead of a resolution. However, all it can *hope* for, so far, is a union of the divided aspects. One such union is expressed as God's incarnation as Christ. Yet here the division between universality and particularity is emphasized all the more, hardly reconciled. In taking on a material and contingent body, God's immaterial and timeless consciousness becomes even more remote from the consciousness of the religionist. It is as though God, in having placed Christ between himself and man, has placed himself at a greater distance from man. For this reason (i.e., the remoteness of the Unchangeable), the religionist's consciousness must content itself with relating to the temporal embodiment (Christ) as the mere surrogate of the Unchangeable. Inasmuch as the individual consciousness (the believer) gives up the idea of seeking union with the Unchangeable, and seeks union only with its incarnation, such consciousness turns away (at least in part) from the idea of the division of consciousness. The incarnate God therefore provides a solace to the failure that goes inevitably with any attempt to unite with the infinite. As Jean Wahl says,[8] it is here alone, in connection with Christianity, that Hegel will not seek a synthesis (of being and non-being) but will rather emphasize the juxtaposition, which is why the Unhappy Consciousness is a consciousness in a state of becoming.

Yet the individual consciousness can (at least) *seek* union with the Unchangeable in a number of ways, depending on how the Unchangeable is conceived of, and on how the individual consciousness thinks of itself. The two sides are interrelated. Thus, the individual consciousness will think of itself in one of a variety of ways; and it will then project one or more visions of God, according to its vision of itself.

The various shapes of that self-thought are reflected in the trinity—but the persons of the trinity are therefore seen by Hegel as aspects of consciousness, not as self-existent aspects of the godhead. The father, son, and holy spirit are thus translated back into their psychic origins in the individual consciousness. That is to say, the individual has a view of consciousness, either as universal, particular or singular—and each of these views is expressed in objective terms as a mode of the deity, with which the individual consciousness seeks a relation: when consciousness considers itself as universal, the deity is seen as pure consciousness; when consciousness considers itself as particular, the deity is seen as an incarnate individual, active in the world; the unifying singular is seen as a consciousness aware of its own being-for-itself, i.e., the deity as spirit.

There is more here than the different views of the deity, corresponding to the different views that consciousness has of itself. We also find—and this is perhaps the strangest step of all in this bit of dialectical argument—that there is a series of developmental stages within consciousness itself that match the characterization of the trinity. Thus, when consciousness is considered as universal, it itself (not God the father) is seen as pure consciousness; when consciousness is regarded as particular, it is seen as an actual individual that is active in the world; and when consciousness is viewed as singular, as being-for-self, it is spirit. That means that we can actually look to a stage of pure consciousness, that this will be followed by its actualization in external action, and that this will then be followed by a consciousness that has returned to itself. The Christian trinity, then, is an exemplification of an evolutionary process undergone by the Unhappy Consciousness.

As pure consciousness, the deity is of a nature that has not yet entered actual existence. It exists as concept only, and consciousness cannot give it content. The Unhappy Consciousness does, however, provide the contact between the abstract conception of consciousness and consciousness as individuality—because it conceives of the deity as individual. Yet even if it sees the deity *as* individual, the Unhappy Consciousness does not know that the deity *is* the individuality of consciousness.

Thus, the Unhappy Consciousness cannot really grasp the deity in thought; the best it can do is to offer its devotion, which is far removed from the conceptual. It can yearn—and it can conceive (in purely abstract terms) of the deity as individual. What the Unhappy Consciousness *does* know is that the deity is forever beyond—and the Unhappy Consciousness therefore sees *itself* as the deity's opposite.

At this point it must return to itself, since itself is all it has. And then it *visualizes* the deity (instead of conceiving it) as a particular individual. But then, as visible, the deity itself has vanished. Since it has vanished as an individual, it is not genuine individuality, i.e., it is not the universal and the particular, as existing. We have the image of the Crusaders, battling their way to the Holy Sepulchre and opening it (with what expectation?), only to find it empty. The visible Christ must vanish to make way for the deity as universal.

If the Unhappy Consciousness has not conceived the deity as selfhood, it has at least *felt* its own self, although without certainty of itself. Its activity (in desire and work) gives it no sense of certainty. Just as *it* is divided, its work is divided also—e.g., between permanence and change, between the sacred and the profane, between its part in the other world and in this, etc. And because the Unhappy Consciousness is uncertain of itself, it regards nothing as its own achievement or the outcome of its own abilities. All is of God—which means that there is very little to one's own selfhood. And yet, although it could have accepted this if it were to have renounced itself entirely, it has not really done so (since it *has* acted in the world). And therefore the fact that it has not given up its selfhood entirely, yet has very little of it, is a further source of division and unhappiness.

So far, in this bewildering dialectic, we have gone through two stages of the psychic "trinity"—first, that of a pure but unactualized consciousness; and second, that of a consciousness actualized (though inadequately) in external activity. Since that actualization (in desire and work) is never fully satisfying to the Unhappy Consciousness, it returns to itself once more. But now it sees itself as nothing when compared to the deity. Thus, the self-return (which is the usual key to the resolution of an antithesis as far as Hegel is concerned) must fail here.

This is because the Unhappy Consciousness, in its return to itself, sees itself not only in a quantitative but also in an evaluative contrast to the deity: not only is the individual consciousness minuscule where the deity is infinitely great, the individual consciousness also sees itself as being in a state of sin where the deity is holy. The relation is almost necessarily reciprocal, so that the one loses where the other gains. (Indeed, the individual must accentuate the sense of his own sinfulness, as a precondition for approaching God.) This, so far, is a theoretical trajectory. In concrete terms we find a parallel process, as characterized by Jean Wahl:[9] the process begins with religious desire, issues into work and communion in a sanctified world, and ends in desolation and the humiliation of the individual. Life is therefore nothing but emptiness. All activity is weary, stale, flat, and unprofitable—along with all the uses of this world.

The depth of its misery can be gauged by the fact that, for the Unhappy Consciousness, the awareness of its unity with the deity is linked *to* that misery and the sense of sin and emptiness. If it is only in the awareness of one's own sinfulness that one can approach God, then how sad it all is!

The gap (quantitative, evaluative, and other)—between the individual consciousness and the deity—is so vast that it needs a mediator, a priest, to serve as go-between. The individual surrenders his freedom of choice to the will of the priest. By giving up one's ego, one turns one's self-consciousness into a thing—but one thereby has the conviction of having achieved unity with God. Nevertheless, the individual self-consciousness has not genuinely achieved this, since the ego *was* surrendered, and a vacuity cannot engage in a union. (Meister Eckhart will disagree precisely on this point, and insist that God can enter only the "empty" soul. But his "argument" is mystical and therefore counterrational in its fundamental assumptions and criteria.) The deity therefore remains as remote as ever. Yet in one's awareness of the action taken as one's own, there arises a view of one's own reason and selfhood—and this is now glimpsed as the ultimately and absolutely real.

Why should this elaborate transformation take place, and what can we gather from it? The discussion Hegel gives to these matters, in the present section, is so complex and abstruse, operating on so many levels at once, as to cry out for interpretation. The answers to the question (above) are rooted in the division of consciousness itself—as is the difficulty of those answers. As we saw, consciousness knows itself divided as universal *and* as particular, as infinite *and* as finite, etc., etc. In any such division, we feel called upon to choose one side over the other. The choices between these alternatives cannot be simple, cannot be made once and for all time, and cannot be made on merely theoretical grounds—because such merely theoretical choices would be entirely abstract, and the abstract way of thinking is too remote and unsatisfying for the Unhappy Consciousness. For these reasons (and probably for others), the various elements of consciousness work their way out as dimorphic imagery. The image that is "chosen" depends, once again, on whether we are thinking in terms of the universal, particular, or singular.

What all this amounts to is the view that a cultural phenomenon such as religion (but by extension we could apply this view to other areas) is the outward projection of individual psychic elements. This sounds innocuous enough when regarded in a deterministic psychological light. Yet we ought to remember that we are operating on a phenomenological (not psychological) plane. So when we say that a cultural phenomenon, such as religion, is the outward projection of individual psychic elements, what we mean is that we must regard culture as the epiphenomenon of consciousness, in the dialectical clash between its component *essences* (not forces).

Thus, certain essences are attached to certain aspects of psychic functioning; these essences conflict and cannot be reconciled or pacified; the unresolved clash therefore comes out as religion (or another cultural mode). This is because the individual cannot choose between the alternatives with any finality; he cannot decisively say what his essence is or ought to be. And because he cannot say what his own essence is, he decides on what God's essence is. Therefore, what the individual consciousness cannot say about itself, it says about God. Unable to grasp itself in any conclusive manner, the Unhappy Consciousness finds a way of saying what it must on another plane—religion.

We can say, therefore, that what Hegel is presenting (in describing the trajectory from Stoicism to Skepticism to the Unhappy Consciousness) is a mini-theory of culture. This is not *stated* as a theory, to be sure, but is rather *displayed* in terms of the three cultural models. He will go on to amplify the "theory" in subsequent chapters, where it will take a different direction altogether. Here, however, we can restrict ourselves to that theory—tacitly presented in chapter IV.

From what we are given here, we see that culture arises out of human dissatisfaction—but more basically out of the (always) frustrated search for selfhood. That search led to combat and enslavement. Yet what is significant is not so much the situation of enslavement as the slave's *continuing* desire to achieve recognition as human. The fact that this cannot be fulfilled in the circumstances is what leads to his dissatisfaction. It is this dissatisfaction that is at first internalized, then externalized as the epiphenomenon that is culture. Stoicism, Skepticism, and the Unhappy Consciousness are mediated responses to that dissatisfaction—even if they also are responses to the more fundamental need to assert and define one's selfhood.

The dissatisfaction expresses itself in the feeling that we are not at home in the world. The fact that the feeling exists in *slave* consciousness is therefore accidental (in my view). What we are relating to, as the most basic element, is not the enslavement but the desire to be recognized as human. The relevant point is that the individual consciousness feels alienated from its surroundings. With this as a basis, the individual consciousness goes on to universalize that alienation: i.e., to regard it as characteristic of the human situation in general.

In that generalization two things (at least) are emphasized: first, the independence of the human consciousness from its surroundings, its freedom from all physical, social, and economic determination; second, the positing of a higher spirituality to which the human spirit bears kinship (near or remote), and to which it seeks a direct connection. What we are shown, therefore, is one path to the elevation of the human spirit. And, paradoxically, that elevation is the outcome of the negativity, isolation, and alienation of spirit.

Obviously this is not the only path to that elevation. Hegel, in selecting these three outgrowths of the Hellenistic period as the path for the spirit to take in its development, is fully aware of the other paths, equally powerful and suggestive, yet far removed from these.[10] To take only one example, the Athenian polis produced a culture of happiness and person-al fulfillment (for adult-male-citizen-freemen) perhaps unequaled by any other. That culture, too, sought the elevation of human spirituality by way of self-consciousness ("Know thyself"), and Hegel will make much of this in his subsequent writings. Why, then, did he here choose to ignore Athenian culture as an extension of self-consciousness?

The historical answer, of course, is that the Athenian polis, elitist as it was, could in no way be seen as serving the needs of slave-consciousness. That is why Socratic self-knowledge could not be presented in response to the slave's need for internalization. Socratic self-examination, verbalized and externalized, is not what the mute slave can use. I have said, however, that what is basic is the need for recognition, and that the situation of enslavement is irrelevant to this, so it would appear as though this "his-torical answer" is not to the point. It is to the point, however—or would have been—if Hegel had been concerned to show the *master's* subsequent development. That is: given the fact that neither the master nor the slave get the recognition they want, perhaps Hegel should have struck two par-allel paths *at this point:* the slave's evolution via Stoicism, Skepticism, and Christianity; and the master's evolution via Athenian culture, the Roman patriciate, etc. Yet in taking the single path of Stoicism, Skepticism, and Christianity, Hegel places greater emphasis on internalization as the medi-ation of culture—as though self-consciousness must first coil inward in order to store up sufficient energy for its outward recoil. (Obviously, he is not aiming at a comprehensive view of the relation between self-con-sciousness and culture; that is why the view he presents here can be called a mini-theory.)

Perhaps the answer is that the effulgent self-consciousness of the polis—celebrated in Sophocles' marvelous paean to man's intelligence and creativity (in *Antigone*)—could only have led to a dead end. Perhaps no world culture could have emerged from it, no Christianity that would speak to man's universal situation of limitation, fallibility, and doom. The polis is a rare moment and a short one. For the emergence of Western self-consciousness, the polis is essential, certainly—but only as an element, a memory, an ideal that could not be actualized more than once. Christianity, on the other hand, *is* Western self-consciousness.

Christianity, then, is the product of slave-mentality—a fact seen by

Nietzsche in pejorative terms. For Hegel, on the contrary, only such a mentality could have yielded a sensitivity for the human condition in general and thus have served as a basis for a world culture. Stoicism and Skepticism—had the development stopped with them—would have led to a dead end as well, because the values of indifference and unperturbedness would not have given us the essential insight into man's permanent state. (What *culture* could have been built upon them?)

A culture is a projection of a worldview, a vision of man in the world. No culture confined within one ethnic boundary—e.g., Judaic or Hellenic—could have provided that *world*-cultural basis. Christianity undoubtedly spoke to the spiritual depression prevailing in the world as a universal condition (not merely to that prevailing in the Hellenistic world). What Hegel shows is that it is by no means accidental that the most exalted vision of the godhead should have emerged in that spiritual depression, when man's grasp of his own selfhood was so shaky. On the contrary, we have seen that that connection is essential. In elevating God, however, man is elevated only by indirection, not in actuality—and so he must take to the road again, to seek yet another path to that end.

Thus, the insight provided by Christianity is not the ultimate, and is to be surpassed by reason. As far as it goes, however, Christianity speaks to the finitude in which we all find ourselves, as human. For Hegel, its weakness is that it speaks in imagery, not theory—which is why its theorizing (as in Scholasticism) is borrowed largely from Hellenic sources.

After the Unhappy Consciousness, the challenge must be to achieve a broader view of man, universal in scope, in which we grasp the point, in concrete terms, that the rational is real, the real is rational (or *ought* to be). Only then can human life be fully rationalized and fulfilled.

9

AFTER "SELF-CONSCIOUSNESS"

Self-consciousness cannot see beyond itself—this is its limitation. The Unhappy Consciousness, for example, takes its own being-in-itself as the absolute essence, as though this is how consciousness must be, per se. As Hegel says, it sees its being-in-itself *(Ansichsein)* as "its own beyond" *(das Jenseits seiner selbst)*. This is as far as it casts its net.

In these circumstances, we might expect the Unhappy Consciousness to be satisfied with the notion of selfhood that it has put forward. Yet the ironic fact (so astutely observed by Hegel) is that the Unhappy Consciousness has posited a notion of selfhood that cannot be fulfilled—not by anything human. Only God can fulfill its conception of selfhood, for only God is the *complete* self. As a consequence of that viewpoint, the human self must forever see itself as incomplete. The individual ego may even get as far as considering itself at one with God. Yet in order to achieve this union with the universal (in its own eyes), it must negate its own particularity. Thus the individual renounces himself in God's favor, so to speak—although this has the effect of rendering himself and his own world less than real.

Since (in this view) God is the only reality, one's own reality can be no better than abstract and illusory by comparison. This is why things cannot end at this point in the career of selfhood: the medieval Christian view of the self cannot be the final one; there must be progress beyond the

Unhappy Consciousness, if only because a complete grasp of the self has not yet been achieved by self-consciousness at this stage.

There still is a long way to go. Self-consciousness is not yet self-knowledge. Nor is it reason—let alone a higher view of the operation of world reason. This is why there will be newer worldviews. The fact that these will be forthcoming indicates the inadequacies of the older views. Thus, in the *Phenomenology*, the stage called "Self-Consciousness" gives way to the stage called "Reason," and beyond this there is the stage describing "Spirit" at work in culture and morality, leading to the stages called "Religion" and "Absolute Knowing." (Here, I shall discuss only the "Reason" chapter, and in very compressed form.)

At the stage of Self-Consciousness—particularly in Stoicism, Skepticism, and the Unhappy Consciousness—we found the *self* and the *world* in an inverse relation to one another: the sense of self was strengthened only by minimizing the world's reality and importance. Further, a similar inverse relation held between man and God—except that it was one-sided, since man could not minimize God. God *must* come out ahead, and therefore man's selfhood must be diminished by comparison. Yet he still could bolster what sense of self he had by denying the world. Thus, man fortifies his ego by weakening his hold on the world; but then he must weaken himself once again vis-à-vis God. What the human psyche gains in one sphere it loses in the other.

At the stage of Reason, on the other hand, that inverse relation gives way to a direct one: In modern thinking we find the gradually developing view that it is human consciousness that creates the world; that it grasps the world's structure and lawfulness, but that our consciousness imposes upon it a structure and lawfulness emanating from consciousness. This culminates in the absolute knowledge of "the Spirit knowing itself as Spirit" *(der sich als Geist wissende Geist)*. Spirit knows *itself* as producing the world. Thus, consciousness is now at home in the world for the first time, because it sees the world as *its* own. Where self-consciousness had groped toward "the truth of self-certainty," reason now arrives at the certainty that consciousness is *all* reality, and that selfhood is the truth of everything.

It is not at all surprising that this standpoint should emerge in the Renaissance attitude that led to the development of the sciences. We need only think of Leonardo's well-known drawing of the extended human figure standing within a concentric square and circle: there is the suggestion that man is now about to square the circle; there is also the more definite suggestion that in touching the points of intersection, man now reaches to the farthest limits of his world because he is its creator, the source of its meaning.

Of course, the truth that human consciousness has created its world—this is a truth that must be *made* true. It must be given content by our reiterating the entire career of consciousness so far—from the earliest doubts about sense certainty on to the unsatisfying end of the Unhappy Consciousness. That truth is also given content when reason finds itself reflected in the world.

Reason thus observes particular things and events as instances of universals and laws—although the expected necessity is more characteristic of the "laws of thought" than of (say) the biological sphere. There is the attempt to reify the human spirit so that we regard it as something inert (as in the pseudo-sciences of physiognomy and phrenology). The genuine view of spirit, however, grasps rational self-consciousness in its *activity*.

In this light alone can we see the human spirit as projecting itself out into the world—that is, in the value systems and social configurations that it devises. When that devising becomes self-conscious, all systems are threatened, of course. Once we begin to think, there is no knowing how things will end. By comparison, what characterizes ordinary moral life is its uncritical immediacy. This is effectually challenged, weakened, or even destroyed when individuality becomes prominent and seeks to shape its own life by taking thought. It is then that we find the individual pitted against society, and seeking his own fulfillment in contradistinction to it. This self-centeredness can take the form of egoistic hedonism, or a rampant romanticism which Hegel calls "the law of the heart," or even a rather exalted self-dedication to the pursuit of virtue.

Egoistic hedonism is not a genuine fulfillment of self-consciousness: the exploitation of another person for one's own pleasure is *self*-destructive, since the ego is thereby reified and thus weakened, not strengthened. It is a driven individuality, and bases itself on a weak conception of the self: even if it appears to fortify its selfhood in self-gratification at the expense of another, it has surrendered its selfhood to what seems (to it) a natural necessity.

The romanticist—ostensibly ruled by "the law of the heart"—places himself in opposition to social conventions, and thereby seems to strengthen his individuality. Yet to the extent that what guides him has itself become a "law," he must oppose that as well. He therefore confounds what he lives by. Moreover, *my* heart's law might not coincide with the "law" of another romanticist. I am therefore driven by a "law" that I cannot universalize as law. This can lead to the derangement of consciousness. Its only possibility for universalization is if everyone shares in the derangement, a general madness (*Wahnsinn im allgemein*) and self-alienation. But this is obviously a false universalization: shared madness is not sanity.

In contrast to all this, another spiritual dichotomy might be set up: that between individual moral activity and the autonomously functioning moral order of society. Individuals operate on the basis of personal interests, and these go to make up a disinterested moral structure of social values. Yet *conscious* moral virtue aims at a deliberate intervention in society's moral order, an intervention the self-propelling order resists. Paradoxically, the path to individual virtue stresses universalization and the surrender of individuality, while the collective moral order does allow for individuality.

Moral individualism and self-legislation (à la Kant) now become the expression of self-consciousness: that is, individuality is now universalized, expected to conform to a generalized moral standard. Yet this involves a simplification of moral reality and moral choice, in contrast to the complexity of individual character (on the basis of which our choices are made). The Kantian application of reason to that human complexity can only result in its stultification, in Hegel's view. We come up with universal maxims; but these fail in their application to particular individuals and events, because the maxims are too simple while the individuals or events are too complex. At best, the application of reason to morality can keep us clear of self-contradiction. Consistency alone, however, is not a sufficient basis for morality.

Thus the conscious application of reason to moral life must fail—and this would become obvious if we tried to run an actual society on Kantian lines. In view of this inevitable failure, then, what we must rely on is the autonomous functioning of ethical life in society itself—where that functioning is the direct expression of the spirit of a culture, and thus of the spirit of humanity in its endless variety.

EARLY-TWENTIETH-CENTURY
EUROPEAN CRITICISM

The chapter on Self-Consciousness is complex enough to have provoked a variety of interpretations—even *seemingly* conflicting ones. Thus, there have been tendencies to read this chapter in the light of a "Christian" Hegel (Wahl), a "Marxist" Hegel (Kojève), and an "existential" Hegel (Hyppolite). Whatever the differences between these readings, it seems (to me) to be undeniable that Hegel is correct in emphasizing the centrality and fragility of the element of recognition in the formation of personhood. We are our own self-image. To some commentators (Sartre), what is unacceptable in that idea is the vulnerability of our self-image in its dependence on another party—especially in the way Hegel depicts the master and slave as depending on one another for recognition, so that the recognition by another is the *truth* of self-certainty. On the contrary, it is stressed that we make our self-image independently, regardless of whether it is deceptive or truthful, serviceable, or trivial.

Perhaps that dependence (on another person) is unacceptable because it is damaging to our self-image of our self-image-making. Yet we all know to what extent our ego and dignity depend upon inanimate objects such as (say) food, clothing, shelter, soap, etc. In the light of this, our dependence on a human factor, such as our being recognized as human by another human, is that much more vital and critical.

There are various objections we might raise to Hegel's presentation of his views in scenario form. One objection to the master-slave scenario is that it is not discursive or theoretical but descriptive—and not descriptive of an actual state of affairs but of a hypothetical situation. As such it cannot be verified or falsified—no more than any piece of fiction can be. This may seem to be a drawback but it is not. Fiction *is* meaningful, after all. One commentator (Hyppolite) sees the master-slave scenario as a "philosophical novel"—and that remark may provide an answer to the objection. Thus, we readily accept a novel such as William Golding's *Lord of the Flies*, in its depiction of the return to savagery on the part of some English schoolboys. The author purports to *show* (not argue) that the civilizing layer is thin, and that savagery is our essential nature in the absence of the restraining forces of civilization. In reading the novel, that view is *inferred* (uncritically) by us. It is not stated as an empirical hypothesis, to be confirmed or disconfirmed. Its "truth" comes not from its correspondence to a body of experimental data, but rather from its internal coherence or else its coherence with a broader worldview. This coherence theory is Hegel's general approach to truth—viz., his statement in the Preface to the *Phenomenology:* "The True is the whole." (*Das Wahre ist das Ganze*).

Yet the master-slave scenario is not to be relegated to the status of mere fiction. Rather, it is a phenomenological presentation in which we "suspend" verifiability in order to arrive at an exposure of certain necessary and essential relations: e.g., why the two parties *must* come to mortal combat in the first place, why the victor *must* let the loser survive, and so on and on.

With verifiability suspended, we see that there are no right or wrong interpretations, only good ones or bad ones; no truth or falsity in the strict sense, only insight or opacity. In the case of the interpretations we shall discuss here, there are only good or better ones, ranging from insight to brilliance. The difference is in the depth of meaning that each interpretation conveys. And since all these are at least good ones, they contribute to one another by providing shading or chiaroscuro.

We, as well, must approach Hegel's master-slave scenario as nonempirical. We thereby open ourselves to a wider range of interpretations than would otherwise be acceptable. Once we understand this, we see that the various views do not really come into conflict with one another, but supplement one another and thus deepen our appreciation of Hegel's insight into the human animal.

Kojève

The main intellectual effort in France during the middle part of this century was spent in accommodating Existentialism to Marxism. And the primary path along which this accommodation was sought involved the adaptation of Hegel to both, as their common ancestor. The effort involved not only Sartre and Merleau-Ponty but a host of others as well. All of them traced their inspiration to one preeminent power source: the lectures on Hegel's *Phenomenology* given by Alexandre Kojève at the *École des Hautes Études* from 1933 to 1939. It was not until 1947 that these were put together and published,[1] although the impact of the lectures was felt earlier, especially by writers such as Sartre and Merleau-Ponty. A whole generation of intellectuals was raised on the lectures, and the effects are still with us. If the *Phenomenology* has had the profound influence it did have in modern times, this is a tribute not only to the vitality of that book itself but as well to the creative interpretation given it by Kojève.

What he does in interpreting the master-slave passage is to emphasize the element of *work* as the humanizing factor for mankind. Of course, the slave is already humanized (to a degree) by the initial struggle and by the subsequent internalization of his consciousness; yet it is primarily the fact that he is put to work on a thing, the benefit of which he will *not* enjoy, that places him on the path to his eventual humanization.

Following Hegel, Kojève identifies the concept "man" with "self-consciousness." Yet he gives this connection a rather simplistic Hobbesian base by *deriving* it from the concept of desire (which is an animal element, more than a specifically human one). According to Kojève, it is conscious desire that leads one to say "I," and thus leads one to take one's own subjectivity as one's object in self-consciousness. As he says: "The (human) I is the I of a Desire or of Desire" (p. 4). Now, Hegel does speak of desire as a basic element in self-consciousness; yet (in my view) he points to the negating capacity of consciousness as primary, and to desire (qua human) as an *extension* of the self-conscious ego.[2] Kojève, on the other hand, sees human life based in its animal life, as its necessary (though not sufficient) condition. He therefore sees the negating capacity as a function or extension of desire (as in the desire to consume food and thus to negate it), rather than the other way around, as I believe it is for Hegel.

On a number of occasions, Hegel does state that self-consciousness *is* desire. Yet I do not think he intends this statement to be taken as *analytically* true. He does not say we *are* self-conscious by virtue of our desiring something. Nor does he say (as Kojève does) that we *become* self-conscious (and therefore human) by desiring something. On the contrary, it is in self-consciousness that we become aware of our desires *as* human desires (although these preexist as animal functions). That is, we first have to *be* human, and to regard ourselves as human, in order to recognize our (animal) desires as human ones. Thus, it is our self-recognition (involving the negating capacity of self-consciousness) that renders our *desires* human in our own eyes. From there we must take the further step of getting recognition for *ourselves* as human. Yet we cannot achieve this for ourselves: *as* individuals, we cannot give ourselves that recognition. In my isolation, I cannot humanize *myself* by my own efforts!

Why is this so? Why should there be this unbridgeable abyss between the self and its grasp of itself? Is it because *all* consciousness sets its object at a distance from itself, and that this fact makes *self*-consciousness impossible for the (as yet) primitive mentality? If that is the case, then we see how very great an advance toward humanness is achieved by self-consciousness.

In the same way, desire presupposes a distance between the ego and its object, so that the two are juxtaposed. Thus, the desired object exists to tell me that I am incomplete—that in becoming, I am not what I (now) am, and I am what I am not (i.e., not yet). This is why desire cannot give me my self-consciousness or my selfhood. If it could, then I would find my human fulfillment in my solitary desire and in solipsism. Thus, the fact that a confrontation ensues indicates the insufficiency of desire.

It seems to me that the whole thrust of Hegel's view is that there is no "private language" of recognition; that our recognition requires a social situation. Now, if it were *analytically* true that self-consciousness is desire, then by virtue of my solitary desire I would be self-conscious, self-aware to the point of being self-recognizing—and then the *social* need would be altogether obviated. But this is not the case, and it is entirely out of line with what Hegel is saying. It would therefore appear that Kojève is reading into desire a social dimension that is not necessarily there, and that what we need is a *phenomenological* corrective to this approach of his, in order to bring us to the social confrontation.[3]

Thus, my desire is not implicitly social, and must yet be directed outward. When desire is directed to another desire (in another individual), socialization begins. Here is where the need for *mutual* recognition arises. (Kojève accepts this; he merely fails to see that by making desire basic, he will not get to mutuality.) In this way, by recognizing one another's desires as human, desire itself becomes our object—and this leads Kojève to proclaim the motto: "Human history is the history of desired Desires" (p. 6).

Indeed, the mortal combat is directed to the desire of another's desire, from which the desired recognition is expected to emerge. In Kojève's view, it is my need to keep the other person's desire alive that leads me to keep *him* alive. I need him alive not merely so that he may recognize me as human, but also so that he may recognize my *desire* as human. History arises, then, in the dialectic of master and slave, but with the added dimension wherein desire is now being accorded human recognition.

The mortal combat ensues because although recognition must be reciprocal, neither party wants it to be more than unilateral. In other words, we *resist* our socialization and humanization—and this resistance must be overcome if there is to be humanization at all. Recognition must be reciprocal because even if a man seeks recognition *for* himself alone, he can get it only *from* another human—one whom he has already acknowledged as human. The seeker must therefore *accord* humanity to the person from whom he seeks recognition, even while he denies it to that person and imposes his own demand for human status upon him.

Yet couldn't this be seen as a possible start? Although this might be the basis (however inadequate) for a shared societal life, such life is not to come about in this context. This is because the one who can demand recognition denies himself recognition by denying prior recognition to the person from whom he demands it. He therefore gets a "recognition" that is no better than formal and one-sided, since it is not the recognition an *acknowledged person* would give.

As one-sided as the "recognition" is, however, some human identification is created. What is important is that this identification is a non-natural entity—an entirely novel element in the natural world and not a part of the natural inventory. Further, *action* (as distinguished from behavior) is created when it is recognized as human—and it is action aimed at making the natural world hospitable to man. The first human action is the imposition of oneself on another person. Since this is the first *human* action, it reflects the human essence in its entirety—like a secular equivalent to Original Sin.

The introduction of recognition as this non-natural element points to a humanizing of nature itself—a transformation to be continued in the form of work, once the respective states of master and slave have been established. The master has already liberated himself from nature by risking his life for prestige—an action whose content is entirely human and non-natural. Yet as we saw, the action is incomplete because the recognition is demanded from one who is not recognized as human but is regarded as no more than an animal or a thing. (A bit further on, we shall see how the slave liberates himself from nature as he humanizes it.) While the master cannot recognize the slave, the slave does "recognize" the master, sees the master's freedom and autonomy (fallaciously), and thus learns what these are. The master has no need to think about his freedom. The slave does think of it, internalizes that aim, and thereby becomes the source of all eventual human advance!

The master, having risked his life to become what he is, is ready to be master forever. The incomplete recognition he has gained could be made complete if he could transcend his status as master and leave it behind him; but this is impossible for *him* since mastery is all. The slave, on the other hand, knows that slavery is not all, that there are other modes of human life—however unlikely it may be for him to achieve them. The slave is therefore open to change, yearning to be free. As Kojève says, "He is historical becoming at his origin, in his essence, in his very existence" (p. 22).

In being forced to work, the slave becomes the "master" of nature. He thereby frees himself from his own "nature" (whose instinct to self-preservation is what made him a slave). And in being freed from his own nature, he is "free" of enslavement and thereby "free" of the master. By his work he transforms (and thus transcends) the immediate world. He thereby "overcomes" his enslavement, and eventually overcomes the master as well. Thus, if his enslavement is the necessary condition of historical progress, his work is its actualization. (And yet the *reality* of that actualization can be questioned, as I did in my discussion of the Hegel text, above. I have implicitly questioned it here as well: the relevant terms, which I have put in quotation-marks, are not used literally but figuratively.)

It would seem that the opposite is the case: the slave is enslaved to nature, the master is master of nature. Yet the master creates nothing real in nature (however much he may be nominally "in charge" of a piece of it). He can never rise above the world. The slave, on the other hand, has the experience of giving shape to nature, imposing his effort upon it, and thereby "freeing" himself from it. In transforming a thing, he comes to know what it is to transform himself!

The slave's work therefore "realizes" the slave, while he realizes himself as a human being. By doing something to nature he is above nature— he is a *super*natural being. (He is supernatural as well in the fact that in transcending the natural world he "realizes"—i.e., in two senses: coming to know and making real—his own spirituality and his tie to spirituality.) Kojève expresses this in rather oracular terms: "By working, he is 'incarnated' Spirit, he is historical 'World,' he is 'objectivized' History" (p. 25).

What the Hegelian view shares with the Marxist view (according to Kojève) is the insight that culture is a superstructure, of which the substructure is work and action: the complex of events whereby man makes himself what he is and thereby differentiates himself from nature. What distinguishes man, as agent and worker, is that he not only makes his world but also understands it as his, as non-natural and as novel.

This is why, in Kojève's view, the *cogito* is an inadequate springboard for our understanding of ourselves: "I think"—but what am *I?* The answer "I am a thinking thing" is inadequate because it is circular and leaves the ultimate question open. Thus, the existential focus must be on the *I*, not on the *think*. In this, man comes to reveal *his* being—and Being, as such. Man is not only the being who reveals Being, however. He is also the being who (in turning to himself) reveals the being who reveals Being. Thus he reveals, in self-consciousness, what his selfhood is. We can say, therefore, that the most striking innovation brought about by our *super*natural existence—the innovation that amounts to an alien intrusion in the natural world—is the introduction of "I," and the subsequent grasp of this as filling the different meanings of subject and object in the statement "I am I."

According to Kojève, there is no direct transition from consciousness to self-consciousness. Mere contemplation of the object will leave us with the object; it will not automatically lead to self-consciousness. Rather, what serves to produce the break that turns us to the "I" and to reveal its being is desire. Here again I believe he misreads Hegel, and that what turns us in that direction *is* a function of consciousness (as desire itself is)—namely, the negating capacity of consciousness. We see that the contemplation of the object does not lead us as far as we want to go, and so we negate the object and that line of thinking—and we turn to ourselves in self-consciousness.

Kojève says that man—in being impelled by desire—is impelled by the awareness of his emptiness, his nothingness and insufficiency. But beyond this, man finally realizes that he *is* to the extent that he *negates* (p. 38). This means that we *are* only to the extent that we *become*—i.e., become what we are. This is the dimension of action, making, fighting, working, and history. Instead of the *cogito*, therefore, what we have as irreducible givens are: a) the capacity to reveal Being in speech; b) action that negates Being, i.e., action emanating from a desire that is directed toward another desire, a non-being; c) the existence of a multiplicity of desires (in a multiplicity of individuals); d) the possibility of a difference in the desires of individuals, and the survival of the individuals in any conflict resulting from the juxtaposition of those desires.

This entire array cannot be fulfilled simultaneously. These are all elements in our attempt to rise above natural existence. And yet the slave, in choosing survival, surrenders to the demands of that natural existence. What he achieves thereafter is his slow climb out of that surrender by means of his internalization and his consequently broadened self-consciousness. His is the final victory, therefore, and it is greater than he could have hoped for when the fight began. First, the recognition depended upon another person, and whether that recognition was justified or not was never raised as a question. He now ends by giving recognition to himself, and this time it is with a full awareness of its justification. Second, he began by wanting mere *recognition* as human. He now ends by having *created* his own humanity!

Although the master does not master nature, he does elude it, in the initial struggle, by placing his prestige above his biological survival. He further eludes nature by interposing the slave's work between nature and himself. The slave eludes nature by his work for the master. (If the slave were working to fulfill his *own* needs he would be *within* nature. Working for another is non-natural, and therefore humanizing.) And just as history began in their combat, it ends when the status difference between them disappears, so that the master no longer has a slave, nor the slave a master. In Kojève's view, Hegel saw history coming to an end in the battle of Jena, as the *Phenomenology* was being completed: the French Revolution and the Napoleonic War produced the *citoyen* of the universal state, and he is neither master nor slave.

The master has sought a nonbiological end in seeking recognition. Although any explicit recognition the slave may give is inadequate from the master's point of view, the master's superiority is nevertheless materialized in the slave's work. Yet the master wanted express recognition from an equal, and this he cannot have: anyone his equal would sooner die than be subjected, and recognition from anyone else is not worth having. For that reason, mastery is at an "existential impasse," as Kojève says (p. 46).

The slave, living in constant fear of death, and having been at the point of death when he lost the battle, comes up against his own vulnerability, his own nothingness—as Kojève calls it, "a nothingness maintained in being" (p. 48). Yet it is this nothingness that negates time, that acts, that understands man. Only the slave can become other than he is, and can thereby impel history. Having transformed nature, he knows that he can transform himself and his own situation. As we saw, it is by his work for another that the slave overcomes his own nature, and transforms nature itself in relation to a non-natural idea. All this, taken together, provides the reason why the slave alone can bring an end to history.

The subsequent worldviews—Stoicism, Skepticism, and Christianity—are treated by Kojève as *ideologies* (in somewhat of the Marxist sense of false consciousness). They are intended to get the slave to accept his enslavement. In Christianity, for example, the enslavement is magnified into an enslavement to God, the supreme master. This gives me, the slave, the dubious consolation of regarding my earthly master as God's slave as well, and *therefore* as much a slave as I! Yet since this is not true, I must ignore a considerable area of reality in order to convince myself of its truth. In any case, this belief liberates neither of us. On the contrary, the distortion of truth enslaves us to further distortion. Thus, the slavish desire for life at any price now becomes the desire for *eternal* life. In the final analysis, Christianity comes from the slave's terror at having to face his own nothingness and death. To accept death and to accept its finality—this is to accept atheism. The true goal of *Christian* progress, Kojève says, is the *atheistic* awareness of human finitude. In this way alone—i.e., by overcoming Christianity and its promise of life in another world—can man realize his freedom in this world.

Hyppolite

While Kojève was giving his lectures (1933–39), no French translation was as yet available of the *Phenomenology*. The first French translation of the entire work was undertaken by Jean Hyppolite—who knew no German, and learned the language by reading the *Phenomenology!* The two volumes of his translation appeared in 1939 and 1941.

Hyppolite did not come under the direct influence of Kojève, and avoided his lectures "for fear of being influenced."[4] At the time, the interpretations of Hegel were polarized between Kojève's Marxian approach (with the master-slave relation at its center) and Jean Wahl's Christian approach (placing the Unhappy Consciousness at the center of Hegel's thinking). Kojève's aim was to politicize the study of Hegel. Thus, in 1946 Kojève declares that any interpretation of Hegel is a program of political struggle, and that the work of the Hegel interpreter is equivalent to a work of political propaganda (p. xv). Further: "It is possible that in reality the future of the world, and thus the meaning of the present and that of the past, depend, in the last analysis, on the way in which the Hegel writings are interpreted today" (p. xxviii).

In this atmosphere of exaggeration and hyperbole, a level head was needed, and it was Hyppolite's. He saw Hegel and Marx as utterly distinct, even diametrically opposed—and he therefore resisted the temptation to interpret Hegel through a Marxist lens. Thus, the Marxian viewpoint— e.g., that of Lukács—sees Hegel's concept of the alienation of spirit as equivalent to Marx's concept of objectification. Against this, Hyppolite suggests that the two concepts are different: Even in our understanding of man's objectification in culture, the more fundamental fact is that he remains alienated from himself, and that (quite apart from the deterministic effects of capitalist systems) this is a feature of human self-consciousness and human existence.[5]

In addition to his massive work, *Genesis and Structure*, Hyppolite's existential interpretation of Hegel is reflected in three splendid essays in his *Studies on Marx and Hegel*: "The Concept of Life and Consciousness of Life in Hegel's Jena Philosophy," "The Concept of Existence in the Hegelian Phenomenology," and "The Human Situation in the Hegelian Phenomenology." (It is these essays that I shall be discussing here.) Directing himself to the concept of existence, he notes that this concept— as an explicit formulation—is absent in Hegel. Yet this absence is perfectly consistent with Kierkegaard's view that the concept of existence cannot be systematized, i.e., that an existential *system* is impossible (even though Kierkegaard accused Hegel of attempting to present such a system). There is, however, an existential *outlook* in Hegel, and Hyppolite therefore says that the *Phenomenology* reveals "a philosopher much closer to Kierkegaard than might seem credible" (p. 23).

True, the existential aspect is in some ways obscured by the phenomenological emphasis, which seeks the underlying essences in various worldviews. Yet the existential impact is there in Hegel's realization that there is an unhappiness which is implicit in our consciousness of human life, since we place life over against us in order to see it, and then we become aware that our life includes our death and our nothingness.[6] In essence, then, when consciousness stands juxtaposed to the life it contemplates, we see that consciousness as such actually *is* opposed to life.

In natural existence, the relation is simple and one-sided: Consciousness is altogether immersed in existence; it is an untroubled consciousness, even a "truth" of sorts. The fact is, however, that we must step out of life (i.e., out of its immediacy) in order to see it, and then we find its truth outside it, in our consciousness of it. For this, the price we pay is that in seeing life as a totality we negate its particular aspects. A further price is that although we lose our naiveté in the process, we add to our anguish. We stand outside life and now see it as "existence"—and we thereby become aware of death in a new and intense way as we reflect on what it means to exist with the prospect of death before us.

In Hegel's earlier writings, the contrast is drawn between Greek happiness (in harmonizing thought and finite life) and the Jews as the unhappy people of history (the unhappiness exemplified in the departure of Abraham from his original homeland, his detachment from everything finite as though it had no value). Only outside finitude can we conceive the universal. In the *Phenomenology*,[7] Hegel explicitly sets up the contrast between self-consciousness and life: self-consciousness *grasps* the unity of differences, while life *is* that unity.

The wedge between life and self-consciousness is the awareness of death. Organic life lacks that awareness, and thus lacks the element of *existence* (i.e., it does not *know* itself *as* existing). In man, therefore, the consciousness of existence is bound up with the concept of his death—and it is in that awareness that man becomes *for himself.* The price man pays for rising above animal life is this painful awareness.

In man, the desire to live is the counterpart to the awareness of death, and this produces a division in his awareness of life: He sees life as identical to himself, yet as alien to himself; he is in it, yet is estranged from it. The resolution of this dichotomy is that he sees that desire as the unity of the universal life, which expresses itself in a multitude of particular forms. Yet life confronts him in the person of another self, and it is only in this confrontation of selves that we arrive at self-consciousness. The confrontation is actually a conflict between the concepts of *being-for-self* and *being-for-another*, or independence and dependence. Only in the death of the other being do I release myself from my dependence. My *being-for-another* is an estranged mode of being: Because I am nothing but an Other for my opponent, I am not a Self. Otherness stands opposed to selfhood, and therefore stands opposed to self-consciousness.

My awareness of my own death (i.e., its imminence and its inevitability) drives me to seek my selfhood by seeking the Other's death. I therefore stake my life in order to authenticate my consciousness of life.[8] At the same time I prove my independence of life itself. I am ready to *face* death because then it is not merely a biological death, an inchoate death, but a death of

which I am humanly aware. This human awareness of death is the foundation of a humanized world, a historical world. Life and death are no longer
absorbed in time; they are the poles of time itself. Thus, the awareness of
death is the basis of my capacity to negate, and of my freedom.

In turning to consider what Hyppolite calls "the human situation" as
depicted in the *Phenomenology* as a whole, we must first try to characterize the *Phenomenology* in what it aims to do. That characterization would
then show us what possibilities are open to it for grasping the human situation. Hyppolite begins by quoting Haym's remark about the
Phenomenology: "It is a history distorted by transcendental psychology and
a transcendental psychology distorted by history." Of course it is neither
of these—as I hope I have made clear so far. There is an element of history, as a parallel track onto which Hegel's presentation will emerge from
time to time—as when he speaks of the Enlightenment or of the Terror.
Thus the itinerary of consciousness is shown to have gone through certain
points that were not only essential but historically actual. This is not a distortion, as Haym suggests it is—as though the *Phenomenology* were a
palimpsest in which the layers of writing (psychological, anthropological,
historical, etc.) make one another indistinct. The *Phenomenology* is
authenticated by touching on history, but it is not a history. It does not
include historical writing as part of its methodological apparatus (and the
same can be said for its "transcendental psychology").

Hyppolite aims to *show* that chapter IV is neither a history nor a transcendental psychology. But he goes farther and says that it has even less to
do with an analysis of essence. In other words, its aim is not so much phenomenological as existential. In this vein, Hyppolite states: "Hegel wanted to analyze the very *foundations* of human action. He inquired into the
general conditions of *human existence* that constitute the possibility of the
human act as such" (p. 154). Thus there are in every historical situation
certain general conditions, which are constant for every human action.

The "analysis of essence" is rejected, since it suggests that there is a
permanent human nature. According to Hyppolite, there is no unchanging human nature for Hegel. What he is inquiring about is not this but
(in the words of Hyppolite) "the conditions of self-consciousness or of the
very existence of man" as a way of getting to the root of history. What we
are to see is how man's consciousness becomes the condition of his existence, and how his consciousness creates (in Hyppolite's words) "almost a
new dimension of being, generating a history in which conscious being
makes and reveals a rational truth" (pp. 155–56).

One aspect of that human *situation* (as opposed to a human *nature*) is the emergence of human consciousness out of universal life. In that emergence, self-consciousness sees itself confronting a universal life that is the life of consciousness as well—identical with itself, yet other than itself—so that the self-consciousness sees itself as both universal and particular. This nascent contradiction emerges in full force in the Unhappy Consciousness, and it is the permanent contradiction we are called upon (as humans) to resolve. That resolution is what history is all about. Thus (very strangely), self-consciousness negates life by reflecting upon it, and from this it generates new forms of being (e.g., desire, recognition, the "I" that is "We," etc.). One's desire is for the world, for life itself—but then life is seen as an object, external to desire. As a result, desire extends itself into the external world, to establish and to authenticate itself there.

Consciousness *exists* in its interchange with the world, desire *exists* as externalized. Only then does desire discover its own self, mediated by the world. In the same way, the self discovers itself in resisting its negation by another self. Consciousness objectifies what it knows, and it therefore resists being objectified itself in being known by another. This is a demand for a new mode of consciousness. It is the basis of intersubjectivity, on which all human existence depends. I enter your sphere of experience and I ask you to look upon me in a way that is altogether different from the way you have been looking at everything else. In asking you to acknowledge my consciousness, I am asking you to acknowledge my being, my being alive. The eventual struggle is followed by labor and one-sided recognition given by the slave—and these are then the very conditions of self-consciousness for the slave. As Hyppolite says about these conditions, "They *ground* history while making it possible" (p. 163).

What we have, therefore, are three essential elements underlying human history: self-consciousness, the opposition presented by the *other* self-consciousness, and the independent background of universal life. The mediating tie between these elements is work, which humanizes nature and gives it the form of self-consciousness. Nature becomes infused with self-consciousness; it *becomes* self-consciousness. Work also enables man to discover himself, to free himself. Finally, work gives human existence a coherence and universality. In it, we have another dimension of recognition, as the human species makes itself what it is through its work.

In all this, history itself is given a meaning, in the fact that self-consciousness is given an independent status and is seen as operating in history. It is the universal predicate that now becomes subject, as a self-created truth. Thus, the truth is humanly *created*, yet *transcends* its human creation! Hyppolite asks how this is possible, but Hegel presents no answer. Yet although there is no answer, the contribution of the *Phenomenology* is in having exposed the foundations of that creativity.

Hyppolite, in his Preface to the English edition of *Studies on Marx and Hegel*, speaks of the *Phenomenology* as presenting "the saga of the human mind as a terrestrial repetition of Dante's *Divine Comedy*" (p. vi). In my view, the first four chapters of the *Phenomenology* could also be described as presenting a secular retelling of *Genesis* after Eden. The difference is that in Eden man comes to self-knowledge by way of moral judgment: his entrance into good and evil leads to a sense of sin and remorse. The serpent's promise—that man would be like God—has the result of moralizing man's self-knowledge and thereby making him man. In Hegel's world, the slave comes to self-consciousness by a process beginning with aggressive self-assertion. Further progress is slow and painful: defeat, enslavement, fear, self-negation. He does not yet *know* himself. That is in the future, in the Unhappy Consciousness and after. But it is easy enough to adapt the serpent's words to this situation: You will be like God, knowing yourself.

As we noted, Hyppolite's existential orientation leads him to see all this as a clash between life and self-consciousness. (This division, too, can be seen as the punishment for the initial transgression, and we can express the penalty in Kierkegaard's terms: Ye shall live your life forward and understand it backward.) Thus, the division between life and self-consciousness involves an ontology.[9]

As with every other Hegelian dichotomy, so with life and self-consciousness: the poles must be kept apart, even while the division between them is being resolved! The totality of life is never given *in* life itself; it is imposed by self-consciousness, which is mediated by other self-consciousnesses in a historical context. Thus, the totality can only *come* to be, but never be. It never is what it is, and it always is what it is not. Life is self-identity *and* self-difference, immediacy *and* self-consciousness. As we saw, Hegel speaks of life's essence as "the infinitude as the overcoming of all differences, [like] the pure motion around an axis whose self-repose is an absolutely restless infinity. . . ."[10] To this we must add the element of spirit, the ego, which is an intrusion into nature: it is the "nothingness" in contrast to the "being" that is the natural/material reality.

In becoming self-conscious, the problem life faces is to give itself content, to overcome the abstractness of the tautology I = I. Desire does not stay with the pursuit of its object, but points beyond itself to the

reunion of the self with itself. It is a narcissism that is immensely productive, since it takes the indirect route, which generates social life and
culture *by the way*, before it gets back to the self. What self-consciousness
is seeking, by going through life as its medium, is self-consciousness itself.
And yet self-consciousness signifies a break with life—and Hyppolite
reminds us that the full tragedy of this will be experienced by the
Unhappy Consciousness.

In self-consciousness, the object has gone back into itself; and in this
reflection it has taken on the significance of life (for us and in itself). But
in this we divide what cannot be divided, unify what is self-repelling—so
that, once again, we have the standoff between self-consciousness and life.
For modern existentialism, the gulf is insurmountable. Hegel sees that
division overcome—at the level of Absolute Knowledge. Since existentialism rejects all absolutes but its own, life and self-consciousness remain
unreconciled for it.

Sartre and Merleau-Ponty

The influence of Hegel on subsequent thinkers is now recognized as
immense. Merleau-Ponty acknowledged that influence in a sweeping
statement: "All the great philosophical ideas of the past century—the
philosophies of Marx and Nietzsche, phenomenology, German existentialism, and psychoanalysis—had their beginnings in Hegel."[11]

Obviously, so broad an impact cannot have stemmed from one idea
or one contribution of Hegel's. Nor could we easily find a common *doc-
trinal* basis, shared by all these movements, that would be traceable to
Hegel. Yet there is at least one *attitude* shared by Hegel's successors that is
traceable to him: a sensitivity to paradox and dialectic. The world, consciousness, society—all present themselves in a series of divisions that
remain polarized just as they are being overcome and resolved into unity;
the unities themselves are at the same time dualities. Indeed, a thought
that does not display this or a similar many-sidedness lacks some essential
truth element.

Hegel thereby enables us to see the unresolved ambivalence that has
left its mark on human existence. It is what makes possible, even necessary, our speaking of anything that is characteristically human as not being
what it is, and being what it is not. As I pointed out, the difference
between Hegel and modern existentialism is that for Hegel there *is* a *final*

resolution of these paradoxes, but at the highest level: that which he calls Absolute Knowledge. At any level but the highest, therefore, life is incommensurable with strict consistency. And from this we may return to the view—which we can now appreciate as the foundation of existentialism—that life and self-consciousness remain not only distinct but juxtaposed, and not only juxtaposed but in an actual clash.

Hegel enunciated this, as we saw, in the opening paragraphs of chapter IV. That division can be given any number of trite versions. The point, however, is not to opt for the one pole over the other, but to maintain the tension between them. That tension can be eased at any number of points; but the lower down in the cognitive scale the "resolution" is procured, the lesser the insight. Real wisdom keeps its paradoxes in full view—until the irresistible resolution is achieved at the highest level.

The paradoxes of selfhood are precisely of this sort: i.e., we can take them as pointing to a yet higher level of insight where the paradoxicality would be fully resolved, or we can stay with them at the simplest level and see them *there* as the ultimate characterization of the self.

Thus, it appears that Hegel and Sartre[12] are in opposition regarding the essential nature of selfhood: Hegel says that my selfhood depends for its very existence upon its recognition by another self, while Sartre says that in this dependency my self-consciousness is inauthentic, and that whatever is marked by such dependence is the source of what is false. More specifically, although Hegel and Sartre both begin their analyses from the standpoint of the conflicts that underlie the master-slave encounter, Hegel moves beyond this toward an ultimate synthesis, while Sartre sees the conflicts that underlie the encounter as irreconcilable. Thus, it turns out that Sartre, when discussing self-consciousness, is not discussing merely the self-consciousness of the slave, whose selfhood is incomplete because it is dependent; rather, he is discussing consciousness as such, where the primary fact is the mutual exclusion which generates a plurality of consciousnesses. This is why the individualistic *cogito* cannot be the point of departure for philosophy: i.e., because selfhood is multiple, and the ego emanates from a complex relation of mutual recognition and exclusion.

In a nutshell, according to Sartre, we can state Hegel's view as follows: The statement "I am I" is a tautology, with all content drained out of it; but in actuality it is not a tautology at all: first, because the two occurrences of "I" have different meanings (as subject and as object), although their reference is the same; second, because the statement must involve the mediating intervention of another self, so that I arrive at my self-consciousness via the self-consciousness of another. The paradox, however, is that although the other's mediation is needed, my selfhood is achieved through the exclusion of everything but the self. Thus, "I am I" needs the other, yet excludes the other—and it *needs* to exclude the other so that the statement can acquire content. (For Hegel, we at least *attempt* to resolve the standoff by struggling for mastery; for Sartre, this impasse is the permanent and irresolvable condition of selfhood.) The other, in the meantime, is in the same situation—that of interrelated dependence and autonomy. The proliferation of mutual awarenesses, dependencies, and exclusions (e.g., I know you knowing me, who knows you, etc.) leads to a multiple overlay of consciousnesses, an illegible palimpsest. As Sartre says, in characterizing Hegel, "Consciousnesses are directly supported by one another in a reciprocal imbrication of their being. . . . The road of interiority passes through the Other" (p. 236)—and "the other penetrates me to the heart" (p. 237).

In Sartre's view, Hegel spells out the complex interrelation between self-consciousnesses in *cognitive* terms, while what ought to be emphasized is the *existential* aspect. Not only is the master the truth for the slave, the slave's own essential being depends upon the essential *being* of the master (as the Other). Thus (for Sartre), Hegel formulated the interrelation in terms of reciprocal *knowledge*, while it should have been formulated in terms of reciprocal *being* or *reality*. Presumably, it is knowledge that is the measure of being, for Hegel, while the reverse is actually the case. In Hegel's idealism, absolute being is identical to knowledge, and it is this identification that Sartre seeks to dethrone, so as to give primacy to being.

This is, at best, a superficial reading of Hegel. A mark of that superficiality is in the characteristic way existentialism (beginning with Kierkegaard) has accused Hegel of excessive rationalism—although it was Hegel who emphasized reason's inadequacy when removed from concrete reality. Another mark of that superficiality is in the way existentialism has so often ignored its debt to Hegel, so that its perennial problem has been how to criticize Hegel without endangering its dependence on him. That the problem of adapting Hegel to an existential viewpoint is a *problem* for existentialism, is another token of its superficiality. (Will this require standing Hegel on his head?)

The important point, for Sartre, is that self-consciousness is not a form of knowing but a form of being. Thus, self-consciousness is not self-knowledge but self-negation: I dissolve myself into myself *as* a self; and this is not at all a case of the ego *referring* to itself, but of being a being that is independent of whatever it knows, a consciousness that preexists whatever it knows—even (and especially) if what it knows is itself.

In Sartre's view, Hegel can be charged with an unwarrantable "optimism," and this has two sides: First there is an *epistemological* optimism that says that the *truth* of self-consciousness can be manifested in a reciprocal relation (even though the master-slave relation is not reciprocal but one-sided). In risking my life, it seems I can separate my life from my consciousness—even though my life, as it turns out, is utterly inseparable from the other's consciousness, and my own consciousness is fundamentally modified in being known by the other. It is as though, despite everything, I am fixed, penetrated, and objectified by the other.

Against this, Sartre says that the being of self-consciousness is such that its own being is in question, and this self-negation is what *interiority* is. Its being is that of "being what it is not and of not being what it is" (p. 241). My selfhood is therefore independent of all otherness and all objectivity. I am what *I* make myself, and this is not an object for me, nor is it the separable thing that Hegel suggests it is when he speaks of the self as object for the other.

According to Sartre, therefore, Hegel says that my being is as an appearance for the other, although this is not what *I* take as I. In this way, Sartre seeks to reject Hegel's view of the interrelation between autonomy and dependence. For Sartre, autonomy is distinct from such dependence, since my temporal stream of consciousness is accessible to me alone, not to the other. This is why the other cannot know me, and why I cannot see myself objectively from the outside, as the other sees me. For me to see myself *in* the other, I would have to apprehend the other as subject, in his interiority—which I obviously cannot do. I cannot be him in the same subjective sense in which he says "I." For the same reason, I can only be a subject for me.

For Hegel, the notion of self-consciousness includes my self-consciousness *and* the other's consciousness of me. For Sartre, the two are not at all commensurable (but Hegel never said they were!), and they cannot be subsumed under the one heading of "Self-Consciousness." This is why (in Sartre's view) Hegel's epistemological optimism must fail: the subject (experienced by me as "I") and the object (experienced by me as Other) cannot be equated in their meaning. (Does Hegel seek to use their identity of *reference* as a basis for their identity of *meaning*? I think not. On the contrary, he keeps the two apart, and emphasizes their difference.)

The other optimism of Hegel is an *ontological* optimism which says that the truth can be grasped as a whole by the philosophical spectator who stands outside both subject and object, so that the plurality is overcome in the totality. Yet as Sartre sees it, Hegel holds to this view only because "he has forgotten his own consciousness" (p. 243) and he can therefore ignore the problem of the connection between *his* individual consciousness and that of the other, having abstracted from his own. "But if Hegel has forgotten himself, we can not forget Hegel" (p. 243). Our separate consciousnesses could be equated if they could be reduced to knowledge as a common denominator. But this cannot be, as we saw, since the I-subject does not know himself as the Other-object knows him. This means that I cannot transcend my selfhood.

It also means that we must go back to the interiority of the *cogito* after all—and that ultimately this is, for Sartre, the sole point of departure in philosophy—however much the other person may modify my interiority. The multiplicity of consciousnesses cannot be overcome. No totality can include my consciousness (experienced as mine) and the consciousnesses of others (as theirs). *This* is the scandal of philosophy, as Sartre sees it, and no optimism can overcome it.

If Hegel had ever believed that this *is* possible, then it would be true to say of him that "he never grasped the nature of that particular dimension of being which is self-consciousness" (p. 244). Even if we could show the relation between the other's self-consciousness and my own, this would serve to overcome the intermonadal division. Does Hegel indeed aim at overcoming the monadic nature of self-consciousness? I do not think so. In my view, he presents the master-slave scenario as the response but not as the solution to the problem. However that may be, Sartre regards the separation (and conflict) as insuperable—while Hegel finds its resolution at the higher level that is Absolute Knowledge.

Sartre accuses Hegel of having "forgotten consciousness" in having forgotten his own—as though it were the philosopher's task to put himself in the place of human experiences in their multiplicity, and to recapitulate the career of human consciousness by reliving that generalized process in himself. Yet Hegel, in his Introduction, had deliberately eschewed that path (rather than forgetting it, as though by an oversight). Merleau-Ponty refers to that point, made by Hegel. For Merleau-Ponty, it is here that Hegel's existentialism truly begins: the connection (between philosophy and experience) is not in the philosopher's vicarious reiteration of (say) the path from Stoicism to the Unhappy Consciousness; rather, it is in his revelation of "the immanent logic of human experience in all its sectors," as Merleau-Ponty says (p. 65). Thus, the philosopher may well be able to disclose what it means to *be* an Unhappy Consciousness, but his path to this revelation is cognitive and discursive.

The philosopher's aim, as Merleau-Ponty indicates, is to see man in confrontation with the world and to show man's religion, culture, and social system emerging in that confrontation. Only in this way does "experience" take on that "tragic resonance" it has in ordinary language—when we speak of "experience" as something we live through and undergo as a trial.

Hegel does not view man as a fully self-possessed consciousness, but rather as a *life*—entirely responsible for itself while trying to understand itself. This is what is existential in Hegel. As Merleau-Ponty says, "All of the *Phénoménologie de l'esprit* describes man's efforts to reappropriate himself" (p. 65). Man begins in the subjective "certainty" of his beliefs, and he acts in accordance with that certainty, only to find those beliefs confuted by objective "truth." He then modifies that "certainty" to conform to that "truth," only to have that new "certainty" overthrown by yet another "truth." This is repeated, time and again, until subjectivity and objectivity coalesce, when (presumably) man attains spiritual maturity. Yet if he were to attain it, he would be like an animal completely at home in the world. On the contrary, what characterizes man (as Merleau-Ponty sees Hegel's existential view of man) is not the attainment but the movement toward it!

This is what Marx did not see, of course. The sociopolitical revolution would bring about an end to history, but this would also signify an end to humanness, not its fulfillment (as Marx expected), because humanness *is* movement, not stasis. Only the inert object (or the animal in nature) *is* what it is; man is what he is not. This is because man is mind and spirit, and his essence is negation. Human consciousness is the absolute dialectical unrest, seeking to return to itself—but without the self-limiting determinacy that such a return would mean, were it to lead to rest.

Once again, we see the conflict between life and consciousness that marked the opening of chapter IV of the *Phenomenology*. It is also spelled out in Hegel's Introduction, where he says that self-consciousness is driven beyond the "natural" in life and is therefore the death of that life. Consciousness goes beyond the limits of natural life—which means going beyond its own self. Consciousness thereby corrupts whatever temporary satisfaction it finds. It may well seek to avoid such truth and seek rest in an unthinking inertia. But it cannot find it: its own thought disturbs its desire to remain unthinking, as its own unrest disturbs its inertia. Thus, what characterizes man—in this clash between life and our consciousness of it—is man's capacity for negation, for *not* being what he is, for being (as Merleau-Ponty says) "an existence without an essence."

With our consciousness of life a disturbance of life sets in—we become aware of death. "To be aware of death and to think or reason are one and the same thing," Merleau-Ponty says (p. 67), "since one thinks only by disregarding what is characteristic of life [i.e., the natural and inertial] and thus by conceiving death." In addition to living and reproducing, we are aware that we exist rather than *merely* live. (It is interesting how our common parlance reverses the order and value of "existing" and "living": one wants not merely to exist but to *live*.) For Merleau-Ponty human existence supervenes human life, and thus human life "can only be thought of as revealed to a consciousness of life which denies it."

This denial of the natural life and our emergence into existence cannot but be disturbing. It is the price man pays for his humanity—which is why Hegel says (in the *Realphilosophie* that precedes the *Phenomenology* by a year), "Man is a sick animal," i.e., sickened by being no longer *in* nature. Merleau-Ponty expresses this by saying: "All consciousness is therefore unhappy, since it knows it is a secondary form of life and misses the innocence from which it senses it came" (p. 67). It is this sense of separation that Judaism gave to the world—in contrast to the Hellenic "happiness." (Merleau-Ponty recalls that Hyppolite told his students, during the war, that we are all Jews to the extent that we care about the universal, refuse to accept mere being, and want to *exist*.)

Consciousness of the universal is consciousness of our death. Yet this must go beyond itself: In the negation of life is the affirmation of it, because in thinking of how death puts an end to life I assert life. This is why the slave's consciousness, having been closer to death, can grasp life more fully than the master can. This is only a *step* toward maturity, not its attainment—nor anything like a conceptual grasp of existence (which is another reason why Sartre is wrong in taking the master-slave relation as emblematic of the human relation as such).

The slave has learned what death is—and it is here that Hegel ceases to be an existentialist, in Hyppolite's view, since the slave's awareness is not retained as the core but is transformed into *cultural* configurations (e.g. Stoicism). The contradiction between *pour soi* and *pour les autres* is not overcome, merely evaded. The dialectic does not go on but is truncated, as Merleau-Ponty says (p. 69). (It is as though the slave developed Stoicism *instead* of grasping his own existence, or as though Christianity stands in the way of his becoming fully conscious of it conceptually. What this means is that culture is a "false consciousness"—almost in a Marxian sense!) Hegel's phenomenological process may thus lead us to a philosophy of Church or Party [i.e., an ideology?] , but it is no longer (in Merleau-Ponty's view) the philosophy of the individual that is existentialism.

That objection, however, is hardly to the point. Since Hegel is concerned with the dialectic of culture as it emerges from the conflict of individuals, he cannot be expected to have stayed at that personal conflict. Once having shown personhood to be incomplete for both master and slave, there was nowhere to go but beyond these "individuals" and toward culture. That transition—from the personal to the cultural and historical— is a necessary part of the human process. (As Heidegger shows us, in *Being and Time*, our grasp of our own existence, as individual, must lead to a grasp of history.) As Merleau-Ponty seems to indicate, the existentialism in Hegel is in the implications rather than in any explicit formulations: Thus, we see it in the awareness of the universality affirmed or implied by the mere fact of our being; and in the half-hidden sense that our conscious life has lost its innocence merely by having emerged from nature.

From this point of view, Hegel and Merleau-Ponty share the view that (at a certain stage, at least) consciousness must be unhappy. There is this difference, however, in the two views of the Unhappy Consciousness: For Hegel, the Christian consciousness is unhappy because it is not God; for Merleau-Ponty, consciousness (in general) is unhappy because it is no longer Nature. Hegel's Unhappy Consciousness yearns for what it can never become; Merleau-Ponty's unhappy consciousness yearns for what it has been and has lost.

Heidegger

The *Phenomenology* does not aim at presenting a metaphysical world system. Yet there are a number of problems in the *Phenomenology* that could possibly be resolved by reference to Hegel's world system (as presented in his *Encyclopaedia*). This approach is warranted by the fact that the *Phenomenology* itself points to its completion in such a broader context:

thus, the 1807 title page presents the *Phenomenology of Spirit* as Part One of a "System of Science"—presumably more comprehensive than the *Phenomenology* as it now stands.

Let us now turn to one of the fundamental problems in the *Phenomenology* and see whether the reference to a broader science might help resolve it. Earlier, we noted Hegel's uncertain transition from the individual consciousnesses of the master and the slave to the sociocultural consciousness embodied in Stoicism, Skepticism, and Christianity. In this transition there is perhaps a more fundamental chasm than can easily be bridged. Hegel uses the term "consciousness" as though it can be applied as easily to the atomic individual as to molecular society, without further ado. What he does not show is how the "consciousness" that is expressed in a sociocultural configuration emerges (with logical necessity) out of the consciousness that expresses the individual's worldview. That is, he may have succeeded in showing why the slave comes to think about his world and himself in something like a Stoic or a Christian mode; what is not shown is why this should lead us to consider Stoicism or Christianity as the world outlook of an entire cultural era, which is the next inevitable step in the evolution of consciousness per se.

What we are not given, then, is a picture of how societal consciousness emerges (as a matter of logical necessity) out of the individual consciousness. This lack is emblematic of a still more basic one: Hegel does not show us how consciousness and spirit emerge out of the natural setting. The emergence of a cultural spirit out of individual consciousness would certainly be illuminated by the picture of the emergence of Spirit out of Nature. Hegel attempts to present such a continuum in the *Encyclopaedia*, but the attempt is by no means successful, in view of the difference between the two realms—a difference that he himself emphasizes.

Nature and Spirit are as different from one another, ontologically, as space is from time. Granting this difference, how does the individual go from the one to the other—leaving Nature behind him and approaching Spirit—and achieve his humanness in the process? It is an unresolved riddle—and as such it is another philosophic scandal, animating the thinking of philosophers as different from one another as Hegel and Heidegger.

The emergence of humanness—out of Nature and into Spirit, out of inert being and into self-conscious awareness—this is Heidegger's tacit theme, as it is Hegel's. Although neither of them takes up this theme in any great detail, what is common to the two is that the element of time provides the connection between the two realms. Heidegger discusses this in a chapter of *Being and Time*.[13]

What we do not see (in Hegel) is *how* the connection is made. We know only that time is common to both—although the types of "time" in each realm differ as each realm differs from the other. Thus, if natural time differs from spiritual time (i.e., time as we are aware of it in our human experience) then we have not bridged the chasm between Nature and Spirit at all. What we do know is one side of that chasm: human time.

We can almost say that our awareness of time is the necessary condition of our humanization: We come to a conscious grasp of ourselves as human when we realize that our conscious life is temporal in essence. It is this realization that gives our conscious life the dimension of spirit and lifts that life out of the merely natural. Heidegger characterizes Hegel as saying that the actualization of spirit involves its *fall into time*. Is it a "fall" in Merleau-Ponty's sense of a fall from innocence? Or is it a fall out of the immanence of natural life into self-consciousness? However that may be, man's entrance into human time is as fundamental and cataclysmic a "fall" as Adam's, and just as pregnant with meaning for man: it is the beginning of man's self-awareness as human; with that awareness he *sees* that his humanness is in his mortality!

This is one feature we can point to as uniquely human in its ambivalence: it is a realization that is negative in its content but positive in its effects. Indeed, we may say that the most positive aspects of our self-awareness as human arise precisely in such negativity—the negativity inherent in consciousness itself. Consciousness is imbued with negativity in that it grasps its object (out there in the world) as not-I; and when consciousness comes to grasp itself as creating its world, this is a negating of that negativity. That is, consciousness grasps itself as self-conscious and sees this as producing its world—and as a capacity belonging to spirit as such, not to this individual alone. It is a universal that is individual.

At least two consequences flow from this self-reflection of consciousness: its freedom (as revealed in its absolute restlessness) and its self-manifestation (expressing itself in an infinitude of possibilities). Now, it is thoroughly typical of Hegel to speak of a social consciousness in terms that characterize the consciousness of the individual. (For example, since the *individual* consciousness is free and infinite, so is the *sociocultural* consciousness—and in the same way! The characteristics of the one are ascribable to the other. The ultimate extension of this parallelism is to be found in that historic "reason" that orchestrates the social self-consciousnesses of nation-states and is their final arbiter.) Thus, there is no difficulty, for Hegel, in making the connection. Indeed, he does it all too easily, and it is so unproblematic as to be merely assumed, never argued for and demonstrated. The personal self-consciousness and the sociocultural self-consciousness are reflections of the one realm of Spirit. Yet the hiatus remains.

A similar hiatus obtains in chapter IV of the *Phenomenology*. As we noted, Hegel goes from the self-consciousness of the master and slave to the cultural self-consciousness expressed in Stoicism, etc.—as though there were nothing problematic about the transition. Both levels involve the negation of the negation; both display freedom and infinitude.

Heidegger seems to suggest that with a proper analysis of human time-consciousness, the hiatus could be overcome. We need not belabor the centrality of the temporal element in all this. It is enough to point out that (for Hegel) our thoughts follow one another in the concatenation of their logical (nontemporal) connections, while the chain itself has a temporal dimension—as we see in the progression from Stoicism to Skepticism to Christianity. It is perhaps this temporal link that allows Hegel to go so easily from the personal level to the sociocultural. The *logical* connection (between premises and conclusion) is nontemporal; yet my own iteration of that connection occurs as the temporal process that is my thinking. In the same way, a cultural configuration has certain implications immanent within it; yet their actualization occurs in historical time.

The bridge between the two self-consciousnesses (individual and social) is thus provided by certain metaphysical assumptions in regard to time. Time is the dimension in which the individual consciousness operates—as long as time itself is not annulled when self-consciousness grasps itself as being *in* time. Once the individual self-consciousness grasps itself in this way, as being *in* time, its grasp of time itself is an empty intuition— an intuition that is nontemporal! This reveals the ontological chasm between the actual operation of consciousness in time and the nontemporal self-awareness—so pithily expressed by Kierkegaard (in a *Journal* entry of 1843) with the remark that life is lived forward but is understood backward. We might therefore say that the "fall" into the awareness of temporality is a "fall" *out* of temporality as lived. As Hegel puts it, time is the pure self when it is not grasped by the self; and to the extent that the self does grasp itself it annuls its temporal form (i.e., steps out of its temporal form as lived, forward). This supposedly illuminates the close connection—even a reciprocal relation—between time as such and the individual consciousness or spirit.

That nascent connection is made manifest in world history, but it must be seen in contrast to the nonhuman environment (because it is precisely this contrast that unites the individual and the social as founded on human time): While nature is essentially spatial, spirit is essentially temporal. "World history is the development of Spirit in *time*, just as Nature is the development of the Idea in *space*."[14] Whatever may be the ambiguity of "falling" into time for the individual consciousness, the historical consciousness (of a society) becomes what it is by overcoming its natural base and becoming aware of itself in its process. This may begin with the individual who regards his own being as a being-in-process, pointed toward death. He comes to see his individual aims as projects to be fulfilled *in* society, by means of *its* goals. Yet these social goals must themselves be grasped as temporal—spirit itself must "fall" into time as a way of becoming actualized. Parallel, then, to what Hegel says about time and individual consciousness, there is his characterization of social time as the "fate and necessity" *(das Schicksal und die Notwendigkeit)*,[15] besetting spirit in its incompleteness—that is, the necessity to enrich the role of self-consciousness in conscious social life, to activate that social consciousness by taking it out of its immanence so that it is revealed and realized.

Much of what I have said is an enlargement of Heidegger's compressed discussion of Hegel's view of the connection between time and spirit. Heidegger is correct in pointing out that what Hegel omits is an examination of "whether the way in which spirit is essentially constituted as the negating of a negation, is possible in any other manner than on the basis of a primordial temporality" (pp. 485–86)—i.e., why and how temporality enters into the very essence of spirit in the first place.

This seems to point to the need for an *existential* rounding out of Hegel, which Heidegger claims to give. The question to be asked, therefore, is not whether it *can* be given an existential interpretation (which obviously can be given) but whether Hegel's outlook *demands* such an interpretation—as its logical fulfillment.

Hegel's existential outlook manifests itself at a number of important and characteristic points: As we saw, the negating capacity and freedom in self-consciousness leave man's ultimate characterization entirely open. No man can choose, with any finality, what it is to be man—although he does and must choose all the time. Man is what he is not. Yet despite this existential outlook of Hegel's, it is apparently in regard to the question of temporality that Heidegger sees the difference between himself and Hegel.

Heidegger contrasts his existential analytic of *Dasein* with Hegel's analysis of human temporality: Heidegger says that his own analysis *begins* with the human situation of "thrownness" into time, while Hegel must yet *arrive* at that human temporal situation as the logical outcome of spirit's own phenomenology. Thus, Heidegger's analysis shows temporality to be the precondition of human existence qua human. For Hegel (in the view of Heidegger) spirit preexists and then "falls" into time; for Heidegger, spirit already exists as the primordial *temporalizing* of temporality itself.

For Hegel, it is we who humanize time by becoming human ourselves and thereby authenticating time (i.e., making it authentic for us). Thus, time is the dimension of our self-realization. So far, Heidegger seems to agree with Hegel. For Heidegger, however, it is not Spirit that falls into time; rather, in our factical existence (i.e., our self-awareness in our contingency, etc.), it is as if we had fallen away *(verfallen)* from some primordial and supposedly authentic temporality. In this way, Heidegger avoids the metaphysical component that Hegel seems to be introducing here—a world spirit—and rather than speak of a fallen Spirit (cosmic or human), Heidegger would prefer to speak of a human "fallenness" as a feature of the human situation.

Thus, as self-aware human beings, we now see ourselves as *existing* rather than as merely alive, i.e., in a self-awareness that goes beyond the biological. We have wrested the concept of our *existence* out of our immanent *life* by becoming self-conscious. This opens us to unlimited existential possibilities as well as imposing definite limits we have become newly aware of; yet despite this richly dangerous humanization, the one-way transition from an unknowing and uncaring life to a self-concerned existence is like a transition from a primordial life (in which we feel no time) to an existence wherein we have entered a temporalized temporality.

Yet I cannot agree with the contrast Heidegger draws between Hegel's fall of Spirit and his own human "fall." Since Hegel characterizes Spirit as temporal in its very essence, it is already temporal at the outset, before any "fall" can have (or need have) occurred. Temporality is spirit's essential dimension (for Hegel), and this includes human spirituality in a concrete sense. This suggests that Hegel's outlook does not require an existential completion—since it is already existential in its deepest fabric.

The difference has to do with the conception of what the *Phenomenology* itself is. We have seen how a number of critics have characterized the book in dynamic terms (as a universalized biography, as the itinerary of consciousness, as the experience of the species, etc.). Hegel himself speaks in this way in his Introduction, characterizing phenomenology as "the path of natural consciousness pressing forward to true knowledge, or as the way of the soul journeying through the succession of its own configurations," as though this path were ordained by its own nature *(als durch ihre Natur)*.[16] In view of that dynamic approach, the *Phenomenology* must be seen as a continuum that is in the process of disclosing its own implicit content. And in the light of that continuum we can see that Hegel's view of the temporal character of spirit is implicitly and already existential. Heidegger does not see it that way. He explicitly rejects as misleading the idea that the *Phenomenology* is an itinerary, the description of a journey.[17] Such a view, he says, makes an implicit distinction between *merely* phenomenal knowledge and true knowledge as yet to be attained (as though its purpose were to lead us through a museum of the shapes of consciousness, after which we go through a special door into Absolute Knowledge). Rather, what the book really intends is the presentation of phenomenal knowledge in its appearance. Yet Heidegger admits that there is a distance here, between natural consciousness and absolute knowledge, and that the *Phenomenology* oscillates between them.

If that is so, then it would seem possible that Hegel would see modern existential analysis (such as that of Heidegger) as itself an intermediary stage inside the museum, to be left behind eventually. Perhaps this implication is what Heidegger seeks to avoid, in order to accord to his analysis an absolute status of its own, beyond the door.

Gadamer

I now turn to two important essays by Gadamer.[18] The problems they address can be presented as follows:

In our "objective" view of the world, we tend to slight or ignore the role of subjectivity in creating that world. When that happens, our "objectivity" spawns the contradictions that will eventually shatter it. The solution is not simply a matter of striking a "balance" between them—as though we were to say that objectivity without subjectivity is blind, subjectivity without objectivity is empty. That approach does not tell us how they actually are mediated by one another, and thus leaves them as far apart as ever. Rather, what must be revealed is the subjective shaping of the world's objectivity; only then do both "aspects" become genuine as one totality.

To get beyond the falsely isolated "objectivity," we must begin by showing up that objectivity as spurious; this means suspending that objectivity, so that what was first seen as real is now seen as unreal. It is a twofold disillusionment: epistemic and evaluative. Not only is "reality" overturned, but what was valued in the former world picture is disvalued in the new one. This is the dialectical path taken by all enlightenment. There is the temptation to stay with a simple division— e.g., between the sensible and the intelligible world, or between the commonsense world as naively accepted and the world as scientifically understood.[19] The real challenge, however, is to *see* how the two sides are one reality.

What Hegel insists on is that the grasp of that unity must begin by casting the heretofore accepted world into doubt. Thus, in 1802, in writing the opening manifesto of the newly established *Critical Journal of Philosophy* (which he co-edited and co-authored with Schelling), Hegel says: "Philosophy is by its nature something esoteric . . . it is philosophy only in that it is directly opposed to the understanding and moreover to sound common sense. . . . In relation to this, the world of philosophy [i.e., the world as grasped by true philosophy] is in and for itself an inverted world."[20] Is it an antiworld?

What this statement omits is the point made by Hegel later on: that the inversion is overcome by means of a perspicuous return to subjectivity, and that such a return is provided by a phenomenology of spirit. The underlying problem in the *Phenomenology* is how that return is to be conducted. We may go from the self-conscious study of consciousness to the study of self-consciousness itself—but only if we know what it is that impels that transition in the first place.

Thus, the two themes—(a) the philosophically inverted world, and (b) the transition from consciousness to self-consciousness—complement one another. But that complementarity is one of shared problems as well as of shared solutions. In effect, the philosopher loses the world and gains his own soul, but in so doing he regains the world and sees it anew.

As we saw, Hegel made the point that we cannot expect consciousness to turn to self-consciousness on its own, automatically. That is because consciousness is individual and subjective, and what we need is a way of overcoming the individuality in that subjectivity. When I discussed Hegel's chapter III, above ("Before 'Self-Consciousness'"), I spoke of the view that the dialectical reversal transforms (for us) the tranquilly lawful world into a dynamic world of change, so that what we have is a unified supersensible world driven back upon itself, as both the law and its inversion—and *that* is now the real world. This world process of self-recursion runs parallel to the self-reflection on the part of consciousness. Yet the two must not be regarded as distinct or separable, for then we are still at the level of individuality and subjectivity. We must advance to self-consciousness regarded as spirit in general. That is, we must go from *ego cogito* to *spiritus cogitans*.

The transition proceeds dialectically, through contradiction and overcoming. We surrender our self-contradictory *aisthesis* of a particular thing and go on to view its inner essence as universal, by means of pure thinking, *noein*. Through it, we arrive at "what remains in disappearance" *(das Bleiben im Verschwinden)*. And as Gadamer points out, this does not refer to a Platonic supersensible world *opposed* to the world of evanescent appearances, but rather to the truth of the disappearing world itself: i.e., appearance seen *as* appearance, the phenomenal *as* law—what Hegel calls "the stable image of unstable appearance" *(dem beständigen Bilde der unsteten Erscheinung)*.[21]

Yet Hegel does not stay with this, but regards it as a first step, still falling short of reality because it does not comprise all reality. It is still enmeshed in the network of impersonal "forces"—a view he seeks to overcome because it does not give full play to the creative nature of subjectivity.

The perceived world has been seen against the background of the universal, but this renders the perceived world unreal. The philosophic world is still "inverted." Notice that Hegel does not set up a division between an illusory world of mere appearance as against a supersensible world of higher reality. (He brands such a division superficial.) The truth is more complex: the true picture is of a supersensible world that includes both the supersensible and the sensible, so that the opposition is turned back on itself. This is the basis of the inversion. What makes it problematic is, as Hegel says, that the inverted world contains the world it inverts; it is its own inversion, itself and its opposite in a unity. The two are distinguishable because the existing world is never adequate to the world as theoretically conceived. For Hegel, however, the result is not that the existing world is rigidified as inadequate, but that in its inverted form it must be inverted once again, so that the world is reflected into itself, and so that its truth is no longer its opposite but is at one with it: the complete world is the theoretical (lawful) world *and* its imperfect instances, as Gadamer says (p. 47).

How are these to be synthesized? One is tempted to say that the reinversion of the inverted world is a "return to itself," which parallels the return of consciousness to itself in self-consciousness. We would then have an ontological reversion mirrored in an epistemological reversion—except that this neat parallel and distinction is just the sort of simplification Hegel would wish to overcome. The idea that reality has two tandem aspects can never present a final view of reality but only a challenging antithesis to be resolved. Just as he rejects the possibility of another world above and beyond the sensible—but rather insists that the realm of laws does not constitute a second realm, and that the existing world is itself the realm of laws—so he ultimately rejects the idea of two independent reversions, one in the world and another in consciousness. On the contrary, the world returns to itself *by way of* consciousness. As Gadamer says, it is Hegel's aim to show "nature as the real foundation of spirit's actualization of itself" (p. 55). But to this we should add that for Hegel this is the *same* as showing spirit as the basis for the career of nature!

What Gadamer shows us is the Kantian element in Hegel's picture—and the way he overcomes Kant. We need an understanding of Kant in order to understand Hegel; but Hegel himself shows us that there is more to what he says. The Kantian element comes out in Hegel's view that Force is not merely an objective aspect of the world, but that it is itself a function of the understanding, imposed by the understanding. *This* is why, in the ultimate inversion, differences are identities, and identities differences. The supposedly "objective" and independent world is entirely a creation and extension of mind. In the final analysis, therefore, our scientific picture of the world is nothing other than the understanding experiencing itself *(sich selbst erfährt)*, as Hegel says.[22]

In view of this identity of the understanding and the world (rather than a parallelism between them), the transition from consciousness to self-consciousness is achieved. In truly grasping the process of the world we grasp our own shaping of it, and thus we grasp ourselves. Thus, we overcome the Kantian division between the thing as it is in itself and as it is for us. The world goes as mind goes, not because the one reflects the other, but because the two are one dialectical process. One and the same fabric underlies both.

How is this demonstrated? "How is the certainty of consciousness that it is all reality . . . demonstrated?" This is the question to which Gadamer addresses himself in his second essay.

If the purpose of reason is to lay hold of reality, then it certainly would seem a counterproductive policy to divide the two. The Platonic approach is to elevate both to a higher level at which alone they can meet;

but this only attenuates the connection. The gap is in some way bridged in Hegel's idea that since the understanding has created its world, it is in contact with itself when it grasps and understands that world. (I say "in some way," because we must go on to show Reason in this role.)

Chapter III of the *Phenomenology* shows *how* our understanding creates its world and gives it its badge of "objectivity." The Understanding can separate the world from itself only because that process of "alienation" is not itself understood by it. This leads us to construct false dichotomies—and we must remember that for Hegel the presence of a solidified dichotomy is always a sign of the failure (on the part of the Understanding) to achieve the needed resolution. In chapter IV, therefore, we are shown a consciousness symbolically attempting to nullify its Other in combat. (Remember that Hegel speaks of the struggle as occurring between individuals as well as between mere aspects of consciousness.) For the victor, at the first moment of victory, there is nothing but himself— just as for consciousness (were it completely "victorious") there would be nothing but itself. We are shown a consciousness now concerned with itself, and creating views of the world from that self-concern. (Even if the creating consciousness is not the initially "victorious" one, it becomes the "victorious" one in its internalization.)

This should give us an indication of the next stop in the itinerary of consciousness. Self-consciousness is still divided because in its view of the world the Unhappy Consciousness has set up a God as the world's creator—instead of seeing itself in that role. So far, all it can see itself responsible for is its own sinfulness and finitude. Only with the onset of Reason will consciousness see itself as creating the world, all and everything. Thus, Self-Consciousness (as a stage) *begins* to see itself as creative and world creating; it still sets its world apart as its Other (because the victory over it was only symbolic, after all). With the coming of Reason, we see that Other as *identical* to the self, not only as its product. *Then* life and consciousness are no longer in opposition, and that existential impasse (too) is surmounted.

Once they are seen as no longer in opposition, we have arrived at the realm of spirit—the sociocultural domain that *is* life and *is* consciousness, but is neither one of these alone. Further, as Gadamer points out (p. 63), spirit is not individual life or individual consciousness, but a "world." The fabric of that world is recognition (and we are by now acquainted with the dialectical interrelation recognition leads to, between the Self and its Other). What this process involves is the emergence of the self out of an unknowing *life* into self-conscious *existence*. The master and the slave, both, overcome their attachment to life by engaging in the struggle, and this is already a step toward selfhood and autonomy. The fact that neither one achieves full selfhood is a further aspect of the dialectical interrelation. This, too, is an inversion: the master dependent, the slave independent, etc. A similar reversal obtains in regard to the Self and its Other. *This*, then, is the transition from consciousness to self-consciousness. That is, the Self becomes its Other, and this other is itself—which is precisely the pattern of the subject-object relation in self-consciousness.

The fact that whole complexes of society, culture, and history are built upon such ephemeral "material" as recognition and internalization—that is very much to the point. It is a human, mental world constructed of mental material. The material does not become more ephemeral or diaphanous in the process. It is not thinned out by being spread over society. On the contrary, its socialization only makes that spiritual material more concrete, opaque, and resistant to individual manipulation. In other words, the spiritual superstructure that is society takes on a selfhood and autonomy of its own.

As Gadamer implies (p. 70), *each* of these stages gives us "a phase in the genealogy of freedom." Those last three words might be added to our inventory of characterizations of the *Phenomenology*, along with "itinerary of consciousness," "universalized biography," etc. I think Gadamer's the most trenchant encapsulation—as, indeed, I find his analysis of chapter IV the most profound (among the critics we have discussed). Just as the individual "itinerary" is pointed to selfhood and autonomy, the implicit goal for society is the same: to make its selfhood and autonomy explicit, by bringing itself into accord with self-conscious Reason, which now *sees* itself as the creator of the world, all and everything.

Wahl

We have seen an attempt to interpret the master-slave episode in global terms, so that it is taken as Hegel's characterization of human relationships in general. (Of course, this is belied by the fact that Hegel goes on to further stages of characterization, so that the master-slave episode must be seen as just that: an episode, to be surpassed.) One might also wish to take the Unhappy Consciousness passage in global terms—as Hegel's insight into religious consciousness as such (quite apart from its specific setting as early medieval Christian), and then as his insight into consciousness in general ("All consciousness is unhappy . . . ").

This brings us to the work of Jean Wahl, the earliest of the twentieth-century commentators we have been discussing, whose book appeared in 1929.[23] What is central to Hegel's phenomenological outlook is its dialectical nature—and this is a dialectic that is not merely logical but also "*historique et affective*" (p. 119). To understand that historical and affective (i.e., emotive) dialectic, we must see it based upon the fundamental elements of negation, mediation, and time, whereby consciousness has entered into dialogue with itself (p. 121).

Consciousness itself involves duality (and I suppose that consciousness of consciousness is duality squared). In any case, that duality is symbolized *(symbolisée)* by the master and slave—the passage that follows describes the attempt to overcome the duality and reunite consciousness with itself. This leads to a new scenario, culminating in the Unhappy Consciousness—unhappy because it looks to God to bring about that reunion for it, and with God as a mediating factor the attempt at reunion must fail. Perhaps this is because God's infinitude and absolute independence give him a status beyond that of mere mediator in human consciousness, finite and dependent as it is. Thus, whatever unity is achieved is necessarily incomplete. The return of consciousness to itself, in the master and slave, is but a "*faux retour*," because that return is itself divided in the interiorization of consciousness—and this is characteristic of the Unhappy Consciousness. That is, instead of overcoming consciousness, we have come back to it all the more, and with this to an awareness of its division (p. 123).

Consciousness says, simultaneously, "I am what is not," and "I am what I am." These two ideas, implicit in Skepticism and kept apart, are made explicit and brought together in Judaism—together, not in unity but in juxtaposition, so that they are constantly coming apart. "The prophet, at the very moment at which he celebrates God, is a prophet of unhappiness; the hymns change into lamentations" (p. 125). What is more, Jewish consciousness knows this contradiction. Thus the Hellenistic movements of Stoicism and Skepticism go over into Christianity *through* Judaism, for here their contradictory elements are made explicit, although without resolution. These elements, embedded in Stoicism and Skepticism, are the essential and the inessential, the universal and the particular. As metaphysical elements we might have kept them at a distance, so that we would remain undisturbed; but as elements *within* consciousness, they give us an awareness of our own nothingness.

Christianity seeks to overcome this by searching for the Changeless One. In the fact that this One becomes incarnate, that the Father is the Son, we have a direct reflection of the attempt on the part of consciousness to achieve the unity of the universal that is the particular. But when consciousness grasps this, it also grasps the fact that it itself is this opposition, as well as this contact between the two. On one hand, it sees the Father and the Son as objectively there; on the other hand, it sees them as perhaps nothing but it itself (i.e., consciousness). It may try to overcome this also, by speaking of God as present in man, man as present in God. But this only brings consciousness back to "square one," its own nothingness. And then it feels that it *is* the Changeless *and* nothingness! It is Pascal as Christ on the Mount of Olives, Wahl says (p. 126), where the particular is touched by the changeless and vice versa—precisely the fundamental character of consciousness itself.

What we must see, then, are two things: first, consciousness can never "forget" or "ignore" the conflicting elements within itself (i.e., it may try to do this but it cannot conclusively succeed, since these will come to haunt it); second, the "figures" we are dealing with (whether they be the master and slave, or the Father and Son) are themselves "elements" of consciousness—and this follows from Hegel's phenomenological approach. As elements (i.e., particular aspects) of consciousness, they must come into opposition, even antagonism—which is why the Christian consciousness is unhappy, unquiet, and cannot conceive of its repose but in a world beyond. And since this is the situation of consciousness in general, the longing for the beyond is also the tendency of all consciousness as such. Consciousness is forever dividing itself into the essential and the inessential, into the particular and the universal—and thus it is self-contradictory, unhappy. In religion, likewise, consciousness sees its simultaneous grandeur and finitude; it is exalted and humiliated.

This is why the Christian consciousness—divided between being and non-being—is always a consciousness in a state of *becoming*. It is precisely the humiliated consciousness—negated, a nothingness, the opposite of God—that wants (for this very reason) to see itself as one with God. The conflict between the inessential and the essential is now played out as the conflict between the particular and the immutable. Thus, Christianity is man's simultaneous awareness of his own universality and particularity. In this way, the particular consciousness tests the idea that its God is it itself (and perhaps proves it to its own satisfaction, only to have to deny itself that satisfaction, once again). Its Christ is the particularity of consciousness attached to the universal. And because religion and consciousness in general have a parallel aim, Wahl can say that a phenomenological theory is the analogue of a theory of grace, that the revelation of the immutable is born out of the corresponding unhappiness, and that the entire phenomenology is the history of that experience (p. 133).

At one and the same time we can ask: How shall this conclude? What conclusions can we come to? This, the Unhappy Consciousness, does not end in any mode of self-satisfaction. As Wahl says, it is a *"sentiment tout subjectif devant quelque chose qui est tout transcendent"* (p. 139). Thus, consciousness can continue only as the movement of an unfulfilled and infinite longing—"une *Sehnsucht* infinie" (as though only the German word will do in that French phrase, and thereby will have that sense of incompleteness express itself concretely, like a piece of conceptual art). Thus, this consciousness will never arrive at a *conclusive* union of the universal and the particular; it will never succeed in grasping its own essence but can only grope its way toward it—because at the moment this consciousness believes it has grasped that essence it is thrown back upon itself. To grasp itself is to grasp its separation from the Changeless—and from itself. This is its paradox. This is why Christianity and Christian man can never fulfill themselves as they are, but must go on to Reason.

This is why we, dealing with chapter IV, can come to no conclusion—for its conclusion comprises chapters V to VIII. The Unhappy Consciousness should (and must) leave us with an ending that is open and incomplete, like the disturbingly unresolved chord at the very end of Bruckner's Ninth—pointing to all that has gone before it in history, retaining it, yet pointing to a time to come that will bring an end to all the harmonies we have become accustomed to.

PART III

THE DENIAL OF THE SELF: THE REPUDIATION OF HEGELIAN SELF-CONSCIOUSNESS IN RECENT EUROPEAN THOUGHT

by

DAVID SHERMAN

11

OVERVIEW

The early twentieth-century French figures that were just considered had a variety of perspectives on the "Self-Consciousness" chapter of Hegel's *Phenomenology*, but—in varying degrees—all understood themselves as working from within Hegel's problematic. Similarly, "first generation" members of the Frankfurt School in Germany, such as Theodor W. Adorno, Herbert Marcuse, and Max Horkheimer, who were writing at the same time, accepted Hegel's notion of the subject, even as they strained against its limits. In contrast, the two German figures that were considered earlier, Heidegger and Gadamer, essentially rejected Hegel's conception of self-consciousness in favor of what they take to be a less metaphysical approach. Breaking with the humanistic implications that are inherent within Hegel's thought, they claimed that human subjectivity is essentially a function of language. Thus, according to Heidegger, "man acts as though he were the shaper or master of language, while in fact language remains the master of man."[1] Heidegger, who had a significant influence upon virtually all of the early twentieth-century French thinkers, but still failed to wrench them away from a humanistic reading of Hegel, as well as Nietzsche, who influenced Heidegger's work, are the two primary inspirations for the more recent move away from Hegel in France. In contrast, the second and third generation members of the Frankfurt School, who have also moved away from Hegel's notion of the subject on linguistic grounds, have drawn their inspiration from the analytical methods of the Anglo-American philosophical tradition.

The movement away from Hegel in France, which began in the 1950s, was precipitated by a number of factors, not the least of which was the changing historical landscape. Unlike earlier French thinkers, such as Kojève and Sartre, who saw in Hegel's dialectic the possibility of using philosophy for the purpose of bringing about historical change (like the Left Hegelians of the past century), more recent French figures came of intellectual age during the Cold War and the failures of the New Left during the 1960s—both of which suggested the relative intractability of history. Accordingly, for more contemporary French thinkers, history is not an opportunity, but a burden; it is either to be escaped or theorized in its intractability (which amounts to the very same thing).[2] Indeed, this is in keeping with the French poststructuralist attack upon self-consciousness, for if there is an efficacious subject, it would be (in Sartre's terms) "bad faith" to disclaim the ontological possibility of recreating society. The shift away from Hegel in Germany, in contrast, is the result of different factors. Unlike the French poststructuralists, who reject the Enlightenment conception of reason that is intrinsic to Hegel's thought, recent German theorists view the Enlightenment as an unfinished project that must be brought to fruition. But part of this process involves the rejection of the subject-object paradigm, which is operative within the philosophies of Hegel and the earlier members of the Frankfurt School, albeit in a qualified way. For these contemporary theorists, the Enlightenment's notion of the subject must be jettisoned in the name of reason and history—but jettisoned nevertheless.

There are a number of different approaches that French poststructuralists have taken in their attempt to escape from Hegel's orbit, but for the sake of simplicity these might be reduced to two generic types, which are not mutually exclusive. On the one hand, there are those theorists who—ostensibly drawing upon the thought of Nietzsche—renounce the alleged pretensions of a systematizing reason and (hypostatized) subjectivity, which they argue are life-denying, in favor of a theory based upon the liberation of bodily drives. These theorists, such as Bataille and Deleuze, who will be considered below, either attempt to open up a space for the body within or alongside Hegel's dialectic of self-consciousness (Bataille) or seek to "deconstruct" this dialectic altogether (Deleuze and Foucault). On the other hand, there are those theorists who fundamentally draw their inspiration from Heidegger's linguistic and ontological analyses. These theorists, such as Lacan, who will be considered below, and Derrida, basically reformulate the connection between language and subjectivity by subordinating the latter to the former, all the while contending that this dynamic plays itself out within the shadow of death—a fact that Hegel glimpsed in the master-slave dialectic but then supposedly turned from in his desire to establish the historical subject. The approach that is taken by current German theorists has been more or less crafted by Jürgen Habermas, who, like Lacan, draws heavily upon Hegel, even as he rejects Hegel's view of subjectivity. (Even Hegel's most ardent opponents either self-consciously or unself-consciously draw upon his thought in the very process of trying to distance themselves from him). Indeed, like Lacan, Habermas sees the subject as formed within the crucible of language— although, unlike Lacan, Habermas is profoundly critical of the irrational tendencies that are to be found in Heidegger's philosophy, as well as in the poststructuralist movement that he was so influential in spawning.

Choosing which thinkers to examine in a study such as the present one is to some extent arbitrary. In choosing to examine Bataille, Deleuze, Lacan, Habermas, and Honneth (who is trying to incorporate aspects of Hegel's theory of recognition into Habermas's linguistic framework), I have left out a number of extremely influential theorists, most notably Derrida and Foucault. In making these choices, I was guided by the extent to which each thinker explicitly deals with Hegel's theory of self-consciousness, and, more specifically, Hegel's exposition of the master-slave encounter, which is the most influential part of the "Self-Consciousness" chapter.

GEORGES BATAILLE

Alexandre Kojève's reading of Hegel's master-slave parable, which was heavily influenced by Marx and Heidegger, had the effect of revivifying the Marxian subject in the face of "official" Marxism's mechanistic leanings. The slave, an existential prototype of the Marxian proletariat, became the driving force within Kojève's anthropocentric conception of history. Nevertheless, Georges Bataille, who had attended Kojève's lectures, and always considered himself to be very much under Kojève's influence,[1] came to the conclusion that Hegel's notion of the subject took as much away from the possibility for genuine human experience as it offered. Bataille therefore turned to Nietzsche in order to counterbalance Hegel, and it was within the irreconcilable tension between Kojève's Marxist interpretation of Hegel and his own particular interpretation of Nietzsche that Bataille fashioned his own thought, the centerpiece of which was his notion of "sovereignty." For Bataille, who, like Kojève, believed that only the slave moves beyond the contradictions of the master-slave problematic, the slave's increasing mastery can never shake its servile beginnings;[2] indeed, Bataille understands the drive to mastery itself as a manifestation of a slavish mentality. It is only through a noncognitive flight from the entire master-slave dialectic that one can come to experience Bataille's reconstructed Nietzschean sovereignty, thus (provisionally) leaving behind the servile mentality that is inherent within Hegelian mastery.

Before considering Bataille's perspective on Hegel's master-slave encounter, however, it is necessary to briefly consider Kojève's position on Hegel's notion of "Absolute Knowing," which constitutes the endpoint of Hegel's phenomenological "highway of dispair." After moving through the numerous forms of self-consciousness that comprise the *Phenomenology of Spirit*, all of which are superseded as a result of the contradictions that arise within them, the human mind reaches the moment at which it realizes that neither the natural world, which has been domesticated by human labor, nor other human beings, who recognize one another within the context of a homogenous and universal State, stand over and against its projects. In the vernacular, there is an identity of subject and object, an overcoming of alienation. This state of affairs, in which reason has realized itself within history, signals the end of history—a condition that Kojève maintains has actually obtained since the introduction of the Napoleonic Code. Experientially, however, this condition of human reconciliation, which precludes the possibility of further meaningful action, is marked by a passionless satisfaction. Kojève's "end of history" thesis is, of course, controversial (although it has recently been recycled)[3]; nevertheless, for our purposes, what matters is that Bataille took it seriously. Thus, in a 1937 letter to Kojève, an "unreconciled" Bataille writes: "I imagine that my life—or its abortion, better still the open wound that is my life—by itself constitutes the refutation of Hegel's closed system."[4] And, with respect to the ontological consequences of there being no grounds for meaningful action in a posthistorical framework, he writes: "If action ('doing') is—like Hegel says—negativity, the question then arises of knowing if the negativity of one who 'no longer has anything to do' disappears or subsists in the state of 'negativity without employ.'"[5] (According to Hegel, "negativity" means being "other than," and it is particular to human beings, who, unlike animals, are other than their objects. As that which enables us to unify our experience by overcoming deficient ways of seeing the world, it is the ontological foundation of our freedom.) For Bataille, it is the posthistorical status of human negativity, which has come full circle from its birth during the master-slave struggle, that presents humankind with its most pressing existential problems. And, to properly deal with these problems, one must grasp the master-slave dynamic: "no one knows anything of *himself* if he has not understood this movement which determines and limits man's successive possibilities" (IE, p. 109).[6]

According to Bataille, there are three successive "negations" that bring about the human animal's transition from animality to humanity (HoE, p. 53),[7] but Hegel only discussed the first and the third within the context of the master-slave encounter. The first negation, Bataille asserts, is the one by way of which the slave negates the natural world through his labor. But, contrary to Hegel and (especially) Kojève, who extol the slave's labor because it makes him conscious of what he truly is,[8] Bataille accentuates the fact that the slave's labor, which is responsible for creating the whole of concrete reality, is still, ultimately, "the action of the man who, rather than die free, chose to live in servitude" (Sov., p. 283). Bataille underscores the servility of labor's first moment because he believes that it was not merely a contingent matter, but, rather, reflected the essentially servile nature of all human labor. Because labor is oriented toward the future, the "first moment of labor" condemns humanity to servility long after the moment at which the slave outlasts the master. It is a process that necessitates ceaseless deferral in the service of its own dynamic: "From the start, the introduction of *labor* into the world replaced intimacy, the depth of desire and its free outbreaks, with rational progression, where what matters is no longer the truth of the present moment, but, rather, the subsequent results of operations. The first labor established the world of *things*... [and then] man himself became one of the things of this world" (GE, p. 57). Indeed, according to Bataille, this dynamic manifests nothing less than the "essential movement of the *Phenomenology of Spirit*": "the slave frees himself from the master through work . . . but the product of his work becomes his master" (IE, p. 129).

The third negation, Bataille tells us, is that of the awareness of death. While the "problem" of death would appear to be applicable to all living things, it is actually only a human problem, for, as the master-slave dialectic teaches, it is only through the apprehension of his own death that the human animal turns into a self-conscious being. It is only by risking everything in the "fight to the death" that human anguish is experienced, and this anguish, which leads to the realization that the human being can be separated from his natural environment—that he is other than the "positivity" of what just exists—is the distinctive mark of humanity. Indeed, what anguish reveals is that the human being is essentially a "Nothingness"—or, in Heideggerian terms, a "being-unto-death"—that manifests itself in the world as "negating" action: "man is death living a human life" (HD&S, p. 10).[9] But, once again, Bataille will remind us of the slave's response to this moment in which he first grasps his own finitude: he shrinks from it, and, in submitting to his nemesis, he postpones the moment of his death at the price of postponing the time in which he can live in the moment. In postponing the "moment of death," however, the slave does not merely forget about death, for the continuing fear of death is the impetus for a self-effacement that continually reinserts him as a thing back into "the order of things"; rather, after that initial moment in which the slave stares death in the face, death itself becomes an increasingly abstract representation. For Bataille, this reflects a fundamental contradiction:

> The privileged manifestation of Negativity is death, but death, in fact, reveals nothing. In theory, it is his natural, animal being whose death reveals man to himself, but the revelation never takes place. For when the animal being supporting him dies, the human being himself ceases to be. In order for Man to reveal himself ultimately to himself, he would have to die, but he would have to do it while living —watching himself ceasing to be. In other words, death itself would have to become (self-) conscious at the very moment that it annihilates the conscious being. (HD&S, p. 19)

Death, which does not neatly fit into the "order of things," is therefore, paradoxically, a transcendent moment. Moreover, as this quotation shows, it refers us back to our own animality, which, in turn, suggests the "second negation" in the transition from animality to humanity. This negation, which Hegel "shuns" (HoE, p. 53), is the one through which the human animal denies its own animal nature to distinguish itself from an animal. Along these lines, Bataille maintains that by sacrificing certain of his animalistic prerogatives through the institution of various universal prohibitions (on, for example, incest, necrophilia, the putrefaction of the corpse, menstrual blood, excrement, and nudity), the human animal brings about a negation "so radically negative that it is not even spoken of" (ibid.). And, according to Bataille, it is ultimately the observance of these "radically negative" prohibitions, not philosophy's vaunted reason, that gives human beings the feeling that they are not animals (cf. Sov., p. 339). But despite the "unspeakable" nature of that which is proscribed by the prohibition, the prohibition gets its vehemence from the fact that on infrequent occasions it is transgressed, just as the transgression gets its extraordinary intensity from the fact that the prohibition generally induces compliance. Indeed, because transgressions of the various universal prohibitions are no more assimilable by the "order of things" than is death, they, too, provide the grounds for a transcendent moment, but are not otherwise subject to the paradoxes that exist with respect to death. However, since Hegel does not acknowledge this "second negation," and therefore unreflectively submits to the universal prohibitions, the grounds for this transcendent moment do not exist within his "system." Bataille argues, in fact, that there is no transcendent moment within Hegel's philosophy.

"Absolute Knowing," which is the culmination of the movement of self-consciousness, is viewed by Bataille not as the moment of human transcendence, but, rather, as the potential death knell for the human spirit. Drawing upon Nietzsche's characterization of "the last man," who is the quintessential utilitarian, Bataille regards the consciousness that would "absolutely know" as one that is inextricably caught up in "the order of things"; all that it does is inevitably geared toward some "useful" purpose. But it is precisely action that is "geared toward some useful purpose" that is anathema to Bataille, who then projects this outlook onto Nietzsche: "the refusal to serve (to be useful) is the principle of Nietzsche's thought, as it is of his work" (Sov., p. 368). Knowledge "in itself," Bataille maintains, as well as discourse, which is the medium through which knowledge develops, points back to that first moment when the slave, stepping back from the abyss of death, opted to conserve himself by subordinating that moment, and, unknowingly, the overwhelming majority of all moments that were to follow, to the dynamic of useful labor:

> Hegel saw very well that, were it acquired in a thorough and definitive way, knowledge is never given to us except by unfolding in time. It is not given in a sudden illumination of the mind but in discourse, which is necessarily deployed in duration. Knowledge, and the most profound knowledge, never appears to us in full except, finally, as the result of a calculated effort, an operation useful to some end. Knowledge can't in any way be confused with the last moment or the end of the operation; it is the entire operation.... To know is always to strive, to work; it is always a servile operation, indefinitely resumed, indefinitely repeated. Knowledge is never sovereign. . . . (Sov., p. 202)

Thus, from Bataille's perspective, what is "absolute" about "Absolute Knowledge" is not the idea that all knowledge has been acquired, nor even Kojève's idea that that there is no longer any basis for meaningful action; rather, knowledge is in some sense "absolute" when the underlying servility that characterizes it constitutes humanity's very self-conception. It occurs when sovereignty, which is Bataille's transcendent moment, is no longer a possibility.

Although he is an avowed atheist, Bataille thinks that Hegel's philosophy denies humanity transcendence because the notion of transcendence has been dragged into the finitude of history: "Before Hegel's 'absolute knowledge' the Christian myth was already based precisely on the fact that nothing divine is possible (in the pre-Christian sense of sacred) which is finite" (HD&S, p. 13). In other words, because Hegelian "transcendence" emanates from the stuff of history, which is servile at its base, "absolute knowledge," which is nothing more than the totality of the moments that have comprised history, must be servile as well. ("But what if knowledge, at least the first impulse of knowledge, were servile"? [Sov., p. 225].) It is for this reason that Bataille emphasizes humanity's inherent animality ("the second negation"), which is not given its due within either the master-slave encounter or any of the subsequent forms of self-consciousness that lead to "absolute knowing." Bataille, who thinks that Hegel's philosophy is a "closed system" that is cut off from the material basis of life, sees in our animality the very notion of "the sacred"—a notion that his atheism would otherwise seem to deny. Drawing upon the work of Emile Durkheim, who stresses the importance of the sacred as a unifying force within the context of social life, the materialistic Bataille apprehends "the sacred" in those moments in which the impetus of animality leads to the transgression of prohibitions: "What is sacred is precisely what is prohibited. But if the sacred, the prohibited, is cast out of the sphere of profane life (inasmuch as it denotes a disruption of that life), it nevertheless has a greater value than this profane that excludes it. It is no longer the despised bestiality; often it has retained an animal form, but the latter has become divine" (HoE, p. 92). The transcendent moment for Bataille is therefore the one in which the human animal (in some sense) pays homage to the material world of which it is inextricably a part.

Indeed, for Bataille, who in an inverted way is no less a dualist than Kant, there are two worlds, or, to use his terminology, "economies," that the human animal problematically straddles. The "General Economy," which is simply another name for the material world, is characterized by an ever-expanding, albeit pointless, expenditure of energy. Using the sun as an archetype, Bataille says that this energy "must necessarily be lost without a profit" (GE, p. 21). Of course, this is not to suggest that elements of the general economy cannot suffer from a lack of energy (or resources); rather, his point is that scarcity exists only from the particular perspective. The general perspective is always marked by a superabundance. In contrast, there is the "Restricted Economy," whose operating principle is that of scarcity. This economy—the economy of the human world—which encompasses but is not limited to the "dismal science" (economics), is typified by the accumulation of allegedly scarce resources, as opposed to their useless expenditure (consumption) and, above all, the drive to realize a profit. And it manifests itself not only in the hoarding of wealth, which is anathema to the proper functioning of "the economy," conventionally understood, but by a sort of conceptual hoarding as well, which Bataille believes is exemplified by the drive for mastery within Hegel's dialectic. (Fittingly enough, from the standpoint of someone like Bataille, Hegel himself refers to this process as "the *labor* of the concept.") Indeed, according to Bataille, by conceptually appropriating everything that it encounters (including, and perhaps especially, the notion of the sacred) in order to first bestow meaning and then limit its play, as well as by reappropriating all of its prior moments (by being *aufgehoben*), Hegel's dialectic is the model of the restrictive economy. Contrarily, sovereignty, which constitutes the transcendent moment for Bataille, occurs only when the human animal, having transgressed the limiting prohibitions of the restrictive economy, acts in accord with the material laws of the general economy by dissolutely consuming his accumulated resources. The human being acting sovereignly is no longer just a thing intertwined in the "order of things." For the human being acting sovereignly, knowledge, meaning, discourse, utility, and the future—and thus Hegel's dialectic—do not exist.[10]

The relationship between the general economy and the restrictive economy, the sacred and the profane, and, ultimately, Bataille's sovereignty and Hegel's mastery is exceedingly thorny. On the one hand, Bataille views the general economy as the substrate upon which Hegel's restrictive economy functions, and he believes that humanity's failure to acknowledge this fact is what leads to catastrophic consequences: "Man's disregard for the material basis of his life still causes him to err in a serious way. . . . Beyond our immediate ends, man's activity in fact pursues the useless and infinite fulfillment of the universe. . . . No doubt these ends and this movement may not be entirely irreconcilable; but if these two terms are to be reconciled we must cease to ignore one of them; otherwise our works quickly turn to catastrophe" (GE, p. 21). So, too, with respect to the relation between the sacred and the profane he says: "The object of the prohibition was first marked out for coveting by the prohibition itself . . . [Erotic life] was given rules, but these rules could only assign it a domain outside the rules. . . . It is quite clear, then, that man's sexual life cannot be considered as a simple datum, but rather as *history*" (HoE, pp. 48–49; emphasis added). Comprehended in this way, there is a dialectical relationship between the general and restrictive economies, the sacred and the profane, and if humankind faces a "catastrophe," it is not because it has approached the world dialectically, but, rather, because it has broken off the dialectic. Yet, on the other hand, Bataille is determined to disconnect his idea of sovereignty from the dialectic altogether. Along these lines, sovereignty is not even the result of a "break out" from the dialectic; to the contrary, it is always-already beyond its pale. Accordingly, Bataille contends that "there ought not exist any *means* by which man might *become* sovereign: it is better for him to *be* sovereign" (Sov., p. 226).

This irreconcilable tension is manifested in Bataille's discussion of the "potlatch," the American Indian festival in which surplus resources are expended through profligate gift giving and consumption. For Bataille, potlatch, in which a chief offers to his rival considerable riches "for the purpose of humiliating, challenging, and obligating him" (GE, p. 67), complements the movement of the general economy. But can it truly be said that potlatch constitutes an expenditure without reserve, especially when its aim is to obligate? Bataille himself recognizes this paradox: inasmuch as potlatch inures to the benefit of the one who gives—he is repaid with a larger stock of goods by the one whom he has obligated and with an enhanced ranking by his social group—"it places the value, the prestige and the truth of life in the negation of the servile use of possessions, but at the same time it makes a servile use of this negation" (GE, p. 73). Nevertheless, Bataille equivocates by refusing to see potlatch as merely one more phenomenon within the profane world. First, he argues that "rank," as an initial matter, is essentially sacred, and that it is only afterward that it is turned into a useable thing to make a profit. Second, he claims that even if potlatch is not actually sacrificial, it still withdraws wealth from productive consumption. At this point, however, we must ask: How is sovereignty, at least as it plays out within the context of the Indian potlatch, any different than the drive for mastery within the context of the master-slave encounter? Is the Indian chief's desire to attain a higher rank any different than the master's desire to be recognized? Moreover, since the master no more labors nor seeks to accumulate in order to realize a profit than the Indian chief—indeed, the master virtually remains at the level of animality—how can it be said that the master-slave encounter initiates the restrictive economy, while the Indian chief is deemed to still partake in the movement of the general economy? The Indian chief would appear to be caught up in the historical movement of Hegel's dialectic, and the otherness of sovereignty would appear to be ontologically out of reach. It would thus seem that not only can one not *become* sovereign, but one cannot *be* sovereign either.

It is for this reason that Bataille's revolt is not just against capitalist society—although from the perspective of his theory of sovereignty, it is the most troubling social form since its underlying principle is one of unremitting accumulation and productive consumption. (Even feudalism, which was aptly coming to an end in Germany as Hegel dashed off the last lines of the *Phenomenology*, consumed some of its wealth nonproductively.) Instead, Bataille's revolt is against nothing less than history itself. To be sure, unlike Hegel, for whom the movement of history brings about social forms that have steadily increasing mastery, Bataille sees in the movement of history an ever diminishing chance for sovereignty: "Every day the sovereignty of the moment is more foreign to the language in which we express ourselves, which draws value back to utility" (Sov., p. 380).[11] Nevertheless, as the paradox of potlatch shows, in his search for that moment of *pure* sovereignty in which there is no socially conditioned (utilitarian) expectation of a return on one's expenditure, Bataille must ultimately go behind history; he must analyze what he sees as that moment of (self-)consciousness gone awry that precedes all social forms— *viz.*, the master-slave encounter—and then reinscribe the fabled consciousness that exists just prior to that moment back into the modern problematic by holding it out as a transcendent moment in which the individual breaks with history itself. And, indeed, this is what Bataille attempts to do in *Inner Experience*, in which he seeks to "recommence and undo Hegel's *Phenomenology*" (IE, p. 80). As one commentator correctly puts it: "The writing of *L'Expérience intérieure* objectifies Bataille's doubt that anyone but an individual can achieve the sovereign experience. . . ."[12]

As Jacques Derrida indicates in his influential essay "From Restricted to General Economy: A Hegelianism without Reserve," "taken one by one and immobilized outside their syntax, all of Bataille's concepts are Hegelian,"[13] and nowhere is this more evident than in *Inner Experience*. In this work, Bataille talks in terms of concepts such as subject and object, immediacy and mediacy, recognition, and negativity, all of which are, of course, essential in the master-slave dynamic. But in each case, Bataille reverses the direction of the movement. Whereas the master-slave encounter undermines the self-certain immediacy of each participant with respect to his environment and his "Self," and thus provides the impetus for the recognition that all things stand in a mediated relation, Bataille stresses the ultimacy of immediacy: "Experience leading to the extreme limit is accessible to the extent that existence successively strips itself of its middle terms" (IE, p. 116). Whereas the master-slave encounter is understood in terms of the binary relationship between subject and object (ego and alter-ego, humanity and nature), Bataille dispels the tension that holds the terms together, which causes him to alternately describe the relationship between them as "dissolved" or "fused": "There is no longer subject-object, but a yawning gap between the one and the other and, in the gap, the subject, the object, are dissolved" (IE, p. 59). Or, alternatively, "experience attains in the end the fusion of subject and object . . ." (IE, p. 9). Whereas the master-slave encounter initiates the entangled "problems" of recognition and selfhood, and the movement to "absolute knowledge" is a movement towards greater degrees of reciprocal recognition and more secure self-conceptions, Bataille contends that "if one proceeds right to the end, one must efface oneself, undergo solitude, suffer severely from it, renounce being *recognized*" (IE, p. 155). And, whereas the master-slave encounter initiates the outward movement in which the human being objectifies his existence in the world (through work), which is a necessary condition for knowledge, Bataille would initiate an inward movement toward "inner experience," which he takes to be the necessary condition for the intuition of "non-knowledge." According to Bataille, non-knowledge is beyond the extreme limits of absolute knowledge, and destabilizes it (cf. IE, p.52).

The only concept emanating from the master-slave parable that Bataille ostensibly embraces is that of "negativity." But, technically, even this is not the case. With the exception of "pure and simple negativity," which is an indeterminate, abstract, formless otherness that is what it is only in virtue of being other than all its objects (like Kant's transcendental ego, to which it tacitly refers), Hegel fundamentally views "negativity" in a determinate or concrete fashion. In other words, the "negativity" that is the human being stands in a relational way to its objects, such that even when we negate or reject certain ways of viewing or relating to these objects, as we perpetually do, we then embrace other ways of viewing or relating to them—ways that ostensibly get us closer to apprehending the truth. For Bataille, on the other hand, the only negativity worthy of the name is pure, "unemployed" negativity. In contrast with the subject in the mode of a servile "I," which employs its negativity to simultaneously accumulate knowledge and project it(s)-self into the world (thereby, according to Bataille, capitulating to "positivity"), Bataille offers the subject in the mode of "wild *ipse*," which rarefies itself by negating its relationship to all objects, especially it(s)-self. Indeed, so stringently "negative" is this wild *ipse* that even a fellow traveler such as Nietzsche, who "knew barely more of Hegel than a standard popularization" (IE, p. 109n), runs afoul of it. Thus, ostensibly referring to Nietzsche, Bataille asserts that the "pure will to power (to growth for its own sake) . . . [while] outwardly contrary to the servile spirit, is basically only its complement" (GE, p. 137). In its particularity, the Nietzschean subject projects itself into the world, but thereby gives up on the totality, which is ultimately the aim of the self-effacing, wild *ipse*:

> As long as *ipse* perseveres in its will to know and be *ipse*, anguish lasts, but if *ipse* abandons itself and knowledge with it, if it gives itself up to non-knowledge in this abandon, then rapture begins. In rapture, my existence finds a sense once again, but the sense is referred immediately to *ipse*; it becomes my rapture, a rapture which I *ipse* possess, giving satisfaction to my will to be everything. (IE, p. 53)

This moment, in which the subject extricates itself from the "order of things" by abstractly negating everything—including (especially) it(s)-self (as object)—in order to fuse with everything and thereby have immediate, "inner" experience, is the moment of "sovereignty." The *notion* of this phenomenon, however, is extremely problematic, even for those thinkers such as Derrida who are otherwise sympathetic to Bataille's (non-)philosophical commitments. Like Bataille, Derrida is preoccupied with the split between living a mediated existence within Hegel's dialectic (within the limits of knowledge, meaning, and language) and living immediately, or, as Derrida articulates it, with "self-presence." For Derrida, however, there is ultimately no escape from Hegel's dialectic; it represents the limits of our horizon. Of Bataille's *notion* of sovereignty, he therefore asserts: "All the attributes ascribed to sovereignty are borrowed from the (Hegelian) logic of 'lordship'. . . . The sign 'sovereignty' itself, in its opposition to servility, was issued from the same stock as that of 'lordship.'"[14] But Derrida does believe that Hegel's "theory of the subject" can be left behind, for Derrida sees no self-determining subject at the end of the dialectical road—just the recognition that subjectivities are produced within the linguistically overdetermining dialectic. Therefore, in virtue of Bataille's preoccupation with the subject, Derrida thinks that he ultimately falls back into the trap of classical thought: "One could even abstract from Bataille's text an entire zone throughout which sovereignty remains inside a classical philosophy of the subject . . . which Heidegger has shown still to be confused, in Hegel and Nietzsche, with the essence of metaphysics."[15]

We need not agree with this Heidegger-cum-Derrida conclusion that Hegel and Nietzsche had confused notions of the subject in order to conclude that Bataille did. But, for our purposes, Bataille's confusions are particularly instructive in that they evidence a key transition point in the twentieth-century reception of Hegel's master-slave encounter (which, after all, engenders the very notion of the subject that postmodernists rail against). While he still operates with one foot in the dialectical framework initiated by the master-slave encounter, Bataille's other foot is already in the postmodern. Thus, when he says that "the object of [his] research cannot be distinguished from the subject at its boiling point" (GE, p. 10), it is only a short step in one of two directions, both of which find no distillates in the wake of Bataille's project. One can either move farther away from history toward a materialism that is even more thoroughgoing than Bataille's (Deleuze), or move wholly into history, thus rejecting the idea that a subject can exist as anything other than a "thing" enmeshed in "the order of things" (Foucault, Derrida). As for Bataille, who sought to do justice to the misguided idea that what is essentially "human" is pure, indeterminate negativity, we would do well to recall Hegel's observation (with respect to the French Terror) that "the unfilled negativity of the self changes round in its inner Notion into absolute positivity,"[16] for this is really the condition of Bataille's subject in its transcendent moment. Collapsing the "positivistic" animal that precedes the master-slave encounter and the positivistic "sovereign" human that stands on the other side of absolute knowing (and thus above history) into the "transcendent moment," Bataille, in rejecting the determinacy of the Hegelian *aufhebung*, leaves the subject in history just as he finds him.

13

GILLES DELEUZE

Although much of Bataille's thought was geared toward rupturing
Hegel's master-slave dialectic, which he believed had accreted the very
notion of human transcendence to servile labor, Bataille never doubted
that it accurately delineated the nature of human self-consciousness.
Indeed, his doubts were more concerned with the possibility of ever
effectuating such a rupture, for, in many respects, Bataille took the master-slave dialectic to be inexorable. Furthermore, although Bataille
refashioned particular aspects of Nietzsche's philosophy for the purpose
of bringing about those transcendent (sovereign) moments that would
(at least temporarily) break out of the constricting contours of the master-slave dialectic, he was not of the opinion that Nietzsche himself had
actually understood Hegel's thought. Bataille thus asserts in *Inner
Experience* that

> Nietzsche knew barely more of Hegel than a standard popularization.
> The Genealogy of Morals is the singular proof of the ignorance in which
> the dialectic of the master and the slave has been held and remains to be
> held, of which the clarity is dazzling (it is the decisive moment in the
> history of the consciousness of self and . . . to the extent that we have to
> distinguish between each thing that affects us, no one knows anything
> of himself if he has not understood this movement which determines
> and limits man's successive possibilities). (IE, p. 109)

179

While many poststructuralist thinkers, such as Jacques Derrida and Jacques Lacan, share this kind of ambivalence with respect to Hegel, Gilles Deleuze is not one of them. According to Deleuze, Hegel's master-slave dialectic constitutes nothing less than the quintessential wrong turn in the history of philosophy, and it would not be an exaggeration to say that even though he rarely focuses upon Hegel directly, Deleuze's entire oeuvre is motivated by a virulently anti-Hegelian bent. Indeed, in his extremely influential *Nietzsche and Philosophy*, which comprises Deleuze's most sustained encounter with Hegel's thought, he does nothing less than project this very outlook onto Nietzsche himself. Ostensibly referring to Bataille, Deleuze states that "it has been said that Nietzsche did not know his Hegel. In the sense that one does not know one's opponent well" (N&P, p. 8).[1] Indeed, he contends that one cannot even begin to understand Nietzsche's thought without referring back to Hegel: "We will misunderstand the whole of Nietzsche's work if we do not see 'against whom' its principle concepts are directed. Hegelian themes are present in this work as the enemy against which it fights" (N&P, p. 162). Moreover, in contrast with Bataille, Deleuze heavily relies upon Nietzsche's *Genealogy of Morals*, as well as his conceptions of the "will to power" and "eternal recurrence," in order to construct an alternative theory of both the initiation of the master-slave dynamic and the history that unfolds from it. Thus, although it was Bataille who set himself to the task of "recommenc[ing] and undo[ing] Hegel's *Phenomenology*" (IE, p. 80), it is actually Deleuze who more radically attempts to bring the job to fruition.

Deleuze attacks Hegel's rendition of the master-slave dialectic by embracing an even more thoroughgoing materialism than Bataille—one that fundamentally rejects not only such Hegelian notions as recognition, mediation, knowledge, and negativity (both determinate and indeterminate), but also rejects the very notion of selfhood. There is no (purely negative) self to be given its due on Deleuze's account; rather, human beings are basically a "play of bodily forces." Thus, Deleuze claims, there are two criteria by which our bodily forces can be identified: the degree to which they are active (noble) or reactive (slavish), and the degree to which they are affirmative or negative. The difference between these two pairs is that "active and reactive designate the original qualities of force but affirmative and negative designate the primordial qualities of the will to power" (N&P, pp. 53–54). In other words, given the ultimate balance of internally conflicting forces, a given person is either active (that is, a master, who ratifies his own existence by evaluating in accordance with his own strengths, i.e, "I am good, and therefore you are bad" or "I shall do. . .") or reactive (that is, a slave, whose life-denying morality emanates from his weakness in regard to the master, i.e., "You are evil, and therefore I am good" or "Thou shalt not do. . ."), but it is only when a person actually *acts* on these qualities that he can be described as either affirmative ("becoming active") or negative ("becoming reactive"). Clearly, active and affirmation have "deep affinities," as do reactive and negative, but, according to Deleuze, these couplings are not exclusive, and herein lies the problem. In section 10 of the first essay in the *Genealogy of Morals*, Nietzsche says that "the slave revolt in morality begins when *ressentiment* itself becomes creative and gives birth to values"[2] (in Deleuze's terminology, this is when reaction [the slave] becomes affirmative), and this leads to a situation in which reaction (the slave) can turn the tables on action (the master): "an active force becomes reactive (in a new sense) when reactive forces (in the first sense) separate it from what it can do" (N&P, p. 57). Thus, when the slave's resentment becomes creative, two new predominant couplings emerge: reactive-affirmative (the slave acting upon his resentment to create a new set of values that limit the ability of the superior master to imperiously act) and active-negative (the master succumbing to the slave's new set of action-limiting values).

According to Deleuze, this is not the end of the story, however. Just as Hegel's notion of determinate negativity provides the impetus for a process in which self-consciousness successively enriches itself on the path from the master-slave encounter to "absolute knowing" (at which time human beings become "reconciled"), Deleuze's Nietzsche depends upon the notion of the "eternal recurrence" to provide the impetus for a process in which active force (the master) successively purges itself of the slavish "becoming negative" within it on the path to the Overman (at which time negativity disappears altogether in the face of an uncontaminated "becoming active"). Eternal recurrence "is [therefore] an answer to the problem of passage [to the Overman]" (N&P, p. 48). However, unlike the historical Nietzsche, whose speculations on eternal recurrence alternately took "cosmological" and "psychological" forms—the former implies that all occurrences actually have happened and will happen an infinite number of times in exactly the same way throughout eternity, while the latter simply views eternal recurrence as a litmus test for determining whether what one would will is truly desired—this "ontological" version of Deleuze's Nietzsche incorporates both and augments them with the "will to power." Accordingly, Deleuze, who attributes to Nietzsche the notion that the world's "being" is nothing other than the flux of a "pure becoming," argues that: 1) it is only "the difference" innate to becoming that can actually recur (cosmological thesis); 2) it is only the master who has the kind of fertile will that can will this difference (psychological thesis); and therefore 3) it is only the master who can overcome himself through his willing. Or as Deleuze puts it, the eternal recurrence "is the moment or the eternity of becoming which eliminates all that resists it. It releases, indeed it creates, the purely active and pure affirmation. And this is the sole content of the Overman; he is the joint power of the will to power and the eternal return. . . ." (N&P, p. xii).

As an initial matter, what is striking about Deleuze's metaphysical rendition of Nietzsche's thought is its form, which shares more in common with certain caricatures of Hegel's "system" than it does with the philosophies of either Hegel or Nietzsche. While Hegel's historical dialectic is teleological, the goal of "absolute knowing" is by no means a logical necessity; to the contrary, its realization depends upon contingent historical circumstances, which give rise to structures of self-consciousness that could have always been otherwise. With Deleuze's self-styled "selective ontology," however, it is necessarily the case that only the active can return, which is a teleological thesis that is not only logically "harder" than Hegel's, but which also runs completely contrary to Nietzsche's own perspective. Indeed, for Nietzsche, the allure of the notion of eternal recurrence is that its circular view of history cannot be reconciled with a teleological viewpoint, Christian or otherwise. Thus, even a relatively sympathetic critic such as Jean Wahl, from whom Deleuze took the view that Hegelian self-consciousness is typified by "the unhappy consciousness" (cf. N&P, p. 196), is constrained to point out that Deleuze's interpretation of Nietzsche is "essentially abstract and formal."[3] But, unlike Nietzsche himself, Deleuze's Nietzsche (as Wahl again correctly points out) is "resentful" of Hegel's philosophy,[4] and if Hegel's so-called "anthropologism" is viewed as culminating in a form of human reconciliation, then Deleuze's ontology, which rejects the Hegelian conception of selfhood, must do the same on its own anti-Hegelian terms (even as it resists being viewed as the antithesis of Hegel's thought, and thus amenable to being sublated by his "system"). Thus, whereas Hegel's thought culminates in more profound forms of recognition and negativity—that is, in a more profound form of self-consciousness in which human beings realize that they are both collectively and individually free, self-determining beings—it is necessary for Deleuze's anti-humanistic ontology to be objectively "selective" so as to make good its own commitment, which is to the destruction of these Hegelian concepts in favor of the affirmation of pure unconceptualized difference. Accordingly, "in and through the eternal return, negation as a quality of the will to power transmutes itself into affirmation, it becomes an affirmation of negation itself, it becomes a power of affirming, an affirmative power," and, in this manner, "affirmation changes nuance and becomes more and more profound" (N&P, pp. 71–72). Notwithstanding Deleuze's claim that "the concept of the Overman is directed against the dialectical conception of man" (N&P, p. 9), can it possibly be said that this process is not dialectical in its own way?

If, in certain formal respects, Deleuze's teleological approach superficially parallels Hegel's while it simultaneously embraces a content that is diametrically opposed to it, the same can be said of his alternative rendition of the master-slave dynamic. Both renditions portray circumstances in which subjectivity becomes alienated from itself, and in which each party comes to see itself in a mediated way through the eyes of the other. Deleuze's mixed couplings of the reactive-affirmative (slave) and the active-negative (master) thus have the same kinds of existential predicaments that exist with Hegel's master and slave. The Deleuzian master, who becomes the slave of the slave in virtue of the latter's transvaluation of values, is like the Hegelian slave in that he seeks recognition on the other's terms. Conversely, the Deleuzian slave, who becomes the master of the master in virtue of his transvaluation of values, is like the Hegelian master in that he is disconnected from the performance of deeds: the Deleuzian slave is incapable of doing the deeds that the master (active force) can do, and thus defines himself in a mediated way in relation to them (in the sense that he self-righteously defines himself as the person who does not do these deeds), just as the Hegelian master, who chooses not to labor (because it is a slave's work), defines himself in a mediated way in relation to the slave's work product.

More importantly, however, these differing renditions have neither the same ontological nor ethical significance for each thinker. As an initial matter, in Hegel's parable the fight that culminates in master and slave began as a struggle between two beings of exactly the same "type," and it is only the outcome of the fight that leads to each combatant's change in status. Moreover, according to Hegel, the master-slave encounter is a necessary occurrence, and while in the short term it leads to the alienation of each combatant from his "self," in the sense that each no longer has the primitive, immediate, tautological self-certainty of I = I, it engenders nothing less than human selfhood, and is thus an indispensable moment on the road to human self-realization. Conversely, according to Deleuze, the categories of master and slave not only precede the moment of the slave's transvaluation of values within his own account, which is readily apparent, but—and this is his fundamental point—they also tacitly precede the moment that constitutes the master-slave struggle within Hegel's account. What Hegel erroneously takes to be the moment in which the categories of master and slave are generated, Deleuze claims, is actually only the moment in which the slave has effectively gotten the upper hand, for, as we have seen, the materialist categories of active and reactive force (master and slave) are irreducible types (cf. N&P, p. 55), not social constructions. Moreover, for Deleuze, such concepts as negativity, recognition, mediation, and selfhood, are not ontological—or, at least, not ontological in the sense that Hegel refers to them—since on Hegel's account they refer to what is essentially human. Instead, negativity, recognition, mediation, and selfhood are concepts that are basic only to reactive force (the slave), although even here the matter is somewhat more complicated.[5] By and large, however, what is pivotal for Deleuze is that these concepts carry "negative" ethical implications, and in two senses. Initially, as Judith Butler points out with respect to negativity, Deleuze views these concepts as ideological: they introduce a "lack" into the social context in order to morally justify an oppressive sameness that is designed to check more masterly drives, which would otherwise found society upon hierarchical orderings.[6] More broadly, however, these concepts, which are part and parcel of "slave morality" (of which Hegel's thought is taken to be the prime example), are actually the foundation of morality as such, which is intrinsically life-denying.

Of all the Hegelian concepts, Deleuze most fiercely attacks the concept of "the negative," which reflects a fundamentally conceptual relationship toward the world in which the concrete differences that exist among living forces are grasped in only an abstract fashion. In contrast with the "positivity" of being, the negativity of the dialectic "manufacture[s] . . . thought being, pure and empty, which affirms itself by passing into its own opposite" (N&P, p. 183). And, in contrast with Nietzsche, for whom "the essential relation of one force to another is never conceived of as a negative element in the essence" (N&P, p. 8), since active force simply affirms its own difference without feeling the need to negate that which it is not, Hegel's dialectic is no more than a reflection on difference that inverts its image. Thus, "for the affirmation of difference as such it substitutes the negation of that which differs; for the affirmation of self it sub-stitutes the negation of the other, and for the affirmation of affirmation it substitutes the famous negation of negation. But this inversion would be meaningless if it were not in fact animated by forces with an 'interest' in doing so" (N&P, p. 196). The type of forces that have such an interest are, of course, the negative, No-saying slaves. And inasmuch as they cannot affirm themselves without placing themselves in a negative relationship to the other, it is only the slaves who seek to be "recognized":

> [T]he famous dialectical aspect of the master-slave relationship depends on the fact that power is conceived not as will to power but as repre-sentation of power, representation of superiority, recognition by "the one" of the superiority of "the other." What the wills in Hegel want is to have their power recognised, to represent their power. According to Nietzsche we have here a wholly erroneous conception of the will to power. This is the slave's conception, it is the image that the man of ressentiment has of power. . . . *Underneath the Hegelian image of the mas-ter we always find the slave.*(N&P, p. 10)(italics added)

What is important to recognize here is that in rejecting Hegel's notions of negativity and recognition, Deleuze is not offering an alterna-tive version of selfhood; rather, what he is doing is far more radical. When he tells us that "in Hegel, consciousness wants to be recognized by anoth-er and represented as self-consciousness" (N&P, p. 80), or, more directly, when he says that "[self]-consciousness is essentially reactive" (N&P, p. 41), Deleuze is taking issue with the very notion of selfhood. The looping back of consciousness onto itself, which "interiorizes" the human being and therefore first creates and then thickens the "identity" of the self, is not an active project, but a reactive one; it is the project of a force that can-not otherwise manifest itself outwardly in the world. Active force, to the contrary, can spend itself in the world—it can "exteriorize" itself—and thus it has no need to turn inward. And by profusely spending itself in the world, active force does not acquire a "self-identity"; instead, it is con-stantly changing, or, better yet, "overcoming" its "self." (This is the return of difference that is vouchsafed by eternal recurrence.) Thus, Deleuze maintains, "underneath the Hegelian image of the master we always find the slave" because the Hegelian master is no longer disseminating himself in the world; rather, because he has been infected by the "becoming reac-tive" negativity of the slave, his thin self-consciousness seeks recognition in order to enable him to forge a thicker "self" identity, and this self-identity is anathema to the play of pure difference, which is the Deleuzian ideal.

Although Deleuze seems to reject all conceptions of self-consciousness and selfhood here, matters are far more complicated, for, as we have observed, in opposition to the slave's "negation of the other," he has proffered the master's "affirmation of *self*," which refers to a phenomenon in which the (affirmative) value-positing subject has just itself as its object: "Affirmation has no object other than itself. To be precise it is being insofar as it is its own object to itself" (N&P, p. 186). How does affirmation make an object of itself? Deleuze explains:

> Affirmation is posited for the first time as multiplicity, becoming and chance. . . . Affirmation is then divided in two, difference is reflected in the affirmation of affirmation: the moment of reflection where a second affirmation takes the first as its object. But in this way affirmation is redoubled: as object of the second affirmation it is affirmation itself affirmed, redoubled affirmation, difference raised to its highest power . . . . The will to power as the differential element that produces and develops difference in affirmation, that reflects difference in the affirmation of affirmation and makes it return in the affirmation which is itself affirmed. (N&P, p. 189)

In this fashion, Deleuze rejects the mediacy that is intrinsic to Hegelian self-determination in favor of an immediacy that would seem to be bought at the expense of the external object. This presents problems for Deleuze, however. He accuses the negativity of the dialectic (or the "negation of negation") of manufacturing a reductive "thought being, pure and empty," as opposed to his own "affirmation of affirmation," which knows and affirms difference in its multifariousness. But if the master's "affirmation of self" involves no object other than himself, in what way does Deleuze seek to give difference its due? What is the relationship between this "affirmation of self," which has no object other than itself, and the affirmation of difference, which—at least nominally—does not "negate" the other, but, rather, fosters its particularity?

To grasp the consequences of Deleuze's anti-Hegelian ontology, it is necessary to revisit Hegel's conceptions of "negativity" and "recognition," for in attacking these ontological concepts by giving them an unjustifiably psychological interpretation, Deleuze has unwittingly projected the tendencies of his own philosophy onto Hegel's dialectical thought. Thus, Hegelian "negativity" means that the human subject is other than (or stands in a "negative" relationship to) that which is its object. To claim that the external world is not the human subject, however, is not tantamount to claiming that the human subject says "No" to the external world (as does the Nietzschean slave in section I-10 of the *Genealogy of Morals*). To the contrary, (Nietzsche's) psychological affirmation presupposes ontological negativity. Historical personages that Nietzsche admired (masterly sorts who were not driven by *ressentiment*) attempted to "conquer" the world around them by placing their own imprimatur upon it. (This goes for a Goethe no less than a Caesar.) For Nietzsche, this is the highest act of affirmation. But in Hegelian terms this must be understood as the "negativity" of a self-consciousness striving to assimilate an alienated objectivity in order to reconstitute it into an ever-expanding subjectivity. In other words, the will to act so as to make the objective world one's own (psychological affirmation) is given impetus by the fact that before acting the world is not one's own: the self-affirming subject acts precisely because he stands in a negative relation to the objective world (ontological negativity). Indeed, it is in this process of conceptually mediating his relationship to the objective world that the subject gives himself a determinate content, i.e., this is how he makes himself who he actually is. And this notion stands in absolute contrast with those "slave moralities" that deny the determinacy that the nature of our phenomenal existences impose by positing another realm (the afterworld) that is completely beyond the pale of such particularistic, self-determining mediations.

Conversely, if we regard Nietzsche's "last man," we see the embodiment of psychological negativity. But the last man is not psychologically negative because he is ontologically negative; to the contrary, while he must be ontologically negative because this is what human beings basically are, he refuses to comprehend himself in these terms for psychological reasons. Consequently, the last man does not embrace a philosophy of negativity, which would require him to continuously engage with the world, and thus perpetually remake both it and himself in the process; instead, he embraces its precise opposite, namely, a philosophy of positivity or "positivism." And, Deleuze's wholesale attacks upon Hegelian negativity notwithstanding, in the final analysis it is positivism that Nietzsche himself railed against, and that the last man embraces. According to Nietzsche, it is the positivist who simply accepts both himself and the world as it is.[7] In short, therefore, from a psychological perspective, what

Deleuze refers to as "the dialectical man" (N&P, p. 163) is neither the purely negativistic, No-saying slave nor the positivistic last man—that is, he neither categorically denies nor affirms what is.

In much the same way that Deleuze fails to differentiate ontological and psychological negativity, he fails to differentiate ontological and psychological recognition. When Hegel speaks to the issue of recognition within the context of the master-slave encounter, he is not maintaining that people psychologically need others to recognize them (although, undoubtedly, this is the case). Far more radically, he is maintaining that there cannot even be a notion of the self in the absence of recognition, for, ontologically, a person can only have a reflective sense of self in response to his interaction with other selves (as opposed to a reflective sense of self wholly in response to his own self, as is the case with Deleuze). This fundamental point pertains only to the necessary conditions for the self, not to its psychological constitution. Nevertheless, it is to the psychological make-up of the self that Deleuze implicitly refers when he speaks of the slavish requirement for recognition: "the slave only conceives of power as the object of recognition, the content of a representation, the stake in a competition, and therefore makes it depend, at the end of a fight, on a simple attribution of established values" (N&P, p. 10). Deleuze fails to see that to conceive of power as the object of recognition or the content of a representation, as well as to attribute established values, the one who so conceives and attributes must already have a notion of self, a notion that, according to Hegel, can only arise within the framework of others. In other words, he has misrepresented the point of the master-slave encounter. Our question, of course, is how Deleuze's own second-order conception of a reflective self, which has no object other than the first-order affirming "self" that it affirms, arises within his own ontological framework. And to this question, Deleuze can give no answer. In the absence of another person that would decenter the first-order "self," who, from the Hegelian standpoint, is akin to the primitively self-certain consciousness in which I = I, there is no impetus for consciousness to loop back onto itself. Indeed, to be able to revel in your difference already presupposes the interiorization of the other, which is exactly what Deleuze forecloses by taking this phenomenon to be simply the hallmark of the slave.

In the final analysis, by simultaneously valorizing an "ontology of difference" and making an immediate, presocial idea of self the wellspring of all life-affirming value, Deleuze alternately, albeit unintentionally, embraces what he incorrectly takes to be the life-denying pillars of Hegel's philosophy, namely, an uncritical acceptance of what is (positivism) and an idealistically contrived unity that represses difference (anti-pluralism). In fact, both of these tendencies flow from both his strategic operation for facilitating human overcoming and his own ideal. Accordingly, on the one hand, Deleuze's thought tends to uncritically accept what is because it would dispense with universality in the name of particularity without identifying particularity's universally preformed nature. In other words, as Hegel would maintain, all particulars subsist in a mediated relationship with culturally generated concepts and values, and to the degree that one purports to dispense with the given cultural context, one just inadvertently reaffirms the existing particulars in precisely the way that they have been culturally impacted. Consequently, despite Deleuze's antipathy toward culture, which he takes to have been slavish at its inception (N&P, p. 138), the attempt to give difference its due must (self-consciously) take place within the context of culture itself, regardless of the degree to which the culture deviates from the norm. Furthermore, from the standpoint of the "first moment" of his archetype—the first-order affirming self—Deleuze would uncritically accept what is because in wholly exteriorizing himself, the first order self has no critical standpoint from which to interpret the world, though Deleuze (following Nietzsche, who does not entangle himself in an ontology) still hollowly claims that interpretation is "philosophy's highest art" (N&P, p. 4). Deleuze's first-order subject is wholly at one with the world, and whatever social institutions may exist exercise an unperceived but absolute influence upon the way that he wills within it.[8]

On the other hand, Deleuze's ontology actually represses difference. From the "strategic" standpoint, although Deleuze would negate this world in favor of the world of difference, he is still much like Nietzsche's allegedly dialectical No-saying slave, who conceptually negates this world in favor of the one beyond.[9] Both yearn for a world that historically has never existed, and both have an ontology that cooks the outcome. And, while Deleuze claims that the "immense" negation in *his* system "has broken its alliance with reactive forces" and is, therefore, "under the sway of affirmation" (cf. N&P, pp. 177–79), isn't it the case that from the vantage point of both Hegel and Nietzsche, Deleuze's selective ontology falls in line with Platonism, Christianity, and Kantianism in terms of its discounting of the particularities of this world? Or, as Deleuze says of Hegel, hasn't Deleuze just manufactured this ontology with his own brand of dialectic, which is a product of the negative, and isn't the "becoming" intrinsic to his ontology only a flattening "thought" becoming, pure and empty? (cf. N&P, p. 183). Moreover, as we have already seen, in his "second moment," Deleuze's archetype is a virtually self-identical being. Because this second-order self-affirming "reflective" subject who takes only himself as an object is not "infected" with the negative—on Hegel's account, the negative is the ontological ground upon which the subject fluidly makes itself determinate in the world—he is unable to generate a concrete relationship with that which he is not. Thus, for all purposes, other persons and things share the second-order subject's life world in only the most attenuated sense; they are merely abstract entities, the furniture on the stage upon which Deleuze's masterly forces affirm themselves in any way that they deem fit.

In his two moments, therefore, the ideal Deleuzian subject careens from pillar to post, from positivism to antipluralism. The first-order subject is completely at one with the world, while the second-order subject, who has only himself for an object, is completely at one with himself. There is no mediation of these two existential moments, however, just as there is no mediation anywhere else within Deleuze's ontology. And while this is in keeping with Deleuze's anti-Hegelian agenda, it only reveals the untenable extremes that inhere within his notion of selfhood. The master and the slave in Hegel's master-slave parable are able to move forward because neither affirmation nor negation are hypostatized within Hegel's dialectic; there is neither the static affirmation of what is nor a negation induced nothingness, as Deleuze alternately alleges. To the contrary, by dint of the *aufhebung*, which is at the heart of the dialectic, what exists is both negated and preserved (in the sense of raised up), thus allowing subjectivity to overcome its own contradictions through fluid self-movement. Because affirmation and negation are not permitted to share the same world on Deleuze's account, however, the Deleuzian subject goes to the extremes.

JACQUES LACAN

Although first and foremost a psychoanalyst whose self-styled mission was to facilitate a "return to Freud," Jacques Lacan's psychoanalytic theory, which draws heavily upon Hegel's thought, has had enormous philosophical implications.[1] As an initial matter, Lacan's vaunted "return to Freud" was motivated, in no small part, by his disdain for "ego psychology," which was particularly (but by no means exclusively) prevalent in the United States. According to Lacan, Freud's thought was revolutionary because it showed—in opposition to classical psychology—that the ego was not the seat of an autonomous self, but, rather, was governed by the unconscious, which was perpetually subverting it. The ego psychologists had not grasped this crucial lesson, however, and by failing to see that the ego was irremediably "decentered," they had misinterpreted "the metapsychological work of Freud after 1920," thereby prompting Lacan to contemptuously declare that "our nice little ego is back again. . . . We're now back on the well-beaten paths of general psychology."[2] But in seeking to revivify the revolutionary implications of Freud's work in the face of those who would domesticate it in accordance with the tenets of classical psychology, Lacan does not categorically embrace the underlying premises of Freud's thought either. Indeed, Lacan dissents from what is unquestionably one of the most important aspects of Freud's work—namely, his view that the ego is largely informed by the biologically rooted drives of the libido. Thus, while Freud's thought is grounded in the biological sciences,

Lacan's thought is vehemently antibiological in nature, and is grounded, instead, in a more hermeneutical approach. And, in effectuating this move away from Freud's more naturalistic views, Lacan latches onto Hegel's writings. But Hegel is more than just a counterbalance to Freud, for, in the final analysis, it would only be a slight overstatement to say that a good deal of Lacan's elaborate and varied corpus, which also owes an enormous debt to the anthropological theories of Claude Lévi-Strauss and the linguistic theories of Ferdinand Saussure, revolves around subtle reworkings of the concepts contained in chapter IV of the *Phenomenology*.

Like Bataille, Lacan attended Kojève's lectures on the *Phenomenology*, and, like Bataille, he was heavily influenced by them. According to Mikkel Borch-Jacobsen, who does an excellent job of tracing the theoretical underpinnings of Lacan's positions to Kojève's Heideggerian inspired reading of the *Phenomenology*, there is a fundamental ambiguity that exists in Kojève's rendition: "Kojève proposed a 'humanist' and 'anthropological' interpretation of Hegel in his course, and that was how he ended up stumbling onto the problem of death and finitude, dragging his most eminent listeners into a sort of strange Hegelianism of pure negativity, which rather quickly swerved into a virulent anti-Hegelianism (and anti-humanism)."[3] At the heart of Kojève's interpretation of Hegel, in other words, there was an irreconcilable conflict. On the one hand, Hegel could be interpreted along strictly humanistic lines, which means that Hegel's Absolute is identical to humankind, and that in sublating "the Other" in its movement toward Absolute Knowledge, humankind is basically reappropriating its own essence. This interpretation, Borch-Jacobsen points out, finds expression in Sartre's claim that "existentialism is a humanism" (though Sartre would clearly deny that human beings can ever wholly reappropriate themselves). On the other hand, humankind is characterized by death and finitude, and the "being" of humans (individually or collectively) is not tantamount to transcendent "Being," of which humans constitute only a part. On this antihumanist view, which finds expression in Heidegger's "Letter on Humanism," human beings cannot reappropriate their own Being, and, indeed, living "authentically" depends upon nothing more than the recognition that we are essentially "Beings-unto-Death"—an idea that implies that our so-called possibilities are actually endlessly deferred. Moreover, this ambiguity manifests itself in Kojève's discussion of "Desire" at the beginning of chapter IV of the *Phenomenology*. The negativity of desire can be comprehended as desiring itself through the other, as Hegel maintains, or "by contrast, if desire is defined, in para-Heideggerian terms, as transcendence toward nothing, it is none the less clear that it will desire 'itself' only as nothingness—in other words, as pure negativity and absolute alterity: that Desire (capital D) will desire 'itself' as Other (capital O), beyond itself and every 'ego'."[4] This suggests that humankind is, in some sense, always beyond its own reach, which is the red thread that runs through the numerous theoretical twists and turns that comprise Lacan's five decade long career. In what follows, I shall consider the various stages of Lacan's thought, paying particular attention to the Hegelian implications each step along the way.

The first phase of Lacan's thought, which basically spans from his inaugural presentation to the International Psychoanalytic Association in 1936 to his so-called "Rome Discourse" in 1953, is, more than any other, preoccupied with Hegel's description of self-consciousness. This phase revolves around Lacan's theory of the "mirror stage," which derives from— but takes in an entirely different direction—Freud's theory of biological immaturity. According to Lacan, when a young child between the ages of six and eighteen months looks into the mirror, the image that stares back leads him to jubilantly test the correspondence between his own bodily movements and the movements of his image in the mirror, as well as the relationship between his specular image and those aspects of his surrounding environment that are also captured in the mirror's reflection. But the specular image actually misrepresents to the young child the nature of his own reality, for while his motor skills are largely undeveloped, the specular image appears to him as an integrated whole. As a result, the young child sees himself in an idealized way, and, moreover, comes to anticipate a future in which his current lack of coordination will have been completely overcome. For Lacan, however, the crucial point is not that the young child's apprehension of its future (or even present) physical coordination is mistaken, but that the specular image with which he identifies suggests an underlying, unified/unifying ego structure, which the young child will then immediately internalize as an ideal. And it is in moving toward this unifying ideal, Lacan will tell us, that the developing child is mistaken:

> The mirror stage is a drama whose internal thrust is precipitated from insufficiency to anticipation—and which manufactures for the subject, caught up in the lure of spatial identification, the succession of phantasies that extends from a fragmented body image to a form of its totality that I shall call orthopaedic—and, lastly, to the assumption of the

armour of an alienating identity, which will mark with its rigid structure
the subject's entire mental development. (E, p. 4)[5]

The "alienating identity" to which Lacan refers here is none other
than the subject's notion of his own autonomously derived self-identity,
and Lacan's point is that—in spite of the ultimate maturation of his powers—the child will never feel truly "unified." At this juncture, we have not
moved all that far from Freud, who himself recognized the high psychic
price that we pay for the development of the ego, which is, as it were, an
"alienating identity" that is under relentless attack from our unconscious
drives. (Along these lines, Freud speaks in *Civilization and its Discontents*
of the feeling of oneness with the external world that a baby has at its
mother's breast, an "oceanic feeling" that is irretrievably lost with the ego's
development.) Freud also claimed, however, that this developmental
process was absolutely necessary in order to bring the individual into a
closer conformity with the requirements of the external world; in Freud's
terminology, there needs to be a progressive substitution of the "reality
principle" for the "pleasure principle." In contrast, although there are certain ambivalences in this earliest phase of his thought, Lacan maintains
(or, at the very least, will come to maintain) that this process of ego development does not propel us any closer to "reality"—or, as Lacan will later
come to name it, "the real"—but, rather, moves us farther away from it.
From the viewpoint of Lacan's "mirror stage" thesis, the "important point"
is that the ego, which ostensibly performs a synthesizing function, is nothing more than an "Ideal-I" that "situates the agency of the ego, before its
social determination, in a fictional direction, which will always remain
irreducible for the individual alone . . . whatever the success of the dialectical syntheses by which he must resolve as *I* his discordance with his own
reality" (E, p.2). In other words, unlike Freud, for whom the ego "realisti-
cally" mediated the relationship between the unconscious and the external
world, for Lacan, it would appear, the ego is a pernicious fiction.

Indeed, Lacan even points out that when a monkey is put before the
mirror, it will "master" its specular image and find it "empty" (E, p. 1),
which has led some commentators to contend that Lacan has a "derisory"
view of the child, who simply has a "perverse will to remain deluded."[6] It
seems to me, however, that this misses the point. To be sure, Lacan, as we
shall see, believes that this "fiction" should be put aside, and this is actually one of his basic objectives in psychoanalysis. But this initial moment
of ego formation may well be a necessary stage that must be surmounted,

just as the initial moment of ego formation in the *Phenomenology*, which splinters into master and slave, is an indispensable stage that must be surmounted. Indeed, there is every reason to believe that Hegel's master-slave dialectic was the model from which Lacan formulated his "mirror stage" thesis. For example, Lacan contends that "this development is experienced as a temporal dialectic that decisively projects the formation of the individual into history" (E, p. 4)—a characterization that could be applied to the master-slave parable without changing a word. So, too, Lacan talks in terms of "recognition," or, to be more exact, "misrecognition": "the function of *méconnaissance* . . . characterizes the ego in all its structures" (E, p. 6). And, finally, in his 1948 paper "Aggressivity in Psychoanalysis," Lacan plainly states that Hegel's developmental theory was the "ultimate" one: "From the conflict of Master and Slave, he deduced the entire subjective and objective progress of our history" (E, p. 26). In short, then, the mirror stage is Lacan's psychoanalytic analogue to the master-slave encounter, and like the master-slave encounter, which also "projects the formation of the individual into history," it is not viewed pejoratively, but merely as an initial step that must be gotten past. Indeed, as we saw, Lacan has even called the petrified specular image "orthopaedic."

But even in this initial phase of this thought, as was suggested above, Lacan was far from optimistic about the prospects for any kind of reconciliation between the ego and the outside world, and, in any event, certainly far less optimistic than Hegel. Nevertheless, prefiguring his "linguistic turn," Lacan characterizes the "Ideal-I" as a "primordial form" that exists "before it is objectified in the dialectic of identification with the other, and before language restores to it, in the universal, its function as subject" (E, p. 2). Language would thus appear to be the key because it is essentially intersubjective in nature, which is more or less in keeping with Hegel's attack on the autonomous, "self-identical" self. The reconciliation afforded by language is imperfect at best, however, for it would seem that any self-identity forged by the mediations of language would necessarily pale in comparison with the virtual omnipotence that the young child had prognosticated for himself when initially apprehending his specular image. It is from the viewpoint of this early and persisting ideal that *méconnaissance* "characterizes the ego in *all* its structures."

In any event, it seems relatively clear that in this first phase of his thought, Lacan's attack on the ego is less an attack on all conceptions of the ego than it is on one in particular—namely, the Cartesian one. Thus, in "The Mirror Stage as Formative of the Function of the I as Revealed in

Psychoanalytic Experience," he emphasizes in the very first paragraph that it is to "any philosophy directly issuing from the *Cogito*" that he is "oppose[d]" (E, p. 1). And, in the penultimate page of the paper, he attacks Sartre, who distinguishes between the free "I" of consciousness and the ego ("Me"), which is an object in the world: "that philosophy grasps negativity only within the limits of a self-sufficiency of consciousness, which, as one of its premises, links to the *méconnaissances* that constitute the ego, the illusion of autonomy" (E, p. 6). Lacan has clearly retained—in some ambiguous form—the idea of an unreified subject, who can only be intersubjectively constituted. Nevertheless, it is also clear that he will have no truck with the more teleological aspects of Hegel's thought for the purpose of effectuating this reconciliation. For while the master-slave dialectic is paradigmatic in these early works, Lacan has already made apparent that he sees knowledge (and certainly the drive toward "Absolute Knowledge") as essentially "paranoid." According to Lacan, "the most general structure of human knowledge" entails a "formal stagnation... which constitutes the ego and its objects with attributes of permanence, identity, and substantiality," and this "formal fixation," which "ruptures" the "shifting field" of animal desire, is a "defensive armour" that the ego dons in order to solidify itself (E, p. 17). In other words, from the vantage point of Lacan's Heraclitean "ego/object dialectic," the drive to know is just the underside of the ego's drive to unify itself, which calls into question the possibility of any reconciliation. At any rate, as he shifts into the second phase of his thought, Lacan will address both sides of this dialectic in the same fashion: he will move beyond his attack on the Cartesian subject to reject even a Hegelian subject, and he will reject any correspondence between the so-called "subject," who is now formed in the force field of language, and the objects of the external world that he would purport to know.

The beginnings of Lacan's mature "system" are evidenced in two significant papers from the mid-1950s—namely, "The Function and Field of Speech and Language in Psychoanalysis" (otherwise known as "the Rome Discourse") and "The Agency of the Letter in the Unconscious or Reason Since Freud." In these papers, Lacan ardently embraces a structural analysis in which all humanistic assumptions that might have remained in his thought up to that time are eradicated. In "The Function and Field of Speech," he stresses the importance of the anthropological theories of Lévi-Strauss, who, "in suggesting the implication of the structures of language with that part of the social laws that regulate marriage ties and kinship, is already conquering the very terrain in which Freud situates the unconscious. From now on, it is impossible not to make a general theory of the symbol the axis of a new classification of the sciences where the sciences of man will once more take up their central position as sciences of subjectivity" (E, p. 73). By collapsing "the symbol" into Freud's unconscious and making it the centerpiece of a new theory of "the sciences of man" to boot, Lacan's Lévi-Strauss largely settles whatever ambiguities had remained for Lacan concerning the goal of subjectivity. It is no longer a question of overcoming the vagaries of misrecognition in order to somehow realize an intersubjective ego ideal because the subject itself is nothing more than a function of the overarching linguistic structures: "Man speaks, then, but it is because the symbol has made him a man" (E, p. 65). From an explicitly psychoanalytic vantage point, moreover, this move to language only deepens Lacan's antibiological stance. Thus, language is no longer just a tool for uncovering the nature of the unconconscious drives that give rise to the patient's symptom; to the contrary, now, Lacan tells us, "the unconscious is structured like a language,"[7] and even a patient's symptom will "resolve itself entirely in an analysis of language, because the symptom is itself structured like a language" (E, p. 59).

Despite subsuming the subject within the deep structures of language, Lacan's "technique" is still, nevertheless, informed by "the structuring moments of the Hegelian phenomenology [and,] in the first place, the master-slave dialectic. . . ." (E, p. 80):

> These principles are simply the dialectic of the consciousness-of-self, as realized from Socrates to Hegel, from the ironic presupposition that all that is rational is real to its culmination in the scientific view that all that is real is rational. But Freud's discovery was to demonstrate that this verifying process authentically attains the subject only by decentering him from the consciousness-of-self, in the axis of which the Hegelian reconstruction of the phenomenology of mind, maintained it: that is, that this discovery renders even more decrepit any pursuit of the *prise de conscience* which, beyond its status as a psychological phenomenon, cannot be inscribed within the conjuncture of the particular moment that alone embodies the universal and in default of which it vanishes into generality. . . . But if there still remains something prophetic in Hegel's insistence on the fundamental identity of the particular and the universal, an insistence that reveals the measure of his genius, it is certainly psychoanalysis that provides it with its paradigm by revealing the structure in which that identity is realized as disjunctive of the subject, and without appeal to any tomorrow. (E, pp. 79–80)

For Lacan, like Hegel, there is still the drive for recognition—"the first object of desire is [still] to be recognized by the other (E, p. 58)—although for Lacan this drive is now understood as one that takes place completely within the boundaries of speech. Accordingly, "what constitutes me as subject is my question," and what "I seek in speech is the response of the other" (E, p. 86). (For the slave in Hegel's master-slave dynamic, of course, this response does not come—or at least does not come to him qua slave.) But where Lacan moves even farther away from Hegel, as this lengthy passage suggests, is in the idea that there can be an ultimate reconciliation between the individual and the collective. Even in the early Lacan, as we observed, there will be no movement toward "Absolute Knowledge," which, for Hegel, is the speculative juncture at which there is an identity of "I" and "We," the subject and the objects of its knowledge. This identity, Lacan says, is "disjunctive of the subject" not just because the individual will not be unified in the interpersonal realm, but because the individual himself, as Freud discovered, is essentially "decenter[ed]...from the consciousness-of-self." But if the individual can be intersubjectively recognized in speech, in what sense has Lacan done away with Hegel's *prise de conscience*? The answer, as the passage above suggests, is that he has shifted it to a dialectic that is no longer Hegelian.[8] In the beginning of "The Function and Field of Speech," Lacan remarks that in analysis there are certain times that "the subject seems to be talking in vain about someone who, even if he were his spitting image, can never become one with the assumption of his desire" (E, p. 45). Or, to put it in terms of the mirror stage, *even if* the person looking into the mirror has, in fact, realized his ego ideal, which stares back at him, there still will be no satisfaction for self-consciousness, for the person's desire will always outstrip his ego ideal.

It would appear, strangely enough, that while the initial moment before the mirror for the young child is much like the initial moment for each of the two self-consciousnesses that confront one another in the "state-of-nature" in that a minimal "self" misrecognizes an objectification of itself before it, Lacan will part company with Hegel by travelling, if you will, in the opposite direction. The master and slave, both of whom have lost their self-certainty as a result of their confrontation, will embark upon a path on which each will recover his self-certainty at a higher (intersubjective) level. In contrast, the young child, who begins with only a fragmented body, can never reach his ego ideal and would not identify with it even if he could; he will become mired in the insatiability of his own desire. In other words, while Hegel's dialectic moves forward through a continuous process in which otherness is steadily reappropriated by the subject—a process (as Lacan says of Freud's work) that culminates in "reintegration and harmony, I could even say of reconciliation" (E, p. 171)—Lacan's symbol-driven "dialectic," as will become clear, moves backward toward the ontological root of an absolute Otherness, which is what the subject really desires, but, because of its unobtainability, disappropriates him at every turn.

The young child, therefore, would do better to seek his recognition in the symbolic realm, not the realm of images, which includes within it baneful ideals such as the unified ego structure, for symbols "envelop the life of man in a network so total that they join together, before he comes into the world those who are going to engender him by 'flesh and blood'; so total that they bring to his birth . . . the shape of his destiny . . . *unless he attains the subjective bringing to realization of being-for-death*" (E, p. 68; emphasis added). With this last clause, we can see the inspiration for Lacan's "dialectic," which, as Borch-Jacobsen correctly points out, is nothing other than Kojève's dialectic "intrerpreted from over Heidegger's shoulder."[9] As we shall see shortly, with his move towards structuralism, Lacan has embraced an ontology that is Heideggerian at its core. But at this point, it is important to emphasize that in now unequivocally rejecting a Hegelian conception of selfhood, Lacan is also rejecting a Hegelian conception of knowledge—that is, he is rejecting the notion that a subject can ever actually know the nature of the objects that he apprehends. This "epistemological break," which extends his earlier views on the paranoiac nature of knowledge (in a fashion that, predictably, is parallel to the extension of his views on the nature of the subject), is detailed in "The Agency of the Letter," and the theoretical medium through which he brings it about is a reworked Saussurian linguistic theory.

If "the unconscious is structured like a language," and the subject is ultimately "the slave of language" (E, p. 148), then a correctly articulated linguistic theory is a necessary psychoanalytic tool, and this is precisely what Lacan purports to give us. Lacan begins with Saussure's linguistic theory, but fundamentally transfigures it by attacking his concept of the "sign." Thus, according to Saussure, the linguistic sign is itself arbitrary—that is, any term could have been used to designate the actual thing to which it refers. But once a particular term is selected, the tie between signifier and signified is instituted, and the sign becomes tethered within an elaborate system of signs, each of which has its own meaning within the specific language. In other words, each sign within a language binds together within it both signifier and signified. According to Lacan, however, the signifier does not truly have any relationship to the signified, a point that he graphically brings out with the following "algorithm": S/s. Capital "S" designates the signifier, small "s" designates the signified, and the bar between them suggests that there is actually no relationship between the two. Rather, "the signifier, as such, signifies nothing."[10] And once signification falls out of the picture, we are left with only a chain of signifiers—or what Lacan refers to as a "signifying chain" akin to the rings of a necklace (E, p. 153)—which is basically a "prison house" of signifiers that bears no relationship to the way things "really are." This signifying chain, in which meaning is condemned to slide from word to word— Lacan also refers to the signifying chain as a "metonymical chain"— implies not only that we lose all access to the referent, that is, the "real" objects of our knowledge, but also that our desires, as subjects born and inextricably bound within this interminably sliding chain, can never be satisfied: desire is "caught in the rails—eternally stretching forth towards the *desire for something else*—of metonymy" (E, pp. 166–67). This, according to Lacan, is "the chain of dead desire" (E, p. 167).

I shall elaborate upon Lacan's notion of desire shortly, but first it must be emphasized that he does not just conceive of the human world in terms of this one (symbolic) dimension. Instead, Lacan articulates the existence of three realms—namely, the Symbolic, the Imaginary and the Real. As we just saw, the Symbolic, which was inspired by the works of Lévi-Strauss and Saussure, is the linguistic realm to which we are ontologically condemned. In contrast, the Imaginary, which is what Lacan's thought has railed against from the beginning, is the realm of images with which we are ostensibly driven to identify—for example, the Cartesian and (now) Hegelian ego ideals that we espy in the mirror, and the certainty of knowledge which supposedly flows from them. So far, of course, we have merely retraced old ground. But with the introduction of his idea of the Real, Lacan moves into the orbit of an ontology whose parameters are circumscribed by the ontology of Heidegger-cum-Kojève. Thus, according to Lacan, the Real falls outside the signifying dimension altogether. And while the signifying dimension is characterized by absence, the Real, which itself cannot be signified, is the veiled presence that stands behind it: "There is no absence in the Real."[11] For Lacan, to get to the heart of the matter, the Real is closely linked with Heidegger's conception of Being, and, indeed, we already see the foreshadowings of this relationship in "The Agency of the Letter." He speaks of the human subject's "lack of being" (E, p. 166), and, in the closing paragraph, repudiates "centuries of philosophical bravado," which were carried out in the name of "humanistic man," in favor of his own project, which he says is defined by "the question of being" (E, p. 175).

According to Heidegger, "the question of being" has been obscured by the epistemological questions of the metaphysical tradition, which began with the ancient Greeks, but came to fruition with Descartes. In this sense, human beings, on Heidegger's account, are essentially fallen—that is, their understanding of the world tends to conform to the understanding of the broader collective (*das Man*), which tends to submerge the "question of being" under the commonplace. Heidegger actually equivocates on this notion of "fallenness," however, for he stresses that falling reveals an essential ontological structure of "Dasein" (human beings), although he also distinguishes between an "authentic" and "inauthentic" comportment toward the world. The individual who recognizes that he is essentially a "being-unto-death" (a phrase that we have already seen Lacan use) is the one who will be able to comport himself more authentically. But, under any circumstance, Heidegger argues, being never just reveals itself as such. Instead, it veils and unveils itself, for it is simply not something to be grasped in the manner of the Cartesian tradition. Lacan's approach is more or less analogous. According to Lacan, we are unalterably a part of the fallen Symbolic realm, but the Real both undergirds this realm and has ripple effects within it. And it is only by not attempting to linguistically grasp this ineffable, self-identical realm that we might come to have some fleeting intuition of it:

> Without going to the heart of the issue of the relationship between the signifier, qua signifier of language, and something that without it would never be named, it's noticeable that the less we express it, the less we speak, the more it speaks to us. The more foreign we are to what is at issue in this being, the more it has a tendency to present itself to us, accompanied by this pacifying expression ["the peace of the evening"] that presents itself as indeterminate, lying on the border between the field of our motor autonomy and this something that is said to us from outside, this something through which the world borders on speaking to us. . . . We have now come to the limit at which discourse, if it opens onto anything beyond meaning, opens onto the signifier in the real . . . which organizes all these phenomena.[12]

Practically speaking, however, as is the case with Heidegger's fundamental ontology, in which human beings can have no real access to Being, Lacan's subject can have no real (linguistic) access to the Real. The Real is wholly Other, which means that the "metonymical chain" in the Symbolic realm remains just that—namely, a ceaseless movement toward an unattainable Otherness. This Otherness, moreover, is the place in which the linguistically structured unconscious is found, and it is here that Hegel's problematic is reinscribed within Lacan's essentially Heideggerian ontology: "If I have said that the unconscious is the discourse of the Other (with a capital O) it is in order to indicate the beyond in which the recognition of desire is bound up with the desire for recognition" (E, p. 172). Indeed, as Lacan shifts into the third phase of his thought, he reformulates the basic Hegelian terms from chapter IV of the *Phenomenology* so as to harmonize them with a framework that is both Heideggerian *and* Freudian: the "recognition of desire" will bring about the realization that the "desire for recognition" will never be satisfied.

Lacan's third phase, which begins in the late 1950s and lasts through the mid-1970s, is marked, in some sense, by a return to the issue of sexuality in psychoanalysis, and, consequently, a return to certain Freudian staples, such as the castration complex. (This complex, Freud asserts, is based upon the establishment of the primordial law, which contains within it the punishment of castration for acts of incest.) In returning to the issue of sexuality, however, Lacan is not rejecting the anti-biologism that has animated his thought; to the contrary, he is only reinterpreting Freudian doctrine into the language of his linguistically driven brand of psychoanalytic theory. Accordingly, in "The Signification of the Phallus," Lacan contends that Freud anticipated the emphasis upon the signifier in modern linguistic analysis, but could not fully explicate this insight because it postdated him (which means that neo-Freudians who have maintained that the phallus is nothing more than the penis or clitoris have missed Freud's point). And, in accordance with Freud's "anticipation" of linguistic analysis, Lacan maintains, the phallus is the ultimate signifier: "the signifier intended to designate as a whole the effects of the signified, in that the signifier conditions them by its presence as a signifier" (E, p. 285). What is the concluding effect of this privileged signifier, "in which the role of the logos is joined with the advent of desire"? (E, p. 287). It is an alienation engendered by an unrequited desire for recognition that is ontologically insurmountable.

Lacan's formulation of desire in "The Signification of the Phallus," in which he juxtaposes desire to needs and demands, is essentially at odds with Hegel's own formulation at the beginning of chapter IV of the *Phenomenology*. For Hegel, it will be recalled, the desire of the Fichtean "I" is insatiable: it perpetually negates its other without ever achieving satisfaction. And the reason for this inability, of course, is that ultimately "self-consciousness attains its satisfaction only in another self-consciousness" (para. 10). Thus, when the desire for recognition from the other is gratified, so is individual satisfaction. In contrast, for Lacan, the insatiability of the Fichtean "I"—to stretch the analogy—is never overcome. Of course, Lacan does not begin with the self-certain "I" in his articulation of desire, just as he did not begin with two encountering self-consciousnesses in his articulation of the mirror stage. Rather, he starts with the infant who cries when its physical needs are not met. But as the infant matures, it acquires language, and therefore the ability to formulate demands, which are of a qualitatively different nature. According to Lacan, while the child's never-ending flow of demands are ostensibly for particular things, "demand in itself bears on something other than the satisfactions it calls for. It is a demand of a presence or of an absence—which is what is manifested in the primordial relation to the mother, pregnant with the Other to be situated within the needs that it can satisfy" (E, p. 286). In other words, what the child is seeking through its demands is an unconditional recognition from its mother, who—inhabiting the existential place of the unattainable Other—is clearly in no position to meet them all. Or to put the matter somewhat differently, the mother does not possess a phallus, the ultimate signifier which alone could meet all the child's demands (cf. E, p. 289). Consequently, "demand annuls the particularity of everything that can be granted by transmuting it into a proof of love, and the very satisfactions that it obtains for need are reduced to the level of being no more than the crushing demand for love" (E, p. 286). And what of desire? Desire, Lacan tells us, is the "difference that results from the subtraction of the first from the second" (E, p. 287). It pertains to those demands that exceed the physical needs that can be met—or, conversely, in pertaining to those demands that cannot be met, it reflects the recognition that cannot be given. Indeed, Lacan says, the desire of the one who demands "remains all the more deprived to the extent that the need articulated in the demand is satisfied" (E, p. 263)—a notion that hearkens back to Lacan's earlier contention that desire would outstrip the individual's satisfaction even if he could become the "spitting image" of his specular ideal. The "recognition of desire," in short, entails the recognition of desire's ultimate unattainability: the person from whom recognition is sought also "lacks being" and is thus also "caught in the rails—eternally stretching forth towards the *desire for something else*—of metonymy."

In the final analysis, then, what we see throughout Lacan's corpus is Hegel's dialectic in reverse: rather than move toward more inclusive syntheses, in which mutual recognition becomes increasingly comprehensive and determinate, Lacan's "dialectic" moves toward the indeterminate vanishing point of desire, which, for both Hegel (in his discussion of the French Revolution) *and* Heidegger, is tantamount to death. Indeed, even when Lacan gets around to theorizing about the particular objects that subjects desire, he still will not speak of them as *particular* objects, but will only speak of them generically—namely, as *objet a,* which are those phantasy objects that stand in for the missing phallus. For Lacan, therefore, all objects are death-like specters, as are, ultimately, all subjectivities. For Hegel, of course, history begins with the slave's whiff of death, but Hegel does not fetishize death, even if history is built upon its sublimation; rather, he moves into history, which will include its own satisfactions. In contrast, Lacan, who fetishizes death in every one of his theoretical constructs, will have no truck with history whatsoever; in moving backward from the master-slave encounter, he seeks to avoid the particularity of history in the barely concealed name of Heidegger's fundamental ontology. What is ironic, however, is that Lacan seems to end up in the very place that he sought to avoid. From the mirror stage onward, he seeks to avoid the self-identical subject, but in embracing the pure negativity of an ontology of death, which flattens all possible experience, he has arrived at it through the back door.

15

JÜRGEN HABERMAS AND
AXEL HONNETH

Before writing the *Phenomenology of Spirit*, Hegel had produced other works within which the themes that are taken up in the master-slave parable were considered. These works, *System of Ethical Life* (1802–1803), *First Philosophy of Spirit* (1803–1804), and *Philosophy of Spirit* (1805–1806), which were written for lectures that he gave in the German city of Jena, as well as earlier essays on natural law and Christianity, place concepts such as lordship and bondage, recognition, and labor in varying frameworks that all differ from the one that is present in the *Phenomenology*. Jürgen Habermas, who has been the single most important philosophical figure in Germany since the death of his teacher, Theodor W. Adorno, in 1969, and Axel Honneth, who was a student of Habermas's and is presently Professor of Philosophy at the University of Frankfurt, believe that these earlier writings contain ground-breaking insights into the nature of human sociality that Hegel should have pursued. Hegel discarded these insights in the *Phenomenology*, however, and instead reverted to what Habermas and Honneth alternatively refer to as a "philosophy of consciousness" and a "philosophy of the subject," which is based upon what they take to be the metaphysically-laden "subject-object paradigm." This reversion, they maintain, evidences a missed opportunity that constitutes one of the defining moments in the history of modern philosophy. Habermas and Honneth therefore seek to go back to the intuitions that are at play in the Jena writings in order to draw sustenance for their own projects. In the case of Habermas, whose seminal essay "Labor and Interaction: Remarks on Hegel's *Jena Philosophy of Mind*"[1] gave rise to numerous studies on these writings,[2] this means drawing upon Hegel's earlier insights for the purpose of articulating a theory of communicative action in which the operative paradigm is not one of a subject and object, but, rather, of an ego and alter ego who are always already embedded within a social context and communicatively seek to realize an uncoerced consensus through the force of reason. Habermas contends that this "option of explicating the ethical totality as a communicative reason embodied in intersubjective life contexts" was still viable under the Jena writings.[3] In the case of Honneth, who largely embraces Habermas's ego-alter ego paradigm, but seeks to move past Habermas's formal linguistic model toward a more robust notion of individual subjectivity, this means revisiting the conceptions of recognition that existed in the Jena writings in order to bring them up to date with the aid of the modern social sciences. This is what he seeks to do in *The Struggle for Recognition: The Moral Grammar of Social Conflicts*, a work that was first published in Germany in 1992.[4]

In "Labor and Interaction," Habermas intends to show that between the Jena writings and the *Phenomenology*, Hegel inverted his view of the relationship that exists between various human characteristics and Spirit. As opposed to the Jena writings, in which Hegel "offered a distinctive, systematic basis for the formative process of the spirit" (L&I, p. 142)—that is, he conceptualized Spirit as a function of the dialectical interconnections between language, labor, and interaction—in the *Phenomenology*, he sees language, labor, and interaction as just a function of Spirit's reflection upon its own self-movement (cf. L&I, p. 143). To make his point, Habermas starts by discussing Hegel's view of Kant's synthetic unity of apperception, as well as Fichte's attempt to surmount the theoretical difficulties that it poses. For our purposes, the nuances of this discussion, in which the evolution of the notion of the ego is explicated from Kant through Fichte to Hegel, are not relevant. Habermas's general point, however, is that unlike Kant's epistemologically driven transcendental unity of apperception, which is a contentless "I" that self-referentially stands behind all experience and makes it possible, and Fichte's abstract idea of the self, which takes itself to be the ground on which all practical relations to others in the world are posited, Hegel's initial idea of the self is one that is based upon an initial reciprocity between subjects: "Hegel's dialectic of self-consciousness passes over the relation of solitary reflection in favor of the complementary relationship between individuals who know each other. The experience of self-consciousness is no longer considered the original one. Rather, for Hegel, it results from the experience of interaction, in which I see myself through the eyes of other subjects" (L&I, pp. 144–45). For the Hegel of the Jena period, according to Habermas, spirit is not simply the universal medium in which non-identical subjects are united, though, as far as it goes, this is correct. More importantly, it is the very context within which individuality is produced as an initial matter.

Although Habermas's essay does not make the point very clearly, Hegel's conception of spirit is continually changing from his earliest writings through the last work of the Jena period, *Philosophy of Spirit*, which, predictably, evidences the closest affinity to the model that he relies upon in the *Phenomenology*. And as his notion of spirit evolves in these works, so does his view of the nature of the struggle for recognition, the relationship of domination and subordination that follows in its wake, and labor. Unlike the master-slave parable in the *Phenomenology*, in which two human consciousnesses are sparked to self-consciousness by coming across one another in a minimalist, "state of nature" type setting, in Hegel's earlier works a fully formed social framework is presupposed. And, unlike the basic movement in the *Phenomenology*, in which individual self-consciousness is ever impelled toward more socially elaborate forms of recognition, in Hegel's earliest works the movement is one in which already existing societies are impelled toward more socially elaborate forms of recognition by breaches in the previously existing forms of recognition. Thus, in a fragment from Hegel's *Spirit of Christianity*, an early work that Habermas discusses, we are presented with the relationship between the criminal and the ethical totality that he sunders by his acts. According to Hegel, Habermas tells us, the criminal "revokes the moral basis, namely the complementary interchange of noncompulsory communication and the mutual satisfaction of interests, by putting himself as an individual in the place of the totality" (L&I, p. 148). This leads to the criminal's alienation not only from the rest of society, but also from his own "deficient life." With time, however, there is a reconciliation, for when both parties see that their separation is the outcome of an "abstraction from the common interconnection of their lives—and within this, in the dialogic relationship of recognizing oneself in the other, they experience the common basis of their existence"(L&I, p. 148). Society therefore generates more complex forms of recognition which, ostensibly, obviate the need for criminal acts of the type committed, for the underlying deficiency in recognition that had precipitated the crime has been addressed.

In the Jena writings, Habermas points out, the struggle for recognition is removed from the framework of criminal activity, and is instead placed within the context of a life and death struggle to preserve one's honor. But unlike the struggle for recognition in the master-slave parable, which only first gives rise to the issue of labor, which, in turn, plays a role in enabling the slave to gain self-consciousness through objectifying himself in his work product, the struggle for recognition in the Jena writings stems from another's threat to one's already existing work product—or, to be more precise, the already existing work product of the family that one both heads and symbolizes in one's singularity. Having labored to gain these possessions, the victimized party views them as an extension of himself. Thus, an attack on any minute thing that this person takes to be his own is taken to be an attack on the totality of his person. Or, as Hegel states it in the *First Philosophy of Spirit*, "the single [family head] is one consciousness, only in as much as every singular aspect of his possessions, and of his being, appears bound up with his whole essence, it is taken up into [himself]. . . . The injuring of any one of his single aspects is therefore infinite, it is an absolute offense, an offense against his integrity, an offense to his honor; and the collision about any single point is a struggle for the whole."[5] Indeed, in an earlier version of this work, Hegel contends that

> this injury must occur, for consciousness must advance to this recognition, the single must injure one another, in order to recognize that they are rational; for consciousness is essentially of this sort, that the totality of the single is opposed to him, and in this othering process is yet the same as he, that the totality of the one is in another consciousness, and is the consciousness of the other, and even this absolute subsistence that it has for itself, is in this other consciousness. In other words it gets recognition from the other.[6]

According to Habermas, this early model of recognition (as opposed to the one presented in the *Phenomenology*), in which the concept of the "I" derives "not from the experiential domain of theoretical consciousness, but from that of the practical" (L&I, p. 150), sharply contrasts not only with Kant's synthetic unity of apperception, which is the "I" of Kant's theoretical philosophy, but also with the "I" of Kant's practical philosophy, the equally abstract autonomous will. For Kant, the autonomous will must abstract from the concrete particulars of one's existence in order to act upon the moral law, which is legislated by the individual himself. Thus, at least with respect to what Kant calls "perfect duties," if a person determines that the basic principle (maxim) governing a possible action with moral implications cannot be universalized without the general principle itself becoming logically impossible, then the action ought not be done, regardless of the consequenses for either the person making the determination or anyone who might be affected by it. For Kant, the advantage of this decision-making process, which gives rise to categorical imperatives, is that the morality of an action is ostensibly determined by reason itself. But by making the individual's determination of the coherence of an action the test of its morality, Habermas complains, Kant has taken it out of the dialogic realm: "The intersubjectivity of the recognition of moral laws accounted for a priori by practical reason permits the reduction of moral action to the monologic domain. The positive relation of the will to the will of others is withdrawn from possible communication. . ." (T&I, p. 151).

In contrast with the abstractness of the foundational "I" in both Kant's theoretical and practical philosophies, Hegel introduces a set of foundational categories in the *First Philosophy of Spirit* that provide a concrete foundation for the formation of human self-consciousness. The three categories that he proffers—namely, language, labor, and interaction (which initially occurs within the framework of the family)—are both originary and irreducible. Thus, according to Habermas, "spirit is an organization of equally original media. . . . These fundamental dialectical patterns are heterogenous; as media of the spirit, language and labor cannot be traced back to the experiences of interaction and mutual recognition" (L&I, p. 152). As we will see momentarily, the distinctiveness of these categories, which Habermas sees as fundamental to Hegel's early project, is, more to the point, fundamental to his own project. Moreover, it should be grasped that Habermas is favorably contrasting the relationship between these categories in the *First Philosophy of Spirit* with their interrelationship in the *Phenomenology,* as well as the works that came after it. Beginning with the master-slave parable, Habermas laments, Hegel's thought increasingly tends to view interaction as primary, and labor and language as simply a function of it:

> [T]he [initial] relationship of the one-sided recognition of the master by the servant is overturned by the servant's power of disposition over

> nature, just as one-sidedly acquired by labor.... [Thus] already in the *Phenomenology* the distinctive dialectic of labor and interaction has been deprived of the specific role which was still attributed to it within the system in the Jena lectures. . . . [And] in the *Encyclopedia*, language and labor, once models of construction for dialectical movement, are now themselves constructed as subordinate real conditions. (L&I, pp. 161–62)

Moreover, if Hegel subordinates language and labor to interaction, Habermas asserts, Marx, who had initially rediscovered the connections between labor and interaction, ultimately subordinates language and interaction to labor in his materialist reconstruction of Hegel's dialectic. Or, to put it in Habermas's terms, Marx ends up reducing "communicative action" to "instrumental action" (cf. L&I, pp. 168–69). This will ultimately prompt Habermas, ironically enough, to return to Kant for theoretical inspiration. Thus, while Habermas uses Hegel to get past Kant's abstract "I," and Marx to get past the subordination of labor to interaction in Hegel, in *The Philosophical Discourse of Modernity*, he will rely upon Kant for the purpose of justifying the integrity of different theoretical realms, which he takes to be one of the hallmarks of the Enlightenment. Of course, for Habermas, theoretical inquiries into these discrete realms are not made by Kant's epistemologically inspired transcendental ego, but by the social subject who is formed within the crucible of language, labor, and interaction.

In any case, although it would appear that Habermas is intent upon maintaining the relative sovereignty of these three originary (albeit dialectically interconnected) categories, as "Labor and Interaction" proceeds it becomes increasingly clear that he is interested in privileging language over labor and interaction, and that he understands this to be the early Hegel's position as well. In the *First Philosophy of Spirit*, in which for the first time Hegel hints at a developmental model within which consciousness becomes self-reflective prior to its embeddedness within a fully formed social framework, language and labor are initially considered at an individual level, with language taking precedence; it is only later that interaction comes into play. Thus, at the individual level, Habermas says that (for Hegel) language reflects the "employment of symbols by the solitary individual who confronts nature and gives names to things," a process that causes consciousness to split itself off from nature. "Only with the appearance of language, and within language, do consciousness and the being of nature begin to separate for consciousness. . . . Thus language is the first category in which spirit is not conceived as something internal" (L&I, p. 153). Individual labor also brings about a separation from nature, according to Habermas, for it requires deferring the satisfaction of the subject's animalistic drives. But while the symbols of language, which are utilized by "name giving consciousness," "penetrate and dominate the perceiving and thinking consciousness . . . the [cunning] consciousness [of labor] [merely] controls the processes of nature by means of its tools" (L&I, p. 155). In other words, although the symbols of the "name giving consciousness" and the tools of "cunning consciousness" both subjugate nature, the name giving consciousness, which orders the impressions that it receives from nature, manufactures the conceptual framework that is needed for the tasks of cunning consciousness to be articulated as an initial matter. Without the distance that naming opens up between subject and object, there would be no basis for moderating the natural drives, which is a precondition for labor (cf. L&I, p.159). Furthermore, even after he proceeds to the cultural level, in which interaction enters into the picture through the "recognizing consciousness," Habermas reiterates the primacy of language:

> Under the title *language* Hegel rightly introduces the employment of representational symbols as the first determination of abstract spirit. For the two subsequent determinations necessarily presuppose this. In the dimension of actual spirit, language attains existence as the system of a specific cultural tradition. . . . As cultural tradition, language enters into communicative action; for only the inter-subjectively valid and constant meanings which are drawn from tradition permit the orientation toward reciprocity, that is, complementary expectations of behavior. Thus interaction is dependent upon language communication which has established itself as a part of life. However, instrumental action, as soon as it comes under the category of actual spirit, as social labor, is also embedded within a network of interactions, and therefore dependent on the communicative boundary conditions that underlie every possible cooperation. (L&I, p. 159)

Habermas's interpretation of the *First Philosophy of Spirit* is problematical. Although he acknowledges that Hegel intends to give equal weight to language, labor, and interaction in terms of the role they play in consciousness formation, Habermas is also intent upon making language the first among equals, which significantly changes the implications of Hegel's model. And while *First Philosophy of Spirit* does contain some textual support for Habermas's claim that language precedes labor and interaction, it can also be interpreted as suggesting that language and labor first take place within the framework of the natural family. In the introduction to his translation of *First Philosophy of Spirit*, for example, H. S. Harris states that "the development of language and labor begins in the context of a kinship organization—the family."[7] Moreover, interpretive questions aside, it must be emphasized that Hegel quickly abandoned the model set forth in this work, which is fraught with problems. (Indeed, Habermas actually relies less upon the Jena writings as a whole than upon this particular work.) Habermas's reliance upon it, therefore, may well reproduce the very problems that Hegel sought to surmount. For example, *First Philosophy of Spirit* straddles the Aristotelian inspired naturalism of *System of Ethical Life*, in which spirit matures within the framework of an always already existing "natural ethical life," and *Philosophy of Spirit*, in which consciousness begins in a "state of nature" type setting and moves through different sociopolitical forms as it incrementally develops, but the two positions are not especially compatible. The former is a classical position; the latter, which embraces what Habermas refers to as the "philosophy of the subject," is inspired by the norms of the Enlightenment.

After articulating the primacy of language with respect to interaction and labor, Habermas contends that "more interesting and by no means as obvious as the relation of the employment of symbols to interaction and labor . . . is the interrelation of labor and interaction" (L&I, p. 159). And this relation, according to Habermas, truly is one in which neither term can simply be reduced to the other: "A reduction of interaction to labor or derivation of labor from interaction is not possible" (L&I, p. 159). Contrary to Hegel's conception of the relationship between interaction and labor in the *Phenomenology*, in which the master-slave parable sets the tone for interaction's primacy—the conditions of the slave's labor derive from the terms of the breakdown in interaction between what should have ideally been two recognizing consciousnesses—Habermas contends that the technical rules that govern the subjugation of nature have nothing to do with the communicative rules of interaction, and that it is actually within the legal context that the two paradigms meet. Within the framework of *legal* recognition, Habermas says, "recognition does not refer directly to the identity of the other, but to the things that are subject to his powers of disposition" (L&I, p. 159), namely, to the products of his labor. And what mediates the exchange of the products of the labor process between two legally recognized persons is the contract, which reflects the culmination of a process in which language is given normative force. In this way, Hegel's notion of mutual recognition is brought within an institutionalized framework in which self-consciousness can be comprehended as the result of a linguistically mediated process that includes both the struggle for recognition and labor. Indeed, as becomes increasingly clear in Habermas's subsequent works, language does not just mediate this process. Rather, inasmuch as the deep structures of language contain within them normative standards that presuppose mutual recognition between parties engaged in speech, who should be swayed only by the force of the better reasoned argument, language essentially becomes for Habermas the transcendental ground upon which more rational forms of interaction and labor can come to fruition. It is for this reason that he is so resistant to what he takes to be the Hegelian and Marxian models. If either the prevailing socioethical (interaction) or technical (labor) forms are primary, language would lose its liberating potential; it would merely be a debauched vehicle for transmitting the values of the one or the other.[8]

To preserve his theory of communicative rationality, therefore, Habermas returns to Kant, who also had a model that was based upon a division of reason into three differentiated spheres, each of which is governed by its own logic. And although Habermas would resist the comparison, for he understands his theory of communicative action to be "postmetaphysical," in many respects Habermas's valorization of language in his ego–alter ego model corresponds to Kant's autonomous will in that both provide the transcendental grounds upon which reason can be practically realized. To be sure, unlike Habermas's linguistically embedded community, in which individual subjects are formed within the framework of their communicative relations with others, Kant's autonomous will is disembodied and individualistic (although even here it might be argued that the autonomous will that acts upon its imperfect duties to bring about the "kingdom of ends" is more of a communal being than liberals usually acknowledge). In the final analysis, however, both Habermas's claim that there is an ever-present possibility for reaching an uncoerced communicative consensus (which is allegedly presupposed in the structures of ordinary discourse) and Kant's claim that there is an ever-present possibility for acting upon maxims that oblige us to wholly abstract from our material interests (which is presupposed in our understanding of ourselves as free, self-determining beings) are starkly ahistorical. But, as Hegel would point out, the transcendental grounds that both posit are themselves historically produced, despite the fact that they purport to get outside mere historical contingency. Furthermore, the differentiation of spheres of competencies insinuates a fragmented subject. For Kant, who explicitly recognized this phenomenon, human beings are, in one sense, completely determined, and yet, in another sense, absolutely free. For Habermas, however, who rejects Kant's dualistic metaphysics, communicative relations ostensibly mediate the relationship between the technical and socioethical spheres, each of which has its own language. But what reason is there to think that laborers who are exploited in the technical realm will be either permitted or able to change "language hats" to fully interact in the socioethical realm, or, alternatively, that the refusal to recognize others will not manifest itself in the structuring of the technical sphere, as is the case in the master-slave parable? Referring to the first phenomenon, which he does take to be a problem, Habermas contends that it is simply a matter of exposing the ways in which the reasoning of the technical sphere "colonizes" the socioethical sphere, but such a position implies that in some deep way both the person being addressed and the language that is utilized to convey the message have not themselves been "colonized," which is highly doubtful. Thus, while Habermas correctly points out that technical mastery does not guarantee uncoerced interaction any more than uncoerced interaction guarantees technical mastery (cf. L&I, p. 169)—in this sense interaction and labor are discrete realms—it is likely that substantial breakdowns in either realm will have an impact upon the other. Indeed, it is only a metaphysical view of both the human subject and language itself that would hold otherwise.

Nevertheless, Habermas argues that it is Hegel who takes shelter in metaphysics when he shifts from the model that he uses in the *First Philosophy of Spirit*, in which individuals rooted within concrete social contexts perpetually breach and reconfigure existing patterns of recognition, to the model that supplants it in the *Phenomenology of Spirit*, which Habermas depicts as one in which the self-reflective movement of Absolute Spirit predominates. Indeed, Habermas claims that the Jena lectures themselves contain within them the seeds of this new model, for they presume the identity of spirit with nature—i.e., that nature is spirit because its essence is realized only through humanity's confrontation with it and spirit is nature because it is where spirit completely objectifies itself. If "subjectivity can always be found in what has been objectivized," Habermas says, "then the relationship of the name giving and the working subject to nature can also be brought within the configuration of reciprocal recognition" (L&I, p.163). However, the shift in models is not simply the result of language and labor being subsumed under interaction: "Nature in its totality is [also] elevated to an antagonist of the united subjects" (L&I, p. 164), and the relationship between spirit and nature is made primary. The intersubjective orientation of Hegel's earlier writings, which is characterized by a "dialogical" process, is therefore replaced by the intrasubjective orientation of a solitary Absolute Spirit, which is characterized by a "monological" process of self-reflection (L&I, p. 164). In other words, from the processes of alienation and reconciliation, which concern the relationship between subjects, Hegel moves to the processes of externalization and appropriation, which concern a "macrosubject" and its reflection upon the way in which it has objectified itself in nature. Nevertheless, Habermas asserts, since both sets of processes presume the philosophy of identity, "the processes of externalization and appropriation formally match those of alienation and reconciliation" (L&I, p. 164).

In *The Philosophical Discourse of Modernity*, Habermas revisits Hegel's "metaphysical" turn, as well as some of the other matters that are raised in "Labor and Interaction." As an initial matter, he acknowledges, as was previously suggested, that Hegel's earlier writings evidence "the idea of an ethical totality along the guidelines of a popular religion in which communicative reason assumed the idealized form of historical communities, such as the primitive Christian community and the Greek polis."[9] Inasmuch as Hegel was concerned with grounding enlightenment reason, however, he recognized that this classical model, in which "communicative reason" collapses into unreflective premodern forms, would not work. Given the trajectory of his thinking in the Jena writings, Habermas contends, Hegel might have availed himself of a "communication-theoretic retrieval and transformation of the reflective concept of reason,"[10] which would have done nothing less than set philosophy upon the right path. Instead, Hegel sought reconciling reason in his idea of Absolute Spirit, which "overpowers every absolutization and retains as unconditional only the infinite processing of the relation-to-self that swallows up everything finite within itself."[11] In *The Philosophical Discourse of Modernity*, however, the positing of Absolute Spirit is no longer taken to be the conceptual core of Hegel's "wrong turn." It is merely taken to be symptomatic of a larger mistake in Hegel's thought—namely, his turn to a "philosophy of the subject" or "philosophy of consciousness." On Habermas's new view, it is the subject-object paradigm itself that is flawed: the "act of tearing loose from an intersubjectively shared lifeworld is what first generates a subject-object relationship. It is introduced as an alien element, or at least subsequently, into relationships that by nature follow the structure of mutual understanding among subjects—and not the logic of an objectification by a subject."[12] For Habermas, this analysis holds whether we are speaking of an individual consciousness or Absolute Spirit.

Just as Habermas's neo-Kantian resort to differentiated spheres of knowledge suggests a fragmented subjectivity, his resort to a neo-Kantian theory of communicative rationality suggests an impoverished one. In attempting to ground enlightenment reason in the structures of language, which supposedly provide the regulative notion of an "ideal speech community," Habermas gives short shrift to the phenomenological component within Hegel's thought. For despite Habermas's emphasis upon Absolute Spirit, it is actually our conscious experience of the world that propels Hegel's *Phenomenology of Spirit*, and Habermas's abstract model is simply not up to the task of accounting for its richness. Honneth, who otherwise buys into both Habermas's interpretation of Hegel's Absolute Spirit and his rejection of the "philosophy of the subject," basically agrees with this appraisal. Instead of seeking to ground social theory in the normative demands that allegedly inhere within discourse, therefore, Honneth attempts to ground it "by referring to the normative demands that are, structurally speaking, internal to the relationship of mutual recognition" (SR, p. 92), and the model of mutual recognition that he finds most auspicious for these purposes is the one presented by Hegel in the early Jena writings. Accordingly, Honneth begins *The Struggle for Recognition* with a detailed analysis of these works, but ultimately finds that *System of Ethical Life* is too sketchy with respect to the motivations that would initiate struggles for recognition, and that *First Philosophy of Spirit* and *Philosophy of Spirit* redress this problem only by recourse to the metaphysical notion of Absolute Spirit. Thus, in the remainder of the book, Honneth attempts to supplement Hegel's essential notion of mutual recognition with a schema for subjectivity formation that is based in the social sciences. In this way, he intends to both flesh out Hegel's basic insight and dissociate it from the metaphysical assumptions that allegedly underlie it. Unfortunately, the particulars of this reconstructive work cannot be explored here. Instead, after a cursory outline, I shall confine myself to a consideration of Honneth's understanding of the relationship between the Jena writings and the master-slave parable, as well as the way in which this understanding relates to Habermas's position.

Honneth begins his "postmetaphysical" reconstruction of Hegel's conception of mutual recognition by attempting to reconfigure it in terms of George Herbert Mead's naturalistic social psychology. He then maintains that both Hegel and Mead (at least implicitly) distinguish between three escalating forms of reciprocal recognition—namely, love and friendship (primary relations), rights (legal relations), and solidarity (a communally shared value horizon)—and that these three forms of recognition correspond, in turn, to self-confidence, self-respect, and self-esteem, which constitute the three forms of one's "practical relation-to-self." (In the case of Hegel, these forms of recognition do roughly correspond to the three-part division of *System of Ethical Life* into "Ethical Life on the Basis of Relation," "The Negative or Freedom or Transgression," and "Ethical Life." Mead's adherence to this tripartite model is less clear.) In a wide-ranging discussion that stretches from Donald Winicott's psychoanalytic object relations theory to legal rights theorists such as Joel Feinberg, Honneth attempts to adduce empirical support for his claim that each "practical relation-to-self" is determined by one's intersubjective relations. In other words, escalating levels of respect engender increasingly undistorted self-conceptions. Conversely, "being disrespected," which, depending upon the forms of recognition that obtain in a given context, manifests itself in physical abuse, a denial of rights, or the denigration of a way of life, "can become the motivational impetus for a struggle for recognition" (SR, p. 138). And the cognitive nexus between the experience of disrespect and social engagement—which Honneth claims Hegel and Mead crucially omitted—are "negative emotional reactions, such as being ashamed or enraged, feeling hurt or indignant. These comprise the psychological symptoms on the basis of which one can come to realize that one is being illegitimately denied social recognition" (SR, p. 136). Honneth argues that these feelings of being disrespected are the core of moral experience—as the book's subtitle suggests, they are *the* moral grammar of social conflicts—and that modern social theory has obscured this essential point by viewing social conflicts primarily in terms of pre-given interests. Casting Marx (as well as all others who see economic interests as the primary motivation behind social struggle) as a utilitarian (cf. SR, p. 148f.), Honneth maintains that "the moral force within social reality that is responsible for development and progress is a struggle for recognition" (SR, p. 143), and that the interests that seem to propel social conflicts should not be seen as "ultimate or original" but rather as constituted within a larger framework within which there is a denial of recognition (cf. SR, p. 166). In sum, like Habermas, Honneth proffers "a formal conception of ethical life" (SR, p. 175), the difference being that recognition stands in for communication as the regulative ideal. In Habermasian terms, Honneth declares, "the goal [is] undistorted and unrestricted recognition" (SR, p. 171).

Honneth's attempt to steer a course between Hegel and Habermas reverberates in his interpretation of the struggle for recognition in both the Jena writings and the master-slave parable. As an initial matter, while Honneth largely agrees with Habermas's contention that the early Jena writings reflected a "communication-theoretical alternative" that is subsequently abandoned in favor of a "philosophy of consciousness" that comes to fruition in the *Phenomenology* (SR, p. 30), he disagrees with Habermas's conclusion that this theoretical shift brings labor and language "within the configuration of reciprocal recognition" (L&I, p. 163). To the contrary, Honneth asserts that "already in the *Phenomenology of Spirit* . . . the conceptual model of a 'struggle for recognition' had lost its central position within Hegel's theory" (SR, p. 5). Accordingly, while Habermas believes that Marx rediscovered the appropriate interconnection between labor and interaction by stressing the importance of social labor as interaction's equal in spirit's formation—that is, until he ends up privileging labor over interaction—Honneth contends that the master-slave parable itself already reflects a bias towards labor:

> The *Phenomenology of Spirit* allots to the struggle for recognition—once the moral force that drove the process of Spirit's socialization through each of its stages—the sole function of the formation of consciousness. Thus reduced to the single meaning represented in the dialectic of lordship and bondage, the struggle between subjects fighting for recognition then comes to be linked so closely to the experience of the practical acknowledgement of one's labour that its own particular logic disappears almost entirely from view. . . . As a result, the possibility of returning to the most compelling of his earlier intuitions, the still incomplete model of the "struggle for recognition," is blocked. (SR, pp. 62–63)

This difference between Habermas and Honneth springs from their differing theoretical commitments, which lead them to consider the "communication-theoretical alternative" that the Jena works supposedly opened up in slightly different ways. For Habermas, who embraces a tripartite schema, this notion pertains to the primacy of language, which not only mediates the relationship between labor and interaction, but provides the transcendental grounds for a normative critique as well. For Honneth, on the other hand, this notion refers to the always already embeddedness of social actors in a communicative (i.e., intersubjectivist) context in which struggles for recognition take place against a backdrop of prior recognitive understandings, and move these understandings to more complex levels of mutual recognition. Language does not operate transcendentally on this account, however, for, in Honneth's two-part schema, it is the normative ideal of complete mutual recognition that informs his "formal conception of ethical life." In contrast with Habermas, then, Honneth does not see interaction and labor as heterogenous; rather, he sees interaction as primary, and then understands relations within the instrumental realm of labor as a function of the relations of recognition.

Nevertheless, this difference between Habermas and Honneth is overshadowed by the similarities in their respective approaches. As an initial matter, although Habermas does nominally argue that recognition becomes primary in the master-slave parable because of Hegel's embrace of a philosophy of identity (cf. L&I, p. 164), Habermas also claims that Hegel introduces the idea of a self-relating, solitary Absolute Spirit here, which effectively undermines this argument. In other words, inasmuch as Habermas takes the position that "absolute spirit is absolute morality" (L&I, p. 165), interaction, which for Habermas is the realm of morality, does appear to assume primacy. But because he also views Spirit as solitary and self-relating, Habermas's model, like Honneth's, finally commits him to the view that "the 'struggle for recognition' [between concrete individuals] is blocked." On this score, therefore, the only difference between the two is that the "demise" of the model of the "struggle for recognition" is overdetermined for Honneth—that is, the logic of the struggle for recognition is supplanted by both the introduction of self-relating, solitary Absolute Spirit *and* its linkage with the dynamic of labor. Indeed, although Habermas also emphasizes the need to keep interaction and labor "rigorously separated" (L&I, p. 169), the reason that Honneth stresses the dynamic of labor in the master-slave parable in a way that Habermas does not stems from another similarity between the two. Both have formal models that depend upon maintaining the integrity of a privileged category that would vouchsafe the possibility of transcendence, and since the realm of interaction is this category for Honneth, he must take greater care in separating it out from the start. Honneth's model thus depends upon a separation of labor and interaction that is even more inflexible than Habermas's, for he does not have normative recourse to the structures of language.

In terms of the master-slave parable, then, Habermas and Honneth are more alike than not. Although Honneth takes Habermas's theory of communicative rationality to be overly formal, it is not clear that his own theory of recognition is significantly less so. While, for Hegel, recognition is clearly the first moment in the master-slave parable, and, as such, is the progenitor of selfhood, his treatment of labor correctly belies the notion that self-identity should be understood within the framework of a pure struggle for recognition in which "mere interest categories" (SR, p. 163) are simply to be abstracted from. Our so-called "interests" are not as severable from our self-identities as Honneth's model seems to suggest. To the contrary, Hegel correctly saw that our accumulated interests thicken our notions of self, and cannot be conceptually filtered out in subsequent struggles for recognition (or, for that matter, in the language that we come to use in subsequent attempts to effectuate an "uncoerced" consensus). In fact, even the escalating struggles for recognition in the vaunted Jena works bear this out, for, as we saw, these struggles arose from the failure of others to properly recognize an individual's property. Much like Habermas before him, then, Honneth has an unmediated conception of subjectivity that contrasts poorly with Hegel's richer dialectical version. And, lastly, without sufficiently explaining the distinction, both Habermas and Honneth alternately accuse Hegel of positing a "monological" Absolute Spirit, and, more broadly, of being a "philosopher of the subject." I shall conclude by briefly considering these criticisms in turn.

As we previously saw, Habermas contends in the *Philosophical Discourse of Modernity* that Hegel's Absolute Spirit "overpowers every absolutization and retains as unconditional only the infinite processing of the relation-to-self that swallows up everything finite within itself."[13] And, in *The Struggle for Recognition*, Honneth basically reiterates this view when he alleges that Hegel "views the ethical sphere on the whole as a form of objectivation of Spirit's self-reflection, so that the place of intersubjective relations has to be taken throughout by relationships between a subject and its moments of externalization. Ethical life has become, in short, a form of monologically self-developing Spirit, and no longer constitutes a particularly demanding form of intersubjectivity" (SR, p. 61). On what basis do Habermas and Honneth reach these conclusions? In what sense does Hegel leave the intersubjectivist approach of the Jena works behind in the *Phenomenology* in favor of an all-encompassing, universal Spirit that "swallows up" the particular human beings that comprise it without being affected by them in turn? I think that Habermas and Honneth are wrong to conclude that Hegel gives up his intersubjectivist approach in virtue of the shift that takes place between the Jena writings and the *Phenomenology*. Indeed, from an intersubjectivist standpoint, Hegel has become far more ambitious in the *Phenomenology* in the sense that he does not merely content himself with positing an always already existing social framework, but, rather, seeks to show through the master-slave encounter that self-consciousness is *essentially* intersubjective in nature: "A self-consciousness exists for a self-consciousness."[14] Furthermore, Spirit is not some ontologically discrete entity that orchestrated this encounter so that it might realize itself through human fodder. To the contrary, Spirit itself is engendered by this initial human encounter: "With this [encounter] we have arrived at the concept of spirit."[15] In other words, human beings are not just along for Spirit's "monological" ride, for Spirit is itself nothing more than the result of human perspectives and activities. And, in turn, the way in which Spirit comes to circumscribe our ways of looking at the world and, therefore, the actions that we undertake—that is, the way in which it comes to condition the possible experiences that we can have at any point in time—simply reflects the logic inherent in our own prior attitudes and actions.

Finally, when Habermas and Honneth contend that Hegel's philosophy is a "philosophy of consciousness" or a "philosophy of the subject," they are contending that it is rooted in the subject-object paradigm, which suggests, among other things, that self-consciousness can come to ground its own knowledge of objects—including itself as an object of knowledge. And this perspective, they maintain, pales in comparison with the one that is embraced in the Jena works, for it is first generated by erroneously "tearing loose [the subject] from an intersubjectively shared lifeworld."[16] This reproach, which cannot be given its due here, is a complicated one, for Hegel does, in some limited sense, subscribe to the subject-object paradigm; nevertheless, it is by no means clear that he does so in a fashion that makes him guilty of this charge. As we just saw, the "subject" to whom Habermas and Honneth refer cannot merely be Spirit as some "monological" macro-subject, for this is not a view that Hegel embraced. And if the relevant "subject" is merely the individual, this, too, cannot be right, for the chapters of the *Phenomenology* leading up to the master-slave parable are designed to show that the individual cannot truly come to know either himself or objects in the world on his own; indeed, the master-slave parable and what follows is revolutionary precisely in virtue of the fact that it *does* take the acquisition of knowledge to be an essentially intersubjectivist endeavor. Furthermore, unlike his philosophical predecessors, Hegel was interested in breaking down the subject-object dichotomy, for subject and object, self and other, necessarily stand in a mediated relation.

The limited sense in which Hegel does subscribe to the subject-object paradigm, however, is in his concern with the reconciliation of the individual with his society, but in closing I would like to suggest that within this setting the paradigm is actually a strength, not a weakness. Unlike Habermas's ego–alter ego reconciliation, which is based upon dialogic agreements that are reached in an intersubjectively shared life world— agreements, given language's historically sedimented state, that may be less coercive in form than substance—Hegel's individual can only be reconciled within a rational social context. And this suggests, contrary to the more vulgar readings of Hegel, which see him as a totalitarian, that there is a hardier impetus toward individual freedom within Hegel's thought than those reconciliations that are linguistically based.

NOTES

INTRODUCTION

1. The reference to "(para. 12)" and similar citations elsewhere refer to the enumerated paragraphs of the Self-Consciousness chapter translated by Leo Rauch in this book.

2. Hegel published a large number of works after the *Phenomenology*, the most significant of which are usually taken to be the *Science of Logic*, the *Encyclopedia of the Philosophical Sciences* (which consists of three volumes dealing with his systematized views on logic, nature, and mind), and the *Philosophy of Right*, which has proven to be a highly important and influential political work. In addition, notes from Hegel's university lectures are published in the *Philosophy of History*, whose introductory section is often viewed as a good point of ingress into Hegel's works, and the *History of Philosophy*. Hegel also published works in both aesthetics and religion, which have had their impact. And, finally, as we shall see, his early (pre-*Phenomenology*) writings have recently received a great deal of attention.

3. Karl Marx, *The Economic and Philosophic Manuscripts of 1844*, ed. Dirk J. Struik, tr. Martin Milligan (New York: International Publishers, 1964), p. 177.

4. Karl Marx, *Capital: Volume 1*, tr. Ben Fowkes (London: Penguin Books, 1990), pp. 102–103 (Marx's Preface to the Second Edition).

CHAPTER FOUR

1. I have discussed this in an article, "Hegel's *Phenomenology of Spirit* as a Phenomenological Project," *Thought* LVI—Hegel Commemorative Issue (Fordham University, September, 1981).

CHAPTER FIVE

1. Hans-Georg Gadamer, "Hegel's 'Inverted World,'" in *Hegel's Dialectic* (New Haven and London: Yale University Press, 1976).

CHAPTER SIX

1. Hegel, *The Philosophy of Right,* tr. T. M. Knox (Oxford: Clarendon Press, 1967), para.7.

2. Hegel, *Encyclopaedia,* III, published as *Hegel's Philosophy of Mind,* tr. W. Wallace (Oxford: Clarendon Press, 1976), para. 424.

3. For some of the political ramifications of this, see my book, *The Political Animal* (Amherst: The University of Massachusetts Press, 1981), chapter on Hegel.

4. Quentin Lauer, *A Reading of Hegel's* Phenomenology of Spirit (New York: Fordham University Press, 1976), p. 97.

5. Hans-Georg Gadamer, "Hegel's Dialectic of Self-Consciousness," in *Hegel's Dialectic* (New Haven and London: Yale University Press, 1976), p. 54.

6. Jean Hyppolite, "The Human Situation in the Hegelian Phenomenology" in *Studies on Marx and Hegel* (New York and London: Basic Books, 1969), p. 154.

7. The question is asked by Werner Becker, *Idealistische und Materialistische Dialektik* (Stuttgart: Kohlhammer Verlag, 1970), p. 28.

CHAPTER SEVEN

1. See the Oxford English Dictionary entries for "Lordship" and "Bondage."

2. George Armstrong Kelly, "Notes on Hegel's 'Lordship and Bondage,'" in Alasdair MacIntyre, ed., *Hegel—A Collection of Critical Essays* (New York: Doubleday, 1972), p. 199 f.

3. Jean Hyppolite, *Genesis and Structure of Hegel's* Phenomenology of Spirit (Evanston: Northwestern University Press, 1974), p. 160.

4. Hyppolite, *Genesis and Structure,* p. 170.

5. Quentin Lauer, *A Reading of Hegel's* Phenomenology of Spirit (New York: Fordham University Press, 1976), p. 102.

6. Hegel, *Philosophy of Mind,* para. 424. *Zusatz*

7. The outcry of Faust: "Ah, two souls inhabit my breast!" *("Zwei Seelen wohnen, ach, in meiner Brust!").*

8. Alexandre Kojève, *Introduction to the Reading of Hegel* (New York and London: Basic Books, 1969), p. 19 ff.

9. Kojève, *Introduction to the Reading of Hegel,* p. 29.

CHAPTER EIGHT

1. For Lukács, the *Phenomenology* concerns "the acquisition by the individual of the experience of the species." Findlay speaks of it as a "universalized biography." For Hyppolite, it describes "the itinerary of consciousness." See Georg Lukács, *The Young Hegel* (Cambridge: MIT Press, 1976), p. 470; J. N. Findlay, *Hegel: A Re-examination* (New York: Macmillan, 1958), p. 85; and Jean Hyppolite, *Studies on Marx and Hegel* (New York: Basic Books, 1969), p. 23.

2. Jean Hyppolite, *Genesis and Structure of Hegel's* Phenomenology of Spirit (Evanston: Northwestern University Press, 1974), p. 179.

3. Hyppolite, *Genesis and Structure*, p. 182.

4. See Quentin Lauer, *A Reading of Hegel's* Phenomenology of Spirit (New York: Fordham University Press, 1976), p. 116.

5. Hyppolite, *Genesis and Structure*, p. 190 ff., makes the point that the unhappiness is the result of the development of self-consciousness itself.

6. Maurice Merleau-Ponty, "Hegel's Existentialism" in *Sense and Non-Sense* (Evanston: Northwestern University Press, 1964), p. 67.

7. Jean Wahl, *Le Malheur de la Conscience dans la Philosophie de Hegel* (Paris: Presses Universitaires, 1951), p. 124.

8. Wahl, *Le Malheur de la Conscience*, p. 128.

9. Wahl, *Le Malheur de la Conscience*, p. 146.

10. See Hegel, *Early Theological Writings*, tr. T. M. Knox (New York: Harper & Row, 1961).

CHAPTER TEN

1. Alexandre Kojève, *Introduction to the Reading of Hegel* (New York and London: Basic Books, 1969). In the remaining discussion, page numbers refer to cited English translations.

2. See Hegel, *Philosophy of Mind*, paras. 426–29 (with *Zusätze*)

3. For some further criticisms along these lines, see George Armstrong Kelly, "Notes on Hegel's 'Lordship and Bondage,'" in Alasdair MacIntyre, ed., *Hegel— A Collection of Critical Essays* (New York: Doubleday, 1972), pp. 191–95.

4. Jean Hyppolite, *Genesis and Structure of Hegel's* Phenomenology of Spirit (Evanston: Northwestern University Press, 1974), Introduction by John Heckman, p. xxvi.

5. Jean Hyppolite, "Alienation and Objectification: Commentary on G. Lukács' *The Young Hegel*," in *Studies on Marx and Hegel* (New York and London: Basic Books, 1969), pp. 86–87.

6. See the Hegel text above, para. 44.

7. See the Hegel text above, para. 3.

8. See the Hegel text above, para. 22.

9. Hyppolite, *Genesis and Structure*, pp. 146–77.

10. See the Hegel text above, para. 4.

11. Maurice Merleau-Ponty, "Hegel's Existentialism," in *Sense and Non-Sense* (Evanston: Northwestern University Press, 1964), p. 63.

12. Jean-Paul Sartre, *Being and Nothingness*, tr. Hazel Barnes (New York: Philosophical Library, 1956), pp. 235–45.

13. Martin Heidegger, *Being and Time*, tr. John Macquarrie and Edward Robinson (New York: Harper & Row, 1962), pp. 484–86.

14. Hegel, *Philosophy of History*, tr. J. Sibree (New York: Dover Publications, 1956), p. 72.

15. Hegel, *Phänomenologie des Geistes* (Hamburg: Felix Meiner Verlag, 1952), p. 558.

16. Hegel, *Phänomenologie des Geistes*, p. 67.

17. Martin Heidegger, *Hegel's Concept of Experience* (New York: Harper & Row, 1970), pp. 51–53.

18. Hans-Georg Gadamer, "Hegel's 'Inverted World'" and "Hegel's Dialectic of Self-Consciousness," in *Hegel's Dialectic* (New Haven and London: Yale University Press, 1976), pp. 35–53 and 54–74.

19. "Naive realism leads to physics, and physics, if true, shows that naive realism is false. Therefore naive realism, if true, is false; therefore it is false." Bertrand Russell, *An Inquiry into Meaning and Truth* (Baltimore: Penguin Books, 1962), p. 13.

20. Hegel, *Gesammelte Werke*, Band 4: Jenaer *Kritische Schriften* (Hamburg: Felix Meiner Verlag, 1968), pp. 124–25.

21. Hegel, *Phänomenologie des Geistes*, pp. 114–15.

22. Hegel, *Phänomenologie des Geistes*, p. 128.

23. Jean Wahl, *Le Malheur de la Conscience dans la Philosophie de Hegel* (Paris: Presses Universitaires de France, 1951).

CHAPTER ELEVEN

1. Martin Heidegger, *Poetry Language Thought*, tr. Albert Hofstadter (New York: Harper and Row, 1971), p. 146.

2. These general points are made by Michael S. Roth in *Knowing and History: Appropriations of Hegel in Twentieth-Century France* (Ithaca, N.Y.: Cornell University Press, 1988), pp. 189–91.

CHAPTER TWELVE

1. See Lionel Abel, *The Intellectual Follies: A Memoir of the Literary Venture in New York and Paris* (New York: W. W. Norton, 1984), p. 174.

2. The notion that the master simply drops out of the picture, and that it is only the slave that moves onto Stoicism is highly problematical. It is at odds with Hegel's all-encompassing idea of Spirit. In addition, at the end of the master-slave discussion, the master's sense of his own autonomy is as compromised as his slave's, which suggests that he is equally in need of Stoicism's consolations. And finally, from a historical standpoint, Stoicism was also embraced by the master "class"—for example, Marcus Aurelius, the emperor of Rome.

3. See Francis Fukuyama, *The End of History and the Last Man* (New York: The Free Press, 1992).

4. Georges Bataille, "Lettre à X., charge d'un cours sur Hegel," *Oeuvres completes de G. Bataille*, p. 369.

5. Ibid.

6. References to Georges Bataille, *Inner Experience*, tr. Leslie Anne Boldt (Albany: State University of New York Press, 1988) will be contained in the form "IE."

7. "The History of Eroticism" is the second volume of *The Accursed Share*, which constitutes the most sustained exposition of Bataille's philosophical thought. The three volumes that make up *The Accursed Share* comprise two books: *The Accursed Share: Volume I* (New York: Zone Books, 1988), which contains "An Essay on General Economy," and *The Accursed Share: Volumes II & III* (New York: Zone Books, 1991), which contains "The History of Eroticism" and "Sovereignty." All references to these works will be contained in the text in the form "GE," "HoE," and "Sov," respectively.

8. See, e.g., G. W. F. Hegel, *Phenomenology of Spirit*, tr. A. V. Miller (London: Oxford University Press, 1977), p. 118 and Alexandre Kojève, *Introduction to the Reading of Hegel*, tr. J. H. Nichols (Ithaca: Cornell University Press, 1969), p. 23–25.

9. Georges Bataille, "Hegel, Death, and Sacrifice," *Yale French Studies* 78 (1990), p. 9. References to this article will be contained in the text in the form "HD&S."

10. At this point it should be apparent that while Bataille adheres to Kojève's notion that it is only the slave that moves beyond the master-slave problematic, his perspective on the subject that emerges from the struggle does not depend on retaining this view. After all, while in one sense the master lives an animal-like existence, in that all he need do is consume, his very conception of self, which is ultimately no more secure than that of the slave whom he refuses to recognize, is tied up with the "economy of meaning." The master wants to be "recognized," "acknowledged," and it is the paradox of receiving this "servile" need for recognition from the slave that causes him to go under.

11. Strictly speaking, this is not quite correct. In Stalinism, Bataille saw the possibility for a realization of sovereign values. He acknowledged that the driving force within Stalinism is to flatten difference, which is the basis for sovereignty,

but contends that this "does not just have the negative meaning of an abolition of sovereign values." According to Bataille, it also "cannot help but have a corresponding positive meaning. If every man is destined for complete nondifferentiation, he abolishes all alienation in himself. . . . He attains thinghood so fully that he is no longer a thing" (Sov, p. 301–302). Nevertheless, we need not dwell on this remarkable transvaluation very long. Besides the fact that, historically, Stalinism is a dead letter, it seems to me that this thesis is undermined by Bataille's more radical revolt against history itself.

12. Michele Richman, *Reading Georges Bataille: Beyond the Gift* (Baltimore: The Johns Hopkins University Press, 1982), p. 77.

13. Jacques Derrida, *Writing and Difference*, tr. Allen Bass (Chicago: University of Chicago Press, 1978), p. 253.

14. Ibid., p. 267.

15. Ibid.

16. G. W. F. Hegel, *Phenomenology of Spirit*, p. 362.

CHAPTER THIRTEEN

1. References to Gilles Deleuze, *Nietzsche and Philosophy*, tr. Hugh Tomlinson (New York: Columbia University Press, 1983), will be contained in the text in the form "N&P."

2. Friedrich Nietzsche, *On the Genealogy of Morals*, tr. Walter Kaufman and R. J. Hollingdale (New York: Random House, 1967), pp. 36–37.

3. Jean Wahl, "Nietzsche et la philosophie," *Revue de Metaphysique et de Morale* 68, no. 3 (1963): pp. 352, 379.

4. Ibid., p. 253.

5. In a subsection toward the end of *Nietzsche and Philosophy* entitled "Is Man Essentially 'Reactive'?" Deleuze refers to Nietzsche's ambivalence with respect to this question: On the one hand, "Nietzsche presents the triumph of reactive forces as something essential to man and history. Ressentiment and bad conscience are constitutive of the humanity of man, nihilism is the a priori concept of universal history" (N&P, p. 166). Nevertheless, on the other hand, "Nietzsche speaks of the masters as a type of human being that the slave has merely conquered, of culture as a human species activity that reactive forces have simply diverted from its course, of the free and sovereign individual as the human product of this activity that the reactive man has only deformed" (N&P, p. 167). In some sense, Deleuze splits the difference. He views active and reactive forces as irreducible, but, with respect to the affirmation-negation dichotomy, claims that not only reactive force, but active force as well, is "becoming-reactive" (i.e., negative): "Man's essence is the becoming-reactive of forces" (N&P, p. 169). Ostensibly, this is what makes active force (the master) susceptible to reactive force's (the slave's) transvaluation of values.

6. See Judith P. Butler, *Subjects of Desire: Hegelian Reflections in Twentieth-Century France* (New York: Columbia University, 1987), pp. 205–206. But when Butler claims that Deleuze simply "historicizes the negative formulation of desire," and that "Deleuze's notion of slave morality has no historical necessity," she overstates her case for the reasons discussed in note 5.

7. In *Beyond Good and Evil*, for example, Nietzsche states that "[The] hodge-podge philosophers who call themselves 'philosophers of reality' or 'positivists' . . . are all losers who have been brought back under the hegemony of science. . . . Philosophy reduced to 'theory of knowledge,' in fact no more than a timid epochism and doctrine of abstinence—a philosophy that never gets beyond the threshold and takes pains to deny itself the right to enter." Friedrich Nietzsche, *Beyond Good and Evil*, tr. Walter Kaufmann (New York: Random House, 1966), section 204. Similarly, in the *Will to Power* Nietzsche declares that "brutal positivism reigns, recognizing facts without becoming excited." Friedrich Nietzsche, *The Will to Power*, tr. and ed. Walter Kaufmann (New York: Vintage Books, 1968), section 120. For a portrait of the last man, see *Thus Spake Zarathustra*.

8. In response to Deleuze's *Anti-Oedipus*, a book in which Deleuze continues to pursue both the logic of his notion of the subject in *Nietzsche and Philosophy* and his attack upon existing social structures, Francois Lyotard wrote *Libidinal Economy*, which brought to light the quietistic perspective that is implicit within Deleuze's position. According to Lyotard, you cannot hang onto both the idea of truth (with the attendant standpoint of critique that this idea implies) and extol the play of libidinal forces, which is what Deleuze attempts to do. As a result, Lyotard basically recommends a "high energy" embracement of the world exactly as we find it, which, I believe, simply clarifies the underlying tendencies of Deleuze's own position.

9. Throughout *Nietzsche and Philosophy*, Deleuze adverts to Nietzsche's oeuvre for the purpose of attacking Hegel's dialectic, but frequently the dialectic that Nietzsche is actually attacking is Socrates'. On page 10, for example, he is attacking Hegel's dialectic for representing the speculation of the pleb, but the endnote is to the section of Nietzsche's *Twilight of the Idols* entitled "The Problem of Socrates."

CHAPTER FOURTEEN

1. See, for example, Jean-Luc Nancy and Phillipe Lacoue-Labarthe, *The Title of the Letter: A Reading of Lacan*, tr. Francois Raffoul and David Pettigrew (Albany: State University of New York Press, 1992), p. xxviii, who argue that Lacan's psychoanalytic theory has actually "sublat[ed] philosophical discourse."

2. Jacques Lacan, *The Seminar of Jacques Lacan: Book II—The Ego in Freud's Theory and in the Technique of Psychoanalysis*, tr. Sylvana Tomaselli (New York: W. W. Norton, 1988), pp. 10–11.

3. Mikkel Borch-Jacobsen, *Lacan: The Absolute Master*, tr. Douglas Brick (Stanford, California: Stanford University Press, 1991), p. 12.

4. Ibid., p. 19.

5. This quote is from "The Mirror Stage as Formative of the Function of the I as Revealed in Psychoanalytic Experience," which appears in Jacques Lacan, *Ecrits: A Selection*, tr. Alan Sheridan (New York: W. W. Norton & Co., 1977). References to *Ecrits* will appear in the text in the form "E."

6. See Malcolm Bowie, *Lacan* (Cambridge: Harvard University Press, 1991), p. 23.

7. Jacques Lacan, *The Four Fundamental Concepts of Psychoanalysis*, tr. Alan Sheridan (New York: W. W. Norton & Co., 1981), p. 20.

8. I am indebted to Borch-Jacobsen for this insight. See Mikkel Borch-Jacobsen, *Lacan: The Absolute Master*, pp. 85–87.

9. Ibid., p. 87.

10. Jacques Lacan, *The Seminar of Jacques Lacan: Book III—The Psychoses*, tr. Russell Grigg (New York: W. W. Norton, 1993). This is the title of chapter XIV.

11. Jacques Lacan, *The Seminar of Jacques Lacan: Book II—The Ego in Freud's Theory and in the Technique of Psychoanalysis*, p. 313.

12. Jacques Lacan, *The Seminar of Jacques Lacan: Book III—The Psychoses*, pp. 138–39.

CHAPTER FIFTEEN

1. "Labor and Interaction" appears in Jürgen Habermas, *Theory and Practice*, tr. John Viertel (Boston: Beacon Press, 1973), pp. 142–69. References to "Labor and Interaction" will be contained in the text in the form "L&I."

2. See, e.g., Andreas Wildt, *Autonomie und Anerkennung: Hegel's Moralitatskritik im Lichte seiner Fichte Rezeption* (Stuttgart: Klett-Cotta, 1982).

3. Jürgen Habermas, *The Philosophical Discourse of Modernity*, tr. Frederick G. Lawrence (Cambridge: MIT Press, 1987), p. 40.

4. Axel Honneth, *The Struggle for Recognition: The Moral Grammar of Social Conflicts*, tr. Joel Anderson (Cambridge: MIT Press, 1996). References to this work will be contained in the text in the form "SR."

5. G. W. F. Hegel, *System of Ethical Life and First Philosophy of Spirit*, tr. H. S. Harris and T. M. Knox (Albany: State University of New York Press, 1979), p. 236.

6. Ibid., p. 237.

7. Ibid., p. 195.

8. In *Dialectic of Enlightenment*, for example, Habermas's teachers, Adorno and Horkheimer, assert that "there is no longer any available form of linguistic expression which has not tended toward accomodation to dominant currents of thought; and what a devalued language does not do automatically is proficiently

executed by societal mechanisms." See Max Horkheimer and Theodor Adorno, *Dialectic of Enlightenment*, tr. John Cummings (New York: Continuum, 1991), p. 5.

9. Jürgen Habermas, *The Philosophical Discourse of Modernity*, p. 30.

10. Ibid.

11. Ibid., p. 36.

12. Ibid., p. 29.

13. See page 211.

14. See the translation above, para. 12.

15. Ibid.

16. Jürgen Habermas, *The Philosophical Discourse of Modernity*, p. 29.

INDEX

Emboldened page references pertain to the translated portions of Hegel's *Phenomenology* and the *Propaedeutic* contained herein.

Abraham, 9, 135

Absolute Knowing, 2–3, 122, 168, 171–172

Adorno, Theodor, 163, 205

Alienation, 7; and self-consciousness, 61–63

Antigone, 119

Bataille, Georges, 164, 165, 167–78, 179–80, 192; on Absolute Knowing, 171–72; on death, 169, 170; Derrida on, 175, 177–78; on "General Economy," 172–73, 174; on human animality, 170, 172; on *ipse*, 177; on labor, 169; on the natural world, 169; on negativity, 168, 176–77; on Nietzsche, 179; on non-knowledge, 176; and the postmodern, 178; on potlach, 174–75; on "Restricted Economy," 173, 174; on the sacred, 172; on sovereignty, 167, 173, 174, 177

Being and Time (Heidegger), 146, 148

Borch-Jacobsen, Mikkel, 192, 199

Butler, Judith, 184

Caesar, Julius, 187

Christ, 114

Christianity, 60–61; Hegel and Nietzsche compared on, 62; as product of slave consciousness, 119–20; and Unhappy Consciousness, 60, 111–12; and universal, 111

Civilization and its Discontents (Freud), 194

Dante, 110, 138

Death, **22–23**, 94–95; and self-certainty, **23**

Deleuze, Gilles, 164, 165, 178, 179–90; anti-Hegelianism of, 180; and difference, 189; on eternal recurrence, 181–82; contrasted with Hegel, 183–84; on master and slave, 183–84; materialism of, 180–81; on negativity, 184–86; on Nietzsche, 180–82; on the overman, 181–82; as positivist, 189; on recognition, 185, 188; selective ontology of, 182–83; Wahl on, 182; on will to power, 181–82

233

Derrida, Jacques, 164, 165, 180; on
    Bataille, 175, 177–78
Descartes, René, 82, 201
Desire, **18–19**, **48**; and self-certainty,
    18–19; satisfaction of, **19**
Dialectic (Hegel's), described, 2
Don Juan, 82
Durkheim, Emile, 172

Eckhart, Meister, 117
*Economic and Philosophic Manuscripts of
    1844* (Marx), 8, 62
Ego, 91, 93–94, 103–6
Either/Or (Kierkegaard), 9, 82
Engels, Friedrich, 9
Epictetus, 106
Epistemology, Hegel and, 3, 126

Faust (Goethe), 62
Feinberg, Joel, 217
Feuerbach, Ludwig, 8, 60
Fichte, Johann Gottlieb, 6–7, 203, 206;
    Hegel's criticism of, 6–7
First Philosophy of Spirit (Hegel), 205,
    209, 210–12, 214, 216
Force, 73–74
"Force and the Understanding", 5
"Forms of Consciousness", 2
Foucault, Michel, 164, 165, 178
Freud, Sigmund, 104, 191, 193–94,
    196–97, 198, 199, 202; on "Pleasure
    Principle," 194; on "Reality
    Principle," 104, 194

Gadamer, Hans-Georg, 76, 77, 152–57,
    163; on inverted world, 153–55; on
    objectivity, 152–153, 156
Genealogy of Morals (Nietzsche), 10,
    180–81, 187
Genesis and Structure of Hegel's Pheno-
    menology of Spirit (Hyppolite), 134
Goethe, Johann Wolfgang von, 62, 92,
    187

Golding, William, 126

Habermas, Jürgen, 165, 205–22; on
    Absolute Spirit, 215–16, 219,
    220–21; theory of communicative
    action, 206; and differentiation of
    spheres, 214; on *First Philosophy
    of Spirit*, 211–12; on Hegel as meta-
    physician, 214–15; contrasted with
    Honneth, 218–20; on interaction,
    206–7, 209–12, 215, 219; compared
    with Kant, 213–14; on legal recogni-
    tion, 212–13; on Marx, 210; on
    subject-object paradigm, 215–16,
    221–22
Harris, H. S., 212
Heidegger, Martin, 146–52, 163, 164,
    165, 167, 169, 178, 199, 200–201,
    202; on authenticity, 201; on *das
    Man*, 201; on "fallenness", 201;
    "Letter on Humanism," 192; con-
    trasted with Hegel, 147–48, 150–52;
    on Hegel and time, 148–51
Hobbes, John, 58, 88, 94
Honneth, Axel, 165, 205–6, 216–22;
    on Absolute Spirit, 220–21;
    contrasted with Habermas, 218–20
    on interaction, 219; on Marx, 217;
    post-metaphysical reconstruction of
    Hegel, 216–18; on subject-object
    paradigm, 221–22
Horkheimer, Max, 163
Hume, David, 5, 66
Hyppolite, Jean, 85, 90, 125, 126,
    133–39; on Hegel's anti-essentialism,
    136; on existential component in
    Hegel, 134, 136; on life, 137,
    138–39; on work, 137

Inner Experience (Bataille), 175,
    179
Inverted World (Hegel), 6, 76, 77, 78,
    153–55

Kant, Immanuel, 4, 5–6, 84, 108, 124, 155, 172, 176, 206, 208–10, 213–14; and autonomous will, 208–9; and transcendental unity of apperception, 84, 206

Kelly, George Armstrong, 88, 90

Kierkegaard, Søren, 9, 56–57, 80, 82, 134, 138, 141, 149; and leap of faith, 9

Kojève, Alexandre, 3, 125, 126–33, 164, 167, 168, 169, 192, 199, 200; on Absolute Knowing, 168; on the cogito, 131; and death, 135–36; on desire, 127–28; on the "end of history," 132, 168; and politicization of Hegel, 133–34; on recognition, 129; on the slave's superiority, 130, 132–33; on work, 127

Lacan, Jacques, 164, 165, 180, 191–204; anti-Cartesianism of, 195–96; on desire, 200, 203–4; on ego as fiction, 194; on ego psychology, 191; contrasted with Freud, 191–92, 194; contrasted with Hegel, 198, 202–3; Heideggerianism of, 199, 201–2; on "the Imaginary," 200; linguistic turn of, 197; on the "mirror stage,"193–96, 203; on misrecognition, 195–96; on *objet a*, 204; on the phallus, 202–3; on "the Real," 200–202; on signifier and signified, 200; on signifying chain, 200; on "the Symbolic," 200–202

"Law of the Heart", 123–24

Laws, 75

Left Hegelians, 9, 164

Leonardo da Vinci, 122

Lévi-Strauss, Claude, 192, 196–97, 200

Life, **15–19**, 81–82; as the object of desire, **19**

Locke, John, 88

Lord of the Flies (Golding), 126

Lukács, Georg, 134

Malraux, Andre, 110

Marcus Aurelius, 106

Marcuse, Herbert, 163

Marx, Karl, 8, 9, 134, 139, 144, 167, 210, 213, 217–18

Master Consciousness, **24–25**

Master-Slave Dialectic, **20–28**, **49–50**, 95–99, 104; see also master consciousness and slave consciousness

Mead, George Herbert, 217

Merleau-Ponty, Maurice, 112, 127, 139, 143–46; on relation between death and reason, 145

Nietzsche, Friedrich, 10, 120, 139, 163, 164, 167, 171, 177–78, 179–82, 187, 189; and "the last man," 171, 187; on positivism, 187

Nietzsche and Philosophy (Deleuze), 180

Pascal, Blaise, 159

Perception, 5, 72, 77

Phenomenology, analyzed, 65–67; contrasted with metaphysics, 83–84; as response to metaphysical dualisms, 67–68; contrasted with phenomenalism, 66; movement toward truth, 68

Philosophical Discourse of Modernity (Habermas), 210, 215, 220

Philosophy of Right (Hegel), 8–9

Philosophy of Spirit (Hegel), 205, 207, 212, 216

Plato, 72, 77–78, 88, 99, 109, 154, 155; Hegel contrasted with, 77

Reason, 61, 78, 122–24

Recognition, **20–22**, **49**, 87–92, 94–95, 97–99, 101, 185; and self-certainty, **22**

Right Hegelians, 9

Robinson Crusoe, 50

Rousseau, Jean-Jacques, 88

Russell, Bertrand, 112
Ryle, Gilbert, 56

Sartre, Jean-Paul, 125, 127, 139–43,
145, 164, 192, 196; on being vs.
knowing, 141–42; on the cogito, 143;
contrasted with Hegel, 140; on
Hegel's epistemological optimism,
142; on Hegel's ontological optimism,
143
Saussure, Ferdinand de, 192, 199; on
linguistic sign, 199
Schelling, Friedrich Wilhelm Joseph, 7,
9; Hegel's criticism of, 7
Science of Logic (Hegel), 8
Self-Certainty, 13, 80, 82, 90–91; and
desire, 18–19
Self-Consciousness, 55–63; and alienation, 61–63; contrasted with consciousness, 80–81; as desire, 15,
18–19; generated through opposition, 57–58; impetus for, 55–56; and
life, 57; and overcoming metaphysical
dualisms, 78; and otherness, 14–15,
20–21; as process, 56, 81; and self-
certainty, 79–80; and truth, 14, 84;
as turning point in Phenomenology, 1
Sense-Certainty, 4–5, 72, 76–77
Sickness Unto Death (Kierkegaard), 80
Skepticism, 31–35, 39, 59–60,
108–10; and freedom, 33–34; and
the objective world, 32; as self-
contradictory, 34; as the realization of
Stoicism, 31–32, 108–9; as sophistic,
109
Slave Consciousness, 25–28, 104–6,
118; and alienation, 118; and death,
26; and fear, 27–28; and service,
27–28; and truth, 26; and work, 27
Socrates, 119
Solipsism, 85
Solon, 50

Spinoza, Baruch de, 93, 94
Spirit of Christianity (Hegel), 207; on
criminality, 207–8
Stoicism, 29–31, 32, 39, 59, 106–8; as
abstract freedom, 30–31, 107;
freedom as highest value of, 107; as
freedom of thought, 30; as indeterminate, 31
Struggle for Recognition (Honneth), 206,
216, 220
Studies on Marx and Hegel (Hyppolite),
134
Subject-Object Paradigm, 164, 205,
215–16, 221–22
System of Ethical Life (Hegel), 205, 212,
216, 217

Understanding (the), 75–76, 77, 78
Unhappy Consciousness, 34–46,
110–20; Christianity as expression of,
111–12; and desiring and working,
40–42; as divided against itself, 35,
111–12, 115–16; and the mediating
priest, 44, 116; and the pure heart,
39–40; contrasted with Skepticism,
113; contrasted with Stoicism, 113;
and the Trinity, 114–16; the universal
Being, 43–46

View of Toledo (El Greco), 110

Wahl, Jean, 113, 114, 116, 125, 133,
157–60; on Deleuze, 182; self-
consciousness as unhappy, 157–60
Winicott, Donald, 217
World-in-Itself, 5–6, 74–75

Young Hegelians, 8